BACKFIRE

Also by Geoffrey Regan and published by Robson Books

Let Them Eat Cake!: A Treasury of Historical Anecdotes

BACKFIRE

A history of friendly fire
from ancient warfare
to the present day

GEOFFREY REGAN

ROBSON BOOKS

This paperback edition first published in Great Britain in 2002 by Robson Books, 64 Brewery Road, London, N7 9NT

A member of the Chrysalis Group plc

British Library Cataloguing in Publication Data
A catalogue record for this title is available from the British Library.

ISBN 1 86105 501 3

Typeset by SX Composing DTP, Rayleigh, Essex
Printed in Great Britain by Creative Print & Design (Wales), Ebbw Vale

For Frank Gregory

Contents

Acknowledgements   1
Introduction   3

Part I: Ground Warfare

1 Ancient and Medieval Warfare   29
2 The Early Modern Battlefield   41
3 The Nineteenth Century   57
4 The First World War   86
5 The Second World War in Europe   122
6 The Second World War in the Pacific   141
7 Ground Warfare Since 1945   152

Part II: Air Warfare

8   Air Warfare up to 1939   171
9   The Second World War   177
10 Operation Cobra and Afterwards   200
11 America's Undeclared War With Switzerland   217
12 Air Warfare in East Asia   224

Contents

Part III: Maintaining Discipline

13   Intentional Friendly Fire   247

Afterword   266
Notes   268
Bibliography   271
Index   273

Acknowledgements

I would like to acknowledge the considerable help that I received from a number of British and American military historians in the writing of this book. The greatest debt I owe to Richard Holmes, whose advice, so willingly proffered, gave me the confidence to begin working on the subject of friendly fire, and whose suggestions put me in touch with several experts in the field. Richard has written already — albeit briefly — on the subject of amicide in his books *Firing Line* and *Nuclear Warriors*, and I was able to gain much from his helpful letters. I would also like to thank Paddy Griffith, David Chandler, and Christopher Duffy for their help and advice, as well as Professor Douglas Porch from the Naval War College in Newport, Rhode Island.

I must also acknowledge my considerable debt to the work of Charles Shrader, whose pioneering study of amicide made my own efforts possible. In addition, certain secondary works have proved most helpful to me, including Eric Bergerud's recent study of the 25th Infantry Division in Vietnam, *Red Thunder, Tropic Lightning,* Charles Whiting's *Slaughter over Sicily,* Denis MacShane's *Friendly Fire Whitewash,* John J Sullivan's study of the air support for Operation Cobra, and Dr Jonathan E Helmreich's essay on US bombings of Switzerland during the Second World War.

In producing a book of this kind I have been dependent on the assistance of a number of libraries. I would therefore like to thank the librarian of the Staff College at the Royal Military

1

Academy, Sandhurst, for her help in finding a number of elusive sources. Thanks also must go to the librarians of the University of Southampton, the London Library, and the Hampshire Library Service.

Most of all I would like to thank my wife Gillian and my two children, Andrew and Victoria, for bearing with me during difficult times and giving me the encouragement, advice and assistance without which the whole undertaking would have been impossible.

Introduction

A study of the subject of friendly fire in history can be a humbling experience. For someone living in the first decade of a new millennium to be confronted by so much evidence of human folly and incompetence is enough to shake the foundations of one's optimism in a better future for mankind. Friendly fire has squandered the lives of many thousands of men, notably in the present century, yet as technology has offered us even more refined and sophisticated ways of killing our fellow men we now discover that the problem of blue-on-blue, amicide – call it what you like – is actually growing in leaps and bounds. During the Gulf War, Coalition troops killed many more of each other than the enemy did – undoubtedly a first in military history. And they did so for two reasons, neither of which is very reassuring. In the first place the technology of war has become so advanced that it has passed beyond the capability of men to utilise it effectively and safely. Secondly, human beings are not 'improving' in their capabilities as fast as the machines they create and are subject to the age-old failing of carelessness. Simple human error, exacerbated by innumerable factors, from stress and fear to anger or exhilaration, from drink-induced torpor to drug-created ecstasy, has been at the root of mistakes that have cost lives, sometimes singly but often numbered in hundreds or thousands.

Warfare is far from being as scientific as those with a vested interest in its propagation would like us to believe. My research, limited mainly to secondary sources as it has had to be by the sheer breadth of the subject, has revealed that the activity of war and the environment in which it has taken place are more chaotic than any other in which civilized man has involved himself. The sheer carnage of an ancient clash of phalanxes, or a mêlée involving heavily armoured men-at-arms wielding crushing and slashing weapons like halberds and maces, must have been no more scientific than an abattoir. However one interprets the strategy and tactics of leaders like Alexander of Macedon, Epaminondas of Thebes, Pyrrhus of Epirus, Hannibal, Scipio Africanus or Julius Caesar, one cannot avoid the fact that in the last analysis their skills served only to bring large numbers of men into a position where they had to kill or be killed, using an array of weapons far more varied but no less barbaric than the blades that are used in a slaughterhouse. Even Hannibal, the author of Cannae – that tactical marvel that has inspired commanders right up to the present day – was only manoeuvring his men into a position where they could more easily butcher their Roman opponents. It was not an intellectual exercise or a war game. There was no victory until his Africans and Gauls had plied their swords and spears to good effect. There may have been science in the mind of Hannibal as he studied his maps, but for his men there was just the fear and panic, the blood and faeces, of a very unscientific process: a battle.

While praising ancient commanders for their skills, military historians have tended to scorn the abilities of medieval captains, pointing out that most of their battles were little more than mêlées, great collisions of men, too clumsy to manoeuvre. Although such a view does scant justice to some notable Byzantine and Arab commanders, the truth is that by their nature all ancient and medieval battles were essentially mêlées, involving hand-to-hand fighting with cutting and crushing hand weapons. Even in the sixteenth century, with the advent of cannons and handguns, cultivation of the science of war could not hide the fact that the collisions of pikemen were just as bloody and no more scientific at the sharp end than they had been in ancient Greece. Battles were still chaotic and wholly unpredictable after the combatants had crossed swords:

That this is a truism I do not for a moment deny, but that randomness and pure chance operate to the extent that they do challenges the notion of warfare as a science. Who could have predicted that the man thought to be the most intellectual, the best-educated, the most gifted British soldier of his day, Major-General Sir George Colley, would take a nap while in command of his forces on Majuba Hill in 1881 and would be shot, according to some sources, by a Boer schoolboy just twelve years old? Probably no operation of the entire First World War was as carefully planned as the British Somme offensive of 1 July 1916. All the best military brains available had been involved, yet it was a disaster. The barbed wire had not been properly cut by the artillery and on that one day the British suffered over 57,000 casualties. Friendly fire or blue-on-blue casualties may have been accidental yet, like traffic accidents and bunker cave-ins, they were an inherent part of war. There is no more sense in concealing the truth about blue-on-blue than there is in pretending that serving soldiers will not suffer from diseases as well as from battle wounds, and that a proportion of the diseases will be self-inflicted.

In this book I have not set out merely to be contentious but to try to build on the work of Charles Shrader by taking the subject further back in time in order to illustrate the range of friendly fire incidents that have occurred – on the ground and in the air – throughout history. While there have been many different reasons for individual accidents in battle there has been the consistent presence of human error in all of them, and this is something that everyone – generals included – must learn to acknowledge. This does not mean that one has to accept the problem and not try to improve techniques of identification to reduce the incidence of friendly fire. Instead one needs to come to terms with the existence of the problem, rather than attempt to 'hush it up' or 'sweep it under the carpet', to use the two ghastly expressions that seem best to sum up the recent behaviour of both British and American defence departments over a Gulf War blue-on-blue.

Gulf War spokesmen were wrong to suggest, or even to allow the idea to be suggested, that war can be a precise and surgical activity. As long as service chiefs are seen to condone this attitude and to allow the general public to believe it, war will always be an acceptable alternative to diplomacy. If, however, the truth is acknowledged that war is imprecise and chaotic and that smart weapons will still be unable to tell friend from foe, or civilians from soldiers, or indeed an Iraqi child from Saddam Hussein himself, then men will be less willing to follow their leaders down the road to war.

General Norman Schwarzkopf has made it quite clear that he has heard enough on the subject of friendly fire in Vietnam, Grenada and the Gulf to last him a lifetime. In his recent autobiography he has been at pains to say that there is really no such thing as friendly fire: no fire is friendly. Any bullet that leaves a rifle, any shell that leaves a cannon, any rocket that leaves a plane or helicopter has been designed for one thing and one thing only: to incapacitate its target. To a dead or maimed soldier it does not matter who fired the bullet that killed him – and it never has. Of one thing we can all be sure, no smart weapon is smart enough to differentiate between friend and foe.

Friendly fire – fratricide, amicide, blue-on-blue, or whatever – has been an integral part of military life since men first became civilized enough to kill each other with something other than their bare hands. Yet getting the military profession to accept this in public is a very different matter. Nobody ever goes out of their way to acknowledge friendly fire casualties. Only the tiniest percentage of those that occur are ever reported or officially recognized. The others are shrouded, like so much else that goes wrong in wartime, in what is euphemistically called the 'fog of war'. These incidents are the clearest manifestation of the fallibility of the human element in warfare. Whether the incidence of friendly fire is increasing – as the percentage figures for casualties in the Gulf War would tend to suggest – or merely that their details are more readily available to the general public, we cannot be sure. What is certain, though, is that 'friendly fire' or, in Charles R Shrader's memorable neologism, 'amicide', has provided investigative journalists in both the United States and Europe with a new stick with which to beat the military behemoths. Operation Desert Storm – with its record of 23 per cent of American casualties being self-inflicted and with 77 per cent of US combat vehicles lost being lost to friendly fire – was a high-exposure news item throughout the world for weeks in February 1991. The death of nine British soldiers in two IFVs struck by American Maverick missiles imposed strains on Anglo–American relations at a crucial stage in the struggle against Saddam Hussein. Evidence of a cover-up on both sides of the Atlantic, as revealed by author Denis MacShane in his *Friendly Fire Whitewash,* shows us that however common a feature of modern warfare friendly fire has become, it is no more acceptable to those in authority than it was in the past. Generals are now more accountable for their actions and less shielded from the glare of publicity. They have reputations to preserve, memoirs to write, political careers to pursue, and the last thing they want to hear about is more evidence of the essentially chaotic nature of warfare. Few professionals – either doctors, lawyers or accountants – would enjoy being reminded like four-star generals that their failures were their own fault and their successes someone else's doing.

In this book I would again like to acknowledge the great assistance I have enjoyed from the researches of Charles Shrader, the pioneer in the work on amicide. His notable study has provided me with many modern examples of friendly fire in an American context and has encouraged me to delve into the comparable areas of British and European military history for others. In examining the concept of friendly fire I have been only too aware of the diversity of factors which have contributed to its operation and its growth. One fundamental problem of all warfare – the difficulties imposed by the environment in which a military operation takes place – has made a substantial contribution to friendly fire. Men have taken war to most parts of the world and each – whether the mountains of the Dolomites in the First World War, the deserts of North Africa in the Second or the jungles of Vietnam – has presented unique problems for the soldiers on both sides. As was evident in the Gulf War, identification of ground troops from their support planes was particularly difficult in the dust and sandstorms of the desert, while in Vietnam, Burma and New Guinea the jungle concealed both friend and foe and sometimes made differentiation impossible. In street fighting, often a feature of the fighting in Normandy in 1944 or on the eastern front between Germans and Russians from 1942–4, enemy and friendly forces could become so closely engaged that there was no battle line and it was almost impossible for forward troops to call up artillery support without the risk – indeed the virtual certainty – that there would be friendly casualties. Clearly the problem of identification was a vital one, and poor visibility produced by fog, low cloud or heavy rain was bound to increase the incidence of friendly fire. Total darkness, as in the case of night operations, has inevitably played a large part in causing friendly casualties. Although modern conflicts, including those in Vietnam, the Falklands and the Gulf, have been fought with the technological capacity to operate at night with night sights and thermal imagers, this has not prevented numerous accidents occurring. In earlier conflicts, night operations have sometimes gained less from the obscurity and cover that darkness gave them than from the confusion and accidental casualties that were a frequent consequence.

Another contributory factor to the incidence of friendly fire has been the nature of a military operation, and the speed with which it was conducted. In the case of Operation Desert Storm, where the rapid movement of tanks and light armour across the vast areas of the Iraqi desert resulted in the intermingling of coalition and Iraqi forces, there were many opportunities for misidentification. Decisions by pilots and junior commanders had to be taken immediately in response to the rapidly changing situation that they encountered, and in such cases mistakes were inevitable. And in an age of high technology, the killing power of modern missile weapons allows for no second thoughts. The finality of the A-10 attack on the British Warrior IFVs showed that. The speed of state-of-the-art fighters, equipped with a full arsenal of guns, missiles and bombs, has resulted in the need for split-second decisions on the part of pilots. Any hesitation can be literally fatal. In a high-tech war, well trained flyers on both sides – sometimes, as in the Falklands War, trained by the same people – will have their fingers on a button with their lives depending on their speed of reaction. As Charles Shrader has observed, 'In many respects modern weapons have outstripped the ability of their human users to control them, and the employment of sophisticated camouflage, electronic deception, and other modern defensive technology further compounds the problem.'

In the final analysis, friendly fire is still a human problem. If Shrader is right and technology is taking – or has already taken – weapons beyond the capacity of human beings to use them then the proportion of friendly casualties in any engagement will continue to rise. Historically, however, it has often been the case that it was not so much the technology that was at fault but that the raw material of all human warfare – man himself – had malfunctioned. In simple terms soldiers, like any other workers, were capable of acts of carelessness. In the past, a misdirected spear or arrow could kill as certainly as one fired purposely. There are literally thousands of examples from the Napoleonic Wars and the American Civil War of soldiers double-charging their muskets and rifles and killing themselves or their colleagues. Others have read the wrong map co-ordinates and called down artillery fire on themselves or other friendly units. In the First World War, the French artillery expert, General Percin, records numerous incidents of this sort. According to his research, 75,000 French casualties were caused by faulty artillery support. Whereas such mistakes may be the product of the confusion of war, much of it is increasingly interpreted as the result of stress. It is doubtful if an eighteenth-century drillmaster would have allowed himself to consider the effect of stress on an individual soldier. He could not allow himself to think in individual terms. His task was to concentrate firepower in the opening moments of a battle and, to achieve this, iron discipline was necessary. As we will see, however, once confusion set in, as it did in General Braddock's famous defeat on the Monongahela River in 1755, friendly casualties were inevitable as panicky soldiers lost their discipline and fired randomly. The British redcoats of that period were so thoroughly drilled that they could hardly function effectively when thrown back on their own initiative. Their training was hard but brittle. In the following century, notably during the American Civil War, we find large numbers of civilian soldiers whose training was so inadequate that they did not know how to use their weapons and killed and injured their colleagues through sheer incompetence. One need only add the stress of combat to their inadequate training to produce a 'cocktail of blue-on-blues'.

Charles Shrader echoes General Percin in seeing a lack of co-ordination as a major factor in causing friendly casualties. While it is generally the common soldier – individually or *en masse* – who inflicts the killing blow or the fatal bullet on his comrades, his responsibility sometimes extends no further than to the officer whose own failings have created a situation in which friendly fire can take place. Poor planning is at the root of many incidents: one has only to think of the example S L A Marshal relates of the American attack on Pork Chop Hill in Korea, in 1953, where friendly troops attacking from different sides encountered each other by surprise and opened a fire-fight. Sometimes plans have not been co-ordinated properly, either between two units of the same service or else between ground troops and their artillery and air supports. A lack of information is often the cause of unnecessary casualties.

In 1755 Lieutenant-Colonel James Wolfe, soon to earn immortality on the Heights of Abraham at Quebec, told his father, 'I have a very mean opinion of the infantry in general. I know their discipline to be bad, and their valour precarious. They are easily put into disorder, and hard to recover out of it; they frequently kill their officers through fear and murder one another in their confusion.' For Wolfe, discipline was a quintessential part of military activities for without it, as he says, there is only chaos. While nobody would suggest that the drill of the eighteenth-century Prussian kings was the only way to prepare men for battle, one could hardly avoid the conclusion that all successful armies have been disciplined, according to their own mores. And what I mean by 'disciplined' is efficient and able to operate within a system or 'discipline', to which all have become accustomed by training. When the training has been inadequate, the discipline is easily fractured and needs to be reinforced by a system of punishments. Historically, army discipline has been concerned not just with the training of a soldier to the peak of efficiency. It has also been seen as the most effective way of keeping men in the battle line or the firing line when most would prefer to run away and thereby avoid danger. To enforce this in most armies it has been necessary to make examples of shirkers by shooting them *pour encourager les autres*. Both official executions for desertion or cowardice and unofficial killings, by officers and NCOs on the battlefield, have been a feature of warfare throughout history. This kind of 'friendly fire' – for disciplinary purposes – differs from the random or chance occurrences which make up most of the book by being deliberate. Both Charles Shrader and Richard Holmes feel that this form of enforcing discipline does not really fit into the category of 'amicide', as they would define it. In this book, however, I have included a brief chapter at the end on deliberate 'friendly fire', partially based on the experiences of a British general who actually boasted about the men he had killed in enforcing discipline during the First World War. The reaction of the military authorities to such 'executions', whether public and official or private and spontaneous, has been the same as for unintentional friendly casualties, namely to conceal the details from the public under the heading of 'died in action'. And it is this aspect of friendly fire – the attempt to 'hush up' the details and hide them from the families of the bereaved – that forms the subject of the next section: the 'amicide' incident during the Gulf War that cost the lives of nine young British soldiers.

At 1500 hours on 26 February 1991, the tanks and
armoured vehicles of the British 1st Armoured Division were
speeding through the Iraqi desert as part of the Allied ground
forces involved in Operation Desert Storm. In very bad
weather and poor visibility, two British Warrior infantry
fighting vehicles of 'C' Company of the 3rd Royal Regiment of
Fusiliers were attacked by American A-10 tankbuster aircraft
firing Maverick missiles. During the attack nine British soldiers
– the oldest just 21 years of age – were killed. The fog of war –
or in this case the rain, the high winds and the sandstorms
reported to the grieving parents by the Colonel-in-Chief of the
Fusiliers, HRH the Duke of Kent, as being responsible for the
tragedy – had claimed yet more victims for that most ghastly of
military euphemisms: friendly fire.

Yet at 1500 hours on 26 February, the bad weather of the
previous night had passed. The sun shone brightly, the wind
had dropped and visibility was perfect. The fog of war had
returned to metaphor. Yet not – it seems – soon enough for the
authorities who swung into action, determined to cover up this
tragic incident. A scenario, sketched out in the minds of
politicians rather than soldiers, was concocted as a damage-
limitation exercise. Friendly fire was a fact of military life, yet
civilians could not be expected to understand this. The idea of
men being killed by mistake, by their friends and allies, was
just too much for them to swallow after all the efforts that had
been made to sanitize this war, with talk of surgical strikes and
smart weapons. What made matters worse for a coalition army
was that the Americans had killed their allies by mistake once
again. Much of the criticism of the unprofessionalism of the
American armed forces made by European commentators had
been based on what they regarded as the 'gung-ho' attitude of
American soldiers and airmen, with their supposed 'shoot first
and identify later' tactics that had caused so many friendly-fire
incidents in earlier conflicts, notably Grenada, Vietnam and
Korea. Relations between America and her allies would hardly
be strengthened by revelations of amicide.

For more than a century the convention had been that

soldiers who died on active service were 'killed in action'. During the First World War, this phrase was even used at first to denote those who died in traffic accidents, those who succumbed to weapon malfunctions and even those shot by their own officers. It was easier that way. The parents or families of dead soldiers had a right to the comforting knowledge that their son's or husband's sacrifice had been worthwhile, and that it had occurred in action with the enemy. Like the euphemism 'instantly' used to describe the often long-drawn-out and horrific process of dying, 'killed in action' was a powerful analgesic for grieving families. How, then, should the death of the nine young British soldiers be described to their loved ones? Could bad weather excuse the American pilots? If so, then let it be used. And how did they die, purposelessly cramped inside the steel tomb of their IFV or – as was to be relayed to the parents of one of the young men by his own brigade commander – heroically struggling to rescue his fellows trapped in the blazing vehicle? At moments like this did the truth really matter? The answer – for the parents – was a resounding 'yes'. The truth of their sons' deaths was all that they were left. The lie about the bad weather and poor visibility indicated that a cover-up was in progress.

There are many people – soldiers, politicians and diplomats – who know the truth of what happened to the British Warriors on 26 February 1991, yet so far none of them has been allowed to make it public knowledge. As a result, any description of the events that took place can only make use of evidence limited to such an extent that no conclusive findings are possible, yet further proof – if it were needed – of the old saying that in time of war the first casualty is the truth.

Even before the start of Operation Desert Storm, the British and American commanders, General Sir Peter de la Billière and General Norman Schwarzkopf, had been acutely aware of the danger – indeed the likelihood – of friendly-fire casualties. With thousands of allied tanks, IFVs and APCs in contact with Iraqi armoured vehicles across hundreds of miles of desert and with close air support a vital part of Allied superiority, identification was bound to be a problem. The two generals had discussed identification at great length, particularly after the matter was brought to a head by the Iraqi attack on the coastal town of Khafji, in Saudi Arabia. During the battle to regain the town some US marines in an APC were attacked and killed by American aircraft. As a result, a system of orange and green recognition panels had been introduced for Allied vehicles with huge inverted V markers – at least six feet in height – painted on the sides of tanks and on their turrets. The system was tested for aerial visibility and found to be effective. Naturally, poor weather conditions could always hinder recognition but at the outset of the fighting both Schwarzkopf and de la Billière were satisfied that friendly casualties could be minimized if not entirely eradicated.

In the opening stages of Operation Desert Storm the British 1st Armoured Division, headed by the 7th Armoured Brigade, was part of the American 'left hook' designed to outflank Iraqi forces by a wide sweep north then east before closing in on Kuwait itself. The British had been allocated targets consisting of a series of large Iraqi concentrations of armour given the names of metals by the divisional commander, Major-General Rupert Smith – Bronze, Copper, Brass, Zinc, Platinum and Tungsten. Warrior IFVs, in platoons of four vehicles, accompanied the Challenger battle tanks to provide infantry back-up, clearing trenches and mopping up knots of Iraqi resistance. By 1400 hours on 26 February, 80 Iraqi armoured vehicles had been destroyed at Objective Brass and infantry of the 1st Battalion of the Royal Scots and the 3rd Battalion of the Royal Fusiliers were brought up to clear the Iraqi trenches. This was quickly achieved and soon more than 80 British tanks and IFVs carrying the 800 men of the 3rd Battalion of the Royal Regiment of Fusiliers Battle Group were setting off again across the wide and very flat plain towards Objective Steel. At this stage it is important to consider the problems of identifying Warrior IFVs which, it later transpired, were misidentified by American pilots as Iraqi T54/55 tanks. The most obvious difference, and one so fundamental that it is almost impossible to confuse the two, is the size of the turret cannon. The 30mm cannon of the Warrior is short, stubby and in length hardly reaches the end of the vehicle's body. In contrast the long, heavy gun of the T54/55 projects far ahead of the main body, declaring itself in outline to be the main armament of a heavy battle tank rather than an infantry fighting vehicle. In other respects – size, outline, profile, tracks – the two vehicles are utterly dissimilar. But – above all – the Warriors were carrying brightly coloured fluorescent sheets as well as large, freshly painted V identification signs. Given the high-powered binoculars available to American aircrew for identification of targets it is amazing that such a misidentification in clear weather conditions was possible.

At the head of the RRF Battle Group in its drive towards Objective Steel were the 37 vehicles of 'C' Company, with 8 Platoon commanded by Lieutenant Brett Duxbury in the lead. On arrival, troops of the Royal Engineers dismounted and placed charges to blow up six Iraqi artillery pieces, though their gunners had already fled and there seemed to be no live Iraqi soldiers in the vicinity. The four Warriors had kept up a steady fire as they approached the battery of six Iraqi guns but it was soon evident that they need expect no resistance and they drew up about 50 metres from the guns. While the engineers worked at placing their charges the young Fusiliers disembarked from their IFVs to relieve themselves or have a smoke, but once the charges were primed everyone was ordered back inside their vehicles in case of casualties from shrapnel. Although Duxbury had ordered his men to close their hatches, the driver of Warrior Callsign 22 had apparently left his half open and this simple oversight may have saved his life. No sooner had his men returned to their vehicles than Warrior Callsign 22 was ripped by an explosion, flinging the driver out of the hatch and saving him from the flames that now engulfed the IFV. As he lay wounded, his first thought was that they had struck a mine, though onlookers wondered if they had been targeted by distant Iraqi artillery. Inside the stricken Warrior, shells and grenades were exploding and four men were already dead, with others grievously wounded. As Duxbury raced to help get the survivors out of the burning IFV, he ordered a second Warrior, Callsign 23, to close in to give further help but as it did so it too was struck by a huge explosion, killing five of its occupants and wounding others. To other units of the Royal Fusiliers, it seemed most likely that the Iraqis were mounting a counter-attack. But the tragic truth was that there were no enemy troops within firing distance. Death had come from the skies in the shape of two Maverick missiles fired by either one or two American A-10 tankbuster aircraft. Yet in the confusion of the battlefield this was the last thing anyone looked for and the witnesses were far from united in their description of what happened. Where soldiers, deep within enemy territory and only recently in contact with enemy troops, had good reason to fear mines underfoot or artillery from afar, they hardly looked for danger in the skies where from day one of the operation they had enjoyed the assurance of total superiority. Thus, there was no unanimity in what the soldiers believed they saw as the Warriors were hit. Some of the Fusiliers present claimed they had seen a single A-10 flying low, which gave a victory waggle of its wings after scoring two hits, others claim there were two A-10s at high altitude – American reports speak of 8,000 feet – while still other Fusiliers claim to have picked up the pilot's report of his error on their radio. Curiously, nobody speaks of seeing or hearing an aircraft before the attack, which in view of the perfect visibility and the fact the vehicles had been stationary for the previous fifteen minutes is rather surprising.

The task of the A-10 tankbusters was to provide close support for ground troops in action against enemy tanks and the desert gave pilots almost unlimited visibility. In contrast with the complex terrain of a West European battlefield, where trees, heavy vegetation, hills, rivers and water obstacles, not to mention urban obstructions like bridges, buildings and civilian areas, might obstruct the view of enemy tanks, the Iraqi desert provided the A-10s with a perfect killing ground, as long as they were careful to identify their targets before they fired. As we have seen, Coalition armoured units had anticipated the dangers of friendly fire incidents by carrying coloured panels and the large, black inverted Vs painted on all vehicles. In good weather conditions and where Coalition units were not in direct combat with active Iraqi ones, it should not have been possible for mistakes to be made. But there is the ever-present element of human failing in military affairs and while men engage in war there are always likely to be errors. On 26 February 1991, the pilots of possibly two A-10s made serious and costly mistakes in identification. The subsequent cover-up in both Britain and the United States was curiously perverse in view of the realistic view that most military commanders take of blue-on-blue, that it is an unpleasant but unavoidable fact of military life. It may well be that politicians rather than serving officers were responsible for concealing the truth from the public.

The problem facing the American ground-support planes was that the situation on the ground was so immensely fluid. There was no fixed battle front and the speed of the Allied advance was so fast that Coalition armoured and motorized units were spread across an enormous area of desert. Iraqi formations had been immobilized and left far behind as the American and British tanks roared northwards and eastwards, outflanking the Iraq positions in Kuwait. The A-10s involved in the blue-on-blue had apparently taken off at midday on 26 February and had initially encountered the fag-end of the bad weather that the units of the British 1st Armoured Division had reported, but soon after refuelling from an air tanker, they reported that the clouds were clearing and visibility was good. Once they were fuelled they contacted the air controller in one of the AWACS Boeings, whose job was to find them a target. Unfortunately, their first assignment was obscured by blowing sand and they checked in for another target. Over two hours had already passed when they were ordered by the Air Support Operations Centre to contact a forward air controller, who happened to be a British officer. He was handling the air-ground support in the area of the British 1st Armoured Division. At this moment something happened that may have contributed to the eventual tragedy. As well as contacting the

British air controller, the A-10 pilots also got talking to an F-16 fighter pilot, who was just returning from attacking an Iraqi target. The F-16 pilot suggested that they should fly east until they came to a north/south crossroads. If they then followed the road eastwards they would find the same Iraqi vehicles that he had attacked. The A-10s, following the instructions of the F-16 pilot set off looking for a crossroads as he had described. But the problem was which crossroad was meant. The desert was criss-crossed with roads and they could not have been certain as to which of these the F-16 was referring. Moreover, how close had they really been to the F-16 when they contacted him? One of the pilots claimed to have seen an F-16 close by, but there is no certainty that this was the plane whose pilot had given them the target. Nevertheless, convinced that they had at last found a potential target, the two A-10s found a suitable crossroads, complete with smoking vehicles and apparently 'juicy' targets. According to both pilots, their attack on these Iraqi targets was unsuccessful and so they both flew south until they came upon a target consisting of about 50 vehicles. They claimed that the British air controller had assured them that there were no friendly vehicles within ten kilometres of their area of operations. Naturally the next step should have been to identify these targets by using the binoculars with which each pilot was equipped. According to the official American version the pilots claimed that they identified the vehicles below as Iraqi by using these binoculars and passing over the target twice to ensure correct identification. They were adamant that there were no Coalition markings on the vehicles they attacked. There was nothing now to prevent them from attacking the vehicles below, which they were convinced were Iraqi T54/55 tanks and not the much smaller British Warrior IFVs. Clearly there was no doubt in the minds of the pilots otherwise they would have asked the British air controller for confirmation of the grid reference of the proposed target. Once they had decided not to do this there was nothing to prevent the tragedy that followed.

In his recent book *Storm Command*, the British commander, General Sir Peter de la Billière, recorded his own views on the disaster. As part of a politically sensitive coalition he knew that unity of purpose between the United States and Britain was absolutely essential. Any breach of Anglo-American relations could have been exploited by the Iraqis to weaken the resolve of the entire Coalition and so this particular blue-on-blue, tragic and wasteful as it was, would have to be played down. In a war situation the priority was victory through close co-operation and whatever differences of opinion there might be must be put aside for the duration. According to the diplomatic British commander, however, while he was able to smooth things over with Norman Schwarzkopf, matters were more difficult with the US air chief, Lieutenant-General Chuck Horner, who 'became deeply emotional, and could not agree that the issue needed to be left open until a formal investigation had been carried out.' He apparently insisted that there was no case to answer as the fault lay entirely with the British air controller and no blame attached to the A-10 pilots. His defence of his airmen was emotional and so wide ranging that it could not be justified by the facts. In spite of the magnificent performance by the vast majority of US airmen, there had been a number of friendly-fire incidents involving loss of life and the responsibility for most of these rested fairly and squarely on the shoulders of some of Horner's pilots. So eager was Horner to defend his pilots that he even resorted to blaming mines for the incident. De la Billière records how taken aback he was by Horner's aggression. He writes, 'As I tried to explain to him why we had thought it essential to release news of the incident, he walked backwards out of the room, barely able to speak . . . I did not go after him. Having spent the past five months doing all I could to make the coalition work, I was not going to risk splitting it now, in the middle of the battle.' Nevertheless, he knew that 'the USAF were not in line with our interpretation of events.'

There are many unanswered questions concerning this blue-on-blue tragedy and neither the British nor the American authorities have been prepared to help solve them. There is an obvious conflict of evidence between the official report issued by the pilots and the evidence given by the British air controller and the troops on the ground. Of the three men who knew the truth at the time of the incident, the British air controller and the two American pilots, the former has claimed that before being contacted by the two A-10s he had already given target grid references to American planes which had successfully attacked Iraqi armour some 20 kilometres to the east of the British Warrior IFVs. He asserts that he gave the same grid references to the two American pilots involved in the blue-on-blue, something that they deny. On the contrary, they claim that he gave them a clearance to attack anything within ten kilometres by saying that there were no friendly forces within that area. The pilots claim they selected their targets on the basis of identification. The British Board of Inquiry was told by the air controller that he had also issued a code word with the grid reference to reassure the American pilots that they were not being fed information by Iraqi intelligence, a precaution that may or may not have been necessary in view of the unsophisticated Iraqi defence system, but one that had been agreed at the outset of the fighting by Coalition members. Curiously, the two pilots deny receiving such a code word and furthermore claim not to know its significance. This conflict of evidence is so wide that one is left with no other conclusion than that someone is lying as part of a cover-up. Without a full knowledge of the conversation between the pilots and the air controller we cannot tell at this stage what really happened. However, even if the air controller gave neither code word nor grid reference and merely vaguely mentioned that there were no friendly forces within ten kilometres, how could the pilots have misidentified the Warrior IFVs as T54/55 tanks and have claimed that they carried no markings? Apparently, once the A-10s had carried out their attack on the Warriors they informed the air controller of the grid reference which showed him for the first time that they had attacked a friendly force. He ordered an American reconnaissance plane to overfly the area and received the significant report that, 'fluorescent air recognition panels could be seen from 6,000 feet and the type of vehicles could be identified from 14,000 feet.' This report would seem to demolish the claims by American commanders that dust and sand could have obscured identification signs and perhaps even made the shapes of the vehicles difficult to identify. What is possible, of course, is that some of the Warrior IFVs could have become dirtied by sand or dust, and some others perhaps lost their fluorescent panels in the wind, but 37 vehicles in close proximity do not all suffer identical mishaps and transform themselves in shape into T54/55 tanks.

In public the American air commanders, notably General Horner, have been adamant that the error leading to the blue-on-blue was made by the British air controller. They claim that his comment that there were no friendly forces within ten kilometres gave the A-10 pilots *carte blanche* to attack anything they found within that area. Yet, even if the British air controller is lying when he asserts that he gave the pilots a grid reference, Horner is on record as saying that pilots had been instructed, 'If in doubt, don't drop.' How was it possible for the two pilots to fail to identify any of the hundreds of identifying panels and signs on the 37 Warriors? The desert was swarming with British vehicles, all thoroughly equipped with coloured panels and inverted Vs, as was apparent from television film shown only minutes after the attack.

The blue-on-blue of 26 February 1991 came as a shattering blow to a complacent British public, accustomed to seeing smart American weapons finding their way into the buildings in central Baghdad with all the skills of a cat burglar. The dangers that British and other Coalition troops were facing seemed far less than those that had been ever present in the short, sharp Falklands War. The news that nine British soldiers, all young men aged between 17 and 21 years, had been killed by a mistake seemed particularly shocking as it had been so unnecessary. Friendly fire was a new term in daily newspapers and on television reports. Old soldiers and those still serving knew it for what it was, an inevitable part of service life ranging from an accidental killing when a rifle was being cleaned right up to Operation Cobra, the misdirected bombing raid on Allied troops in Normandy in 1944. But to a public accustomed mainly to casualties in peacekeeping operations, the deaths of nine soldiers in an attack by American planes was something that could not be ignored. Old prejudices surfaced and newspaper articles appeared, dredging up previous examples of American 'gung-ho' behaviour in the Second World War or Korea. Author Denis MacShane, in the most complete survey of the incident in the Iraqi desert, told his readers what he felt to be characteristics of American pilots that might have contributed to the disaster. According to MacShane, the case of another blue-on-blue involving a senior American officer, Lieutenant-Colonel Ralph Hayes, might offer parallels. Apparently Hayes was flying an Apache helicopter that destroyed two US Bradley IFVs, killing two men the day after the British blue-on-blue. Hayes, on leaving the US Army, gave a detailed interview on American television in which he attempted to vindicate himself. Human error clearly played a major part in his incident, as he misread the grid reference while in contact with unidentified vehicles at night. The result was that he believed himself to be over an Iraqi-held area and was immediately ordered by his ground controller to destroy the targets. But something worried Hayes at the time and he felt uneasy about attacking with missiles. He tried to strafe the mystery vehicles but his gun jammed. His uncertainty was manifest as he told the controller, 'Boy, I'm going to tell you, it's hard to pull this trigger.' However, the controller is adamant and continues to order him to 'take 'em out.' In response, he fires first one missile and then another and two American lives are lost. The controller now realizes that a mistake has occurred and informs Hayes that he has just hit American vehicles. In spite of state-of-the-art technology, a senior American pilot misread a number and from that moment onwards no amount of technology could save the lives of those two soldiers.

According to MacShane, the Hayes case reveals the fact that audio recordings are kept of conversations between air controllers and pilots as well as video recordings of targets as seen by the aircraft's weapons system. Thus the conflict of evidence between the two A-10 pilots and the British air controller could easily be rectified by the production of this material. The fact that it has not been produced in public indicates that a cloak of secrecy has been drawn over this particular incident, as was not the case in the Hayes affair. If the British Ministry of Defence has seen the videos and heard the recordings then it has entered into the American cover-up. If not, then the Americans are operating a cover-up on their own behalf. Certainly, the authorities in the United States have gone to some lengths to conceal details of friendly-fire incidents in the Gulf War, of which there were many. At least 35 US servicemen died as a result of blue-on-blue incidents in the Gulf and it is significant that in casualty reports the phrase 'hit by friendly fire' has been replaced at high level by a handwritten 'vehicle hit by enemy fire'. Where US soldiers have tried to speak of their experiences of friendly fire they have been threatened with court martial, according to reports in the *Washington Post*. In fact, it was not until August 1991 that all the families of the 35 American victims of friendly fire had been officially informed of the cause of their deaths. Truth may be the first victim in wartime, but there is no reason why that should continue to be the case once the war has ended. The parents of the nine British servicemen who died deserve to know the truth of the events that led to the deaths of their sons. Nothing is gained by cover-ups except delay: the truth cannot be permanently suppressed.

In the course of the fighting in the Gulf there were three further incidents that involved friendly fire and in which British soldiers were casualties. Though far less damaging than that involving the nine young men in the Warrior IFVs, these cases are further proof of the increasing incidence of blue-on-blue episodes. The first of them occurred on 26 February at 1100 hours. An officer of the 1st Staffordshire Regiment, who had just alighted from a Warrior, was hit by shrapnel during a brief engagement with a Challenger tank of the Royal Scots Dragoon Guards. The Challenger had opened fire in poor visibility on a number of Iraqi tanks, which turned out to be abandoned. The tank then fired at a group of Warriors from the Staffords and although no great damage was done the officer was evacuated for hospital treatment. The poor visibility due to the dust storm was clearly the cause of the incident.

The following day, again at 1100 hours, two units of the Queen's Royal Irish Hussars, travelling in Scorpion armoured reconnaissance vehicles, fell foul of an American M1 Abrams tank, which opened fire on them in spite of the fact that both Scorpions carried the normal Coalition markings and visibility was good. The cause of the confusion may have been that the Scorpions had both stopped to take the surrender of Iraqi troops, and this may have given the American tank crew the impression that they were, in fact, Iraqi vehicles. In any case, the M1 opened fire at a range of 1,500 metres and hit the first Scorpion in the front, injuring one soldier. The other Scorpion was then hit by machine-gun rounds and shrapnel from a main turret round. The gunner in the Scorpion was injured by the shrapnel. On discovering their error the crew of the Abrams helped evacuate the wounded to hospital.

The third incident occurred on the same day, but during the afternoon. Two soldiers from the 10th Air Defence Battery of the Royal Artillery were wounded when their Spartan armoured vehicles were fired on by British Challenger tanks. The tanks were using thermal sights to aid targeting and this prevented the identifying signs on the Spartans being seen. As a result, one of the Spartans burst into flames on being hit, but fortunately it was empty at the time. The other Spartan was damaged, albeit less seriously.

American losses from friendly fire were much greater than those suffered by British or other Coalition forces. In fact, 23 per cent of American casualties were blue-on-blues. Yet the case of the nine British soldiers killed by the mysterious blue-on-blue, 'mysterious' because at least one government is not prepared to release the full facts, has come to symbolize the entire subject for many people. Chuck Horner's reaction to the

the bereaved parents' attempt to get at the truth – that it was 'picking at a scab' – is unhelpful because even if the scab is a sign of healing, normality only returns when the scab is gone and forgotten.

Part I

Ground Warfare

1

Ancient and Medieval Warfare

The wars of antiquity and of the medieval period rarely speak of friendly casualties. Accidents on the battlefield must have been so common that they were scarcely worthy of comment unless they related to a leader of note struck down by mischance. It might be thought that the hand-to-hand nature of battle in these periods would preclude the sort of problems that have bedevilled more recent conflicts and, to the extent that missile fire – from bowmen, javelin throwers, siege engines and even primitive cannon – was directed at a seen target rather than indirect, this could be said to be true. Yet the use of pointed and edged weapons in close order was bound to offer a danger to colleagues as well as to enemies. In his book *The Western Way of War,* Victor Davis Hanson has shown that the ancient Greek battlefield was a place of 'confusion, misdirection and mob violence', with 'no clear demarcation between sides' and where it was sometimes almost impossible to identify friends and allies in the chaotic fighting. If one remembers that uniforms were not generally worn in European warfare until the middle of the seventeenth century, the opportunities for mistakes were great. As Hanson shows, the Greek hoplites from various states were almost indistinguishable from one another. One hardly had time to ask a man's allegiance before falling to blows with him, nor could one be certain that he was telling the truth. Thus, 'hoplite battle was

29

frequently enough a free-for-all of sorts between infantry who looked, dressed, fought and spoke alike, and there is little wonder that often men had no idea whom they were fighting once their phalanxes had crashed and merged. Since the pressure of advancing and retreating lines varied, men might find their own colleagues out in front and nearly in their faces, while pockets of the enemy were at their side and perhaps already to their rear.' Thucydides described the situation that ensued during the Athenian night attack at Epipolae in Syracuse in 413 BC:

> The Athenians now fell into great disorder and perplexity ... seeking for one another, taking all in front of them for enemies, even although they might be some of their now flying friends ... They ended by coming into collision with each other in many parts of the field, friends with friends, and citizens with citizens, and not only terrified one another, but even came to blows and could only be parted with difficulty.[1]

This chaos, even more typical of a medieval mêlée, was naturally productive of much 'amicide'. What is apparent, however, is that neither ancient warriors nor medieval soldiers thought fit to complain about this additional threat to their lives, reinforcing the view that it was viewed as simply an unavoidable part of a soldier's lot. In several other ancient battles – notably at Cannae in 216 BC and Adrianople in 378 – the troops of one army became so compressed by the enemy that they could do little other than strike at their own friends and inflict casualties on their own side. Ammianus Marcellinus, writing of the terrible defeat of the Romans under Valens by Fridigern's Goths at Adrianople, described how 'the different companies became so huddled together that hardly anyone could pull out his sword, or draw back his arm, and because of clouds of dust the heavens could no longer be seen, and echoed with frightful cries.' So confused was the fighting that many Romans fell victim to their own men at the rear and nobody could escape until the frenzied slaughter had thinned the ranks and made more space for men to fight and run.

Thucydides describes the chaos that ensued within the Athenian army during the battle of Delion in 424 BC against the Boeotians and their Thespian allies. The Athenians achieved a kind of pre-Cannae encirclement of the Thespians but when the left wing of the Athenians eventually joined up with the right wing, the hoplites failed to identify each other as Athenians and fighting broke out. Hanson has suggested that the reason for these friendly casualties was that the lust for killing blinded the Athenian soldiers to everything but the so-called enemies around them. Inherent in this is a positional problem. The Athenians assumed that anyone in front of their battle line must be an enemy and therefore must be engaged and killed. In the confusion of hand-to-hand battle this simple assurance was frequently wrong. Nevertheless, where warriors were dressed alike, spoke the same language and were not obviously identifiable, position was the best assurance that the men you were fighting were the enemies you were supposed to be fighting. In the event of the two armies becoming inter-mingled then mistakes were certain.

Besides the positional problems inherent in hand-to-hand fighting in an era before uniforms were generally worn, Hanson has also drawn attention to the propensity for friendly casualties arising from the use of certain pointed or edged weapons. Accidental wounding or killing was an ever-present problem of service in the Greek phalanxes. And what was so in the Greece of the fifth and fourth centuries BC must also have been true of the phalanx formations used by the Swiss and the German *landsknechte* of the fifteenth and sixteenth centuries. The Macedonian *sarissa* reached the extraordinary length of 6.3 metres, according to Polybius, compared to the 5.5 metres of the Swiss medieval pike. This meant that when the Greek phalanx advanced into battle the *sarissas* of the first five ranks projected beyond the foremost men. The problem was that the *sarissa* was pointed at both ends so that when the front ranks drew back to strike the enemy they frequently wounded or killed men further back in the phalanx. As Hanson reasonably explains, 'After all, front line troops are fighting for their lives with leveled spears against the enemy. They could hardly worry about the danger of their own butt spikes to the men behind. At the same time, the men in the front row or two might themselves be wounded on the flank from the spear tips of those in the rank behind.' An additional problem was tripping and trampling, which must have been a very common problem in the confused fighting at the front of the phalanx, while if the front rank fighters were forced backwards they were likely to be impaled on the spears of the men behind them. Although the Roman legionary formations were quite unlike the Greek phalanxes, notably in their flexibility, several times in Rome's history her armies were trapped and so compressed as to cause a panic resulting in many casualties from friendly blows and trampling, particularly at Lake Trasimene in 217 BC and at Cannae the following year.

The almost universal adoption of a butt spike for the long, thrusting spear was not only an important technological addition to the range of weapons available in the battle between the phalanxes in ancient Greece, but a major factor in amicide. The spike was generally squared in shape and was made of bronze, about eight inches in length. Not only did it act as a counter-weight to the spearhead, allowing better balance for the hoplites or later phalangites, but it also enabled the spear to be reversed in the event that the spearhead was broken off during the first shattering impact of phalanxes. As we have seen, this butt spike undoubtedly inflicted many friendly casualties, but it had a sound military purpose. As the phalanx passed over fallen enemies it was relatively easy for the hoplites to administer the *coup de grâce* by a vertical thrust with the butt spike. There is much evidence in the shape of squared holes in Grecian armour to suggest that this was a normal way to dispatch men on the ground.

Several times in the Middle Ages, perhaps at Morgarten in 1315, Roosebeke in 1382 and Morat in 1476, scenes of slaughter and amicide such as occurred at Epipolae, Cannae and Adrianople, were seen again. On a misty day at Roosebeke, a large force of Flemish rebels, commanded by Philip van Arteveld, drew up in defensive formation behind a ditch and a barricade of bushes, awaiting attack by a French army under King Charles VI and the Constable of France, Olivier de Clisson. When the French did not immediately attack, the Flemings lost patience and moved out of their position in an attempt to reach a nearby hill. This manoeuvre proved fatal to an essentially infantry army facing one strong in heavy cavalry. As the mist rose the Flemings were exposed on the march and the French cavalry advanced on both flanks and encircled them. The Flemish pikemen were now hemmed so close together that they could not even reach the French to strike at them. In the press many Flemings fell and were trampled under foot or suffocated, Philip himself dying in this way. The chronicles tell us that the Flemings were 'slain by heaps, one upon another'.

As John Keegan has demonstrated in his account of the battle of Agincourt in *The Face of Battle,* during the infantry struggle the simple art of keeping one's feet becomes a matter of life and death. In the tight scrimmage which was a feature of most ancient and medieval battles, death came quickest to the man who fell and left himself open to being trampled, suffocated or penetrated by a stabbing blow from above. Many an apparently invulnerable knight, clothed from head to toe in armour, died when a lowly archer opened his visor and stabbed him in the face.

Keegan stresses the importance of the press of sheer numbers that was a feature of the battle as the dismounted French men-at-arms came to grips with their English equivalents. Although the French mass was far larger than the English, it did not necessarily increase their chances. 'The unrelenting pressure from the rear on the backs of those in the line of battle [drove] them steadily into the weapon-strokes of the English [and denied] them the freedom for individual manoeuvre which is essential if men are to defend themselves.' The Frenchmen at

the front were thus reduced to helpless impotence, denied room
to swing their weapons or even raise their arms. It was all they
could do to keep their feet without falling. As Keegan explains,

> At Agincourt, where the man-at-arms bore lance, sword,
> dagger, mace or battleaxe, his ability to kill or wound was
> restricted to the circle centred on his own body, within
> which his reach allowed him to club, slash or stab.
> Prevented by the throng at their backs from dodging, side-
> stepping or retreating from the blows and thrusts directed
> at them by their English opponents, the individual French
> men-at-arms must shortly have begun to lose their man-
> to-man fights, collecting blows to the head or limbs which,
> even through armour, were sufficiently bruising or
> stunning to make them drop their weapons or lose their
> balance or footing. Within minutes, perhaps seconds, of
> hand-to-hand fighting being joined, some of them would
> have fallen, their bodies lying at the feet of their comrades,
> further impeding the movement of individuals and thus
> offering an obstacle to the advance of the whole column.[2]

Ironically the only person we know by name who died by
trampling and suffocation was on the English side, the Duke of
York, yet many French knights undoubtedly died in this
fashion unnoticed, trod under foot by their own side. As
Keegan demonstrates, once the front men fell, those behind
would have to try to step over them, for to step on them risked
tripping yourself. 'Once the French column had become
stationary, its front impeded by fallen bodies and its ranks
animated by heavy pressure from the rear, the "tumbling
effect" along its forward edge would have become cumulative.'
    The hacking and slashing weapons used by the men-at-arms
in medieval battles must have inflicted many injuries on their
own colleagues. There simply was not the space in a medieval
mêlée for the use of the Swiss halberd or the English bill
without there being risks for colleagues alongside or those
behind. This must have been a factor taken into account by

medieval commanders, who concluded that the offensive capability of such weapons more than compensated for the friendly casualties they caused. At Hastings in October 1066, and presumably at Stamford Bridge three weeks earlier, where there were axe-men on both sides, the English housecarls, fighting left-handed and swinging huge battleaxes with five-foot helves, cannot fail to have struck friend as well as foe. Although these men were well–trained professional warriors, space alone would have determined how easily they could have swung a weapon requiring such freedom of action. To make matters more difficult for the housecarls, they had been positioned at the front of the English line on the hill at Senlac and had stacked up behind them the mass of the fyrd, four to five thousand men who ranged in quality from the professional housecarls of the numerous English thanes to excitable shire levies, farmworkers armed with flails, spades, hoes and pitchforks. The chroniclers tell us that as they advanced up the slopes towards the English position, the Norman cavalry and infantry were struck by a hail of missiles, hurled by the fyrdmen. It must have been scarcely safer or more palatable to have stood with your back to the fyrd, as did the housecarls, while these missiles, ranging from stones to throwing axes, flew overhead than to be the Normans facing the barrage. That men fell on both sides from the blows and missiles of their comrades was inevitable in such close-quarter fighting.

Missile misdirection must have been a cause of many friendly casualties in the days before firearms became generally employed. Massed archery fire, which was a feature of all English battles of the fourteenth and fifteenth centuries, would have always involved a proportion of accidental killings. Whilst the two armies were well separated the archers could have fired with relative impunity but when the main bodies of men-at-arms became heavily engaged, as against the French at Crécy in 1346, Poitiers in 1356 and Agincourt in 1415, the archers would have had to cease firing at a time when friendly casualties exceeded an acceptable level. At that moment the archer became militarily helpless, unless he were able to turn his hand to the kind of killing that was a feature of the battle at Agincourt, where archers took on the task of dispatching fallen knights, who found it difficult to get to their feet in the muddy and slippery conditions, wearing 60 pounds' weight in armour. Nevertheless, as lightly armed and unarmoured infantrymen, they would have kept firing as long as possible, thereby risking friendly casualties, rather than lose their only advantage over the armoured pikeman or sword-and-buckler man-at-arms.

Missile misdirection was a feature of the battle of Towton in 1461, during the Wars of the Roses. Here high winds driving snow into the faces of the Lancastrians created a visibility problem that was exploited by Lord Fauconburg, one of the Yorkist leaders, who ordered his archers to fire a cloud of arrows 'indirectly' towards the unseen enemy, so that the strong wind carried them far beyond their normal range. Convinced that the Yorkists were well within range – though hidden by the blizzard – the Lancastrian archers fired back into the wind only for their arrows to fall harmlessly short or more dangerously onto the heads of their own forward troops.

A second and even more serious visibility problem occurred at the battle of Barnet in 1471. This time the problem was fog. As we have seen, the lack of uniforms created serious problems of identification, and consequently contributed to accidents on the battlefield. During the Wars of the Roses many men-at-arms and soldiers wore the colours or liveries of their lords and these emblems or devices helped identify friend and foe, even in the heat of battle.

At Barnet, misidentification had profound consequences. The problem arose because of the similarity, or so it might appear in the fog of war – literal and physical – between the banner of the Earl of Oxford, commanding the right wing of the Lancastrian army, and that of the Yorkist king, Edward IV. In the murk it was possible to mistake the radiant star of the de Veres (Oxford's standard) for Edward's device of a brilliant sun with rays. In battle men are frequently governed less by their hopes than by their fears and so as Oxford brought up his wing to the rescue of the Lancastrian centre, under the Duke of Somerset, instead of their thanks he received a volley of arrows from a flank guard of their archers. His cavalry was thrown into confusion and began to shout 'Treason! Treason!' to add to the chaos. With the enemy in front and a host of cavalry emerging from behind them bearing the devices of what looked like the Yorkist blazing sun, Somerset's men assumed the worst and panicked. As the Lancastrian centre collapsed, Somerset's men fought tooth and nail against the troops Oxford had brought to their succour, while the latter, convinced that they were being attacked by men who had changed sides and become traitors fought back equally vigorously. The beneficiaries, Edward's Yorkists, leaving Somerset and Oxford to their internecine struggle, were left with the relatively simple job of routing the Earl of Warwick's remaining reserve and winning a decisive victory.

The most celebrated example of a medieval blue-on-blue must certainly be the destruction of the Genoese crossbowmen at the battle of Crécy by their French paymasters in 1346. As the French army advanced in disorder towards the English, King Philip VI ordered his crossbowmen, 6,000 or so Genoese mercenaries under the command of Odone Doria and Carlo Grimaldi, to open the attack. The Genoese, however, were exhausted after marching for nearly 18 hours and when ordered to fire they complained that their bowstrings had been soaked by the intermittent rain. But the king was insistent and so the Genoese marched ahead of the French army and prepared to open fire on the silent ranks of the English, drawn up on a slight hill before them. The first volley from the Genoese fell short and they never managed a second because they were struck by an astonishing arrow storm of perhaps 60,000 arrows in the next 60 seconds. The Genoese panicked and tried to get out of range of the deadly English longbows, but they could not break through the serried ranks of the French cavalry. The chronicler Froissart continues the story to its ridiculous denouement: 'The French had a large body of men-at-arms on horseback to support the Genoese, and the

king, seeing them thus fall back, cried out, "Kill me those
scoundrels, for they stop up our road without any reason." '3

The result was that lines of French knights commanded by
the Duc d'Alençon charged straight into the Genoese ranks and
tried to trample them underfoot. In the words of Sir Charles
Oman, 'This mad attempt to ride down their own infantry was
fatal to the front line of the French cavalry. In spite of
themselves they were brought to a stand at the foot of the
slope, where the whole mass of horse and foot rocked
helplessly to and fro under a constant hail of arrows from the
English archery.'

As was seen at Agincourt and elsewhere, the cutting and
slashing weapons prevalent during the Middle Ages were a
major source of amicide, in view of the hand-to-hand nature of
much medieval warfare. By the fifteenth century the weapons
wielded by men-at-arms had reached a limit, imposed by the
capacity of individual warriors to wield them. The halberd of
the Swiss was a deadly weapon, but one that required too
much space to employ it. In addition, its length of six to seven
feet was not great enough to keep enemy cavalry out of killing
distance. Its replacement by the pike – 18 to 20 feet in length –
imposed on the Swiss infantry a new and even more successful
adaptation of the ancient phalanx formation. But the halberd
was not totally rejected and when the pike-phalanx failed to
make the initial breakthrough, halberdiers from the centre or
rear of the phalanx emerged, to try to cut their way through the
enemy pikes. To counter the effectiveness of the Swiss pikemen
of the fifteenth century, the Hapsburg emperor, Maximilian I,
created his own bands of German pikemen, known as the
landsknechte. These men, who often fought against the Swiss
as mercenaries, attempted to challenge the Swiss in the 'push of
pike' and wielded weapons of an even more deadly nature, like
the huge six-foot-long double-handed sword, which must have
endangered friendly forces as much as the enemy, or the
halberd, the voulge, the glaive, the partisan or the spetum, all
huge slashing and crushing weapons. In the hands of the
Doppelsöldner, the double-handed sword, known as the

Zweihänder, must have been a fearsome thing, but limited by the space necessary to wield it. In the hand-to-hand fighting that was a feature of fifteenth- and sixteenth-century battles, and before the advent of effective firearms, it is inconceivable that such weapons could have been wielded safely without a significant number of friendly casualties.

Blaise de Monluc, that grim and doughty professional, writes of a friendly-fire incident in which he was involved during the Hapsburg–Valois Wars of the early sixteenth century. During a Spanish siege of Marseilles in 1536, Monluc and a company of men had raided the flour mills at Auriol on which the Spaniards were dependent. But in trying to return to Marseilles he was mistaken for a Spaniard and brought under friendly fire:

> Coming near to Notre Dame de la Garde, the captain of the castle taking us for the enemy let fly three or four pieces of cannon at us, which forced us to shift behind the rocks. From thence we made signs with our hats, but for all that he ceased not to shoot till in the end, having sent out a soldier to make a sign, so soon as he understood who we were he gave over shooting . . .[4]

The introduction of early cannons and handguns greatly increased the incidence of friendly fire. The simple factor of unreliability meant that numerous 'accidents' became a feature of battles and sieges. The untimely death of King James II of Scotland in 1460, during the siege of Roxburgh Castle, was a pointer to the future. James was personally inspecting his pride and joy, a large, hooped bombard, to which he had given the name 'Lion'. When he tried to fire it, it exploded, showering pieces of wrought iron in all directions. A large piece of casing hit the king in the chest and killed him instantly, while other pieces wounded the Earl of Angus and several gunners standing nearby. The fifteenth century was the age of the great cannons, built to satisfy the wildest fantasies of conquerors like Charles the Bold of Burgundy or the Sultan Mahomet II, who used the greatest artillery train in the world at that time to batter the walls of Constantinople in 1453. But the lifespan of these monster guns was very short and they exacted a high price for their services in dead and mutilated gunners.

2

The Early Modern Battlefield

Friendly fire was no less a feature of seventeenth- and eighteenth-century battlefields. The infantry of the day fought in lines, usually three or four ranks deep. The problem of maintaining effective musket fire in such deep formations was such that in the latter half of the century the three-rank formation, first adopted by Frederick the Great of Prussia, became the pattern for Austrian, Russian and French armies. Even so, the danger for men in the front two ranks of having their heads blown off by the fire of the third rank men was considerable. Perhaps the most extreme example of this occurred in the English Civil War, during the siege of Basing House in 1643. The house was a powerfully fortified building and was heavily garrisoned by Royalist troops. Parliamentary regulars, supported by men from the London Trained Bands, were besieging the south face of the building when Lieutenant Archer brought up the men of the Tower Hamlets Regiment, the Green Auxiliaries of London and the redcoated Westminster troops. In spite of their colourful appearance and their impressive names, these men were closer to being militiamen than regulars and were poorly trained, with little experience on the battlefield. Once drawn up, the three lines of infantry forgot their drill completely and there followed a most 'lamentable spectacle'. The front rank had been trained to fire a volley and then retire behind the other two ranks to reload

and fire again when their turn came. Instead, in the excitement
– or stress – of battle, all three ranks fired at the same time and
the front rank was completely wiped out by the fire of the rear-
rank men. Over 70 Parliamentarians were shot down in an
instant by their fellows, one of their officers wryly commenting,
'Some on both sides did well, others did ill and deserved to be
hanged.'

Charles Carlton, in his book *Going to the Wars,* gives a vivid
picture of the experience of the English Civil Wars between
1638 and 1651 for both the soldiers and the general
population of the British Isles. The standard of military
training in England under the early Stuarts was very low indeed
and English armies were generally recruited from the worst
possible material. While planning the expedition to Cadiz in
1625 the Duke of Buckingham raised an army of 10,000 men.
But these were no better than an undisciplined rabble of
pressed men, the dregs of society, untrained, unfed and badly
clothed. One of his senior officers told the Duke that 'the army,
both by land and sea, [was] in a very miserable condition for
want of clothes', but Buckingham paid little attention. For
months the soldiers were not paid and not surprisingly many
deserted or fell sick. In August 1625, a new impressment of
2,000 men was billeted on the farmers of South Devon and
trouble immediately broke out when the farmers discovered
that their guests had no money to pay for their food. The
destitute soldiers took the law into their own hands, roaming
the countryside looking for sustenance, killing sheep and
threatening violence. When a senior officer reviewed the new
recruits he found that of the original 2,000, 200 were quite
unfit for service through ill health, 26 of them being aged over
60, four men were blind, one raving mad and a number of
others deformed or severely maimed. The corruption of the
impressment system produced many anomalies, not least of
which was sending one man who had no toes and another who
had one leg only half the length of the other. It is with no
surprise that one reads the unfortunate history of the
expedition. With such poor manpower it was impossible for its

commander, Viscount Wimbledon, to weld them into a proper military force. Once in Spain, the English soldiers became so drunk that they degenerated into a raging mob, who besieged Wimbledon in his own quarters when he tried to stop them drinking the Spanish wine, shooting each other in their madness. Eventually Wimbledon's personal bodyguard had to shoot some of their own colleagues to save the commander. When they were finally engaged in battle with the Spaniards, Wimbledon wrote, 'They made few or no shot to any purpose, blew up their powder, fled out of their order, and would hardly be persuaded to stand from a shameful flight . . . the landmen were so ill exercised that when we came to employ them, they proved rather a danger to us than a strength, killing more of our own men than they did of the enemy.

Spared the horrors of the Thirty Years' War in Germany and Central Europe, the English saw no need to professionalize their army and as a result in the early stages of their own Civil War incidents of military ineptitude, including friendly fire, were legion. Carlton records that during the First Bishop's War against the Scots the English troops were equipped with faulty muskets, some with no touch-holes or with broken stocks, poorly glued together. In a way the men got the weapons they deserved. One man accidentally fired his during the march north under the Earl of Holland and killed a gentleman's son riding nearby. Other soldiers had less reason to complain when in their drunkenness they fired musket balls through their own officer's tents. On one occasion during the Civil War, the King's own tent had a ball accidentally shot through it by an unruly soldier. As early as July 1642 the records show a soldier shot in the foot by his own gun and another shot in the back by a rear-rank man. Even in the best hands muskets were often unreliable and exacted a high cost in lives among those who used them. Lieutenant-Colonel Arthur Swayne was 'slain by his boy, teaching him to use his arms. He bid the boy aim at him (thinking the gun had not been charged) which he did only too well.' Captain John Francis, we are told, forgetting that his piece was loaded, 'shot a maid through the head and she immediately died.' During an argument with two Oxford undergraduates, Captain Stagger's musket went off accidentally, killing a woman who was shopping at a stall next door. A band of rowdy Royalist musketeers under the command of Sir Ralph Hopton were, according to Charles Carlton, responsible for two accidental killings in the space of a few days. In the first instance, a gentleman volunteer by the name of Christopher Berry was killed by 'the going off of a musket unawares', while two days later one Thomas Hollomor was killed in the same way. In February 1645, we are told that Thomas Hills was killed by his own musket and Lieutenant Vernon also killed when two balls from pistols were accidentally discharged by Captain Gibbon's groom. A Royalist officer confirmed the amount of accidental damage caused by seventeenth-century firearms when he commented, 'We bury more toes and fingers than we do men.' Misfires, it has been estimated, could reach as high as 18 per cent. Even the doughty Parliamentarian, John Hampden, succumbed to his own overloaded pistol at the Battle of Chalgrove Field.

At the siege of Farnham Church in November 1642, Parliamentarian pikemen trying to force their way into the building became so congested in the church graveyard that a number of them were impaled on the pikes of their rear-rank comrades. Yet if problems in raising good pikemen and musketeers were great, getting skilled gunners was of an entirely higher level of difficulty. And allowing unskilled louts to work with heavy guns and barrels of powder was just asking for trouble. Some of the first casualties of the Civil War were the six Royalist gunners killed when their gun burst during an early skirmish. At the siege of Limerick in 1642 Master Gunner Beech, unwisely relying on his unskilled assistants, died when they overloaded a cannon with powder. When Beech fired the gun the barrel exploded blowing him and – one hopes – the culprits to Kingdom Come.

Accidental explosions were always a danger in the age of gunpowder. Eighty barrels of powder had been stored in Torrington Church during the English Civil War, and their accidental explosion killed more than 200 of the garrison guarding the town. It was not always possible to blame a malign fate for such a fiery intervention – sometimes it was just plain stupidity. The Earl of Haddington and some of his staff officers were blown up when they called for candles and one of their servants set them up on a nearby barrel of gunpowder. One powder manufacturer, Edward Morton, died with his entire household except his wife, while mixing powder for the King. Other accidental friendly fire involved the foolish Captain James Hurcus 'hoist by his own petard' when, during the siege of Gloucester, he climbed out of his trench to see if the grenade he had just thrown had exploded. It had not, but it did once he retrieved it.

The literal fog of battle in the age of pike and musket was very severe. In a large battle of the English Civil War, such as Marston Moor in 1644, hundreds of cannon and perhaps 20,000 men firing muskets at the same time produced great billows of sulphuric smoke, reducing visibility for everyone on the field. In such conditions mistakes through misidentification were inevitable. And if one remembers that it was not until the mid-seventeenth century that identifiable uniforms became common the chances of friendly fire were very high. In May 1645, at the small battle of Crewkerne, Royalists under General Goring fought for nearly two hours against each other, entirely mistaking their colleagues for Parliamentarians. In place of uniforms identification was limited to battle signs – sometimes coloured cloth or heather – but this was so easily acquired and discarded that it was worse than useless. The Parliamentarian general, Sir Thomas Fairfax, actually rode through the entire Royalist army at Marston Moor without being recognized merely by removing the white cloth that the Parliamentarians had been wearing in their hats for identification. Slipping it in a pocket he escaped capture and simply replaced it as he regained friendly lines. This worked well as long as you remembered which side was wearing what. At Edgehill in 1642, Sir Faithful Fortescue – belying his name – deserted the Parliamentary army and led his troop of soldiers over to the King's side. But, failing to remove their 'orange tawny scarves', they were attacked by their new allies, and 18 men were cut down and killed.

The closing stages of the Duke of Marlborough's victory at the battle of Oudenarde on 11 July 1708, contained elements of such confusion between General Overkirk's Dutch troops and General Cadogan's British command that it was finally necessary to allow many of Marshal Vendôme's trapped French soldiers to escape in order to avoid a catastrophic blue-on-blue incident. Like the Athenians at Delion in 424 BC, Marlborough's allied army was in the process of encircling their opponents, and the trouble began when the troops of each encircling flank began firing on each other. To add to the confusion visibility was poor as dusk was setting in rather early for midsummer and a light rain was beginning to fall. In the deepening gloom Marlborough and Prince Eugene felt they had no alternative but to order a general ceasefire as Overkirk's and Cadogan's troops were by now thoroughly intermingled and mistakes were certain.

The only way through this maze of military incompetence was through discipline and drill, and the eighteenth century was the great age of the drillmaster. The model for all European – and American – armies was the one established by the Prussian kings. But even Prussian-trained armies had difficulties in the heat of battle. While commanders saw advantages in having the strongest, tallest and fiercest fighters in the front-line – for bayonet and hand-to-hand struggles – the taller the front line men the greater the chance of them being shot by the shorter men in the rear rank. The way out of this apparent impasse was to drill the men so thoroughly that they worked with machine-like efficiency. At least that was the theory. Moreover, provided that the troops kept in close formation the musket barrel of the third rank men was supposed to project a few inches beyond the heads of the front rank men, thus removing the danger of friendly casualties, except perhaps through deafness. However, although the first volley in a battle might have been fired in such a co-ordinated fashion, later volleys were fired in the confusion of battle. Once men began to fall from enemy musket or cannon fire, the formation became disordered and, when it was necessary to repel a cavalry charge, even the most well-drilled soldiers lost their sense of formation. It was at this point that mistakes were made. What had seemed so easy on the parade ground became unattainable even for the automatons of Frederick's Prussian army or the Austrians of Marshal Daun. Writing of poor fire discipline among eighteenth-century soldiers, Christopher Duffy says:

> In the excitement and noise of action there was no guarantee that the soldier would notice that his musket had failed to fire and in such a case he loaded round after round until five, six or more charges were superimposed. If the first round now took fire the barrel exploded like a Bangalore torpedo. The barrel was also liable to burst when the muzzle was obstructed by dirt or snow, when a bullet happened to stick in the bore or if the ramrod was left in the barrel after loading.[5]

At the battle of Kolin in 1757 an Austrian officer noted that, '. . . many a brave lad fell dead of wounds inflicted from the back, without having turned tail to the enemy . . . The surgeons were later ordered to inspect the battlefield, and it transpired that these mortal wounds had been delivered by men of the rearward ranks, who carelessly mishandled their muskets in the heat of the fire.' In fact, Kolin saw another outbreak of friendly fire which Christopher Duffy has described as a *feu de joie*. So delighted were the Austrian rank and file after defeating the Prussians and reversing a long string of defeats that many soldiers broke ranks and fired their muskets in celebration, careless of where their bullets went.

The disintegration of formal lines which was a normal consequence of the chaos of battle often followed after the first two or three volleys of the fire-fight. Even the Prussians sometimes succumbed to a 'general blazing away', so that as the adrenalin flowed men began to load faster and faster and fire with less thought as to consequences. Whereas the front rank alone was often ordered to kneel when it fired, soon men at the rear began to kneel for safety and found their own comrades blocking their aim at the enemy. At Zorndorf in 1758, retreating Prussian troops ran straight into their own rear ranks taking heavy casualties from their own infantrymen. So great was the confusion that previously well-ordered units panicked and began to fire this way and that, inflicting more casualties than the pursuing Russians.

At the battles of Parma and Guastalla in 1734, the French and Austrian front-rank infantry both fired from a kneeling position. But, no doubt feeling safer close to the ground, many of them refused to stand up to reload and it was observed that soldiers on both sides lay full length, firing 'in the manner of the Croats' from a prone position. With their aim obscured by the legs – if not the bodies – of many of their colleagues, they could not fail but to shoot many of them in the back. In the heat of battle, it may be suggested, many of the soldiers were scarcely aware of what they were doing.

The discipline thought essential in the eighteenth century was thus a two-edged weapon. Its positive virtue was to bring order to an essentially chaotic situation and give the individual soldier the certainty of being part of a much larger machine, in which he was merely a cog – and an unthinking one at that. It maximized firepower at the beginning of a battle but could do little to check the speedily developing chaos that was bound to take over as the battle progressed. Frederick the Great admitted as much to his friend Catt at the battle of Zorndorf. He first asked Catt if he had understood what was going on during the battle, to which Catt replied that he could make no sense of the various movements. Frederick reassured him, 'You were not the only one, my dear friend. Console yourself, you were not the only one.' Thus for any commander it was vital for the first two or three volleys to be administered with parade-ground precision, after which matters began to move into the realm of chance.

The obverse side of producing well-drilled automatons on the Prussian model was that, deprived of the power of initiative or flexibility, European armies of the eighteenth century were often at a disadvantage when fighting in unfamiliar conditions and against unconventional opponents. This had a significant bearing on the incidence of friendly fire, which was essentially a product of the disintegration of discipline in the infantry fire-fight. One of the best examples of this can be seen in General Edward Braddock's disastrous campaign on the Monongahela River in North America against the French and their Indian allies in 1755. Here the formalized manoeuvres and rigid linear formations of the British troops were unsuccessful against the mobility and flexibility of the woodsmen, who used conceal-ment and scattered alignments to reduce the effectiveness of enemy firepower and discipline. Nor could the officers, however brutal their application of punishment to their men, ever recapture in the forests of North America the parade-ground qualities that were the essence of European warfare.

The two regiments with which Braddock marched to Fort Duquesne were made up of relatively poor material, good enough perhaps to exchange volleys with their French counterparts, but low on initiative and, what was far worse, low on morale. The 44th Foot, under Colonel Sir Peter Halkett, and the 48th, under Colonel Thomas Dunbar, had seen no recent wartime service and were taken directly from their peacetime cantonments in Ireland. Both were to sail from Cork under strength – with just 340 men out of a usual strength of 700. In fact, the plan was for them to be made up to full strength on arrival in America, by recruiting from the colonial population. This was a very unwise plan as the new recruits would have no time to accustom themselves to European standards of discipline. In recognition of this a last-minute decision was taken to increase the British element to 500 in both the 44th and the 48th by calling in men from other regiments. The result was that Braddock's army became a dumping ground for the 'undesirables' that other regiments did not want. By the time he led his force to Fort Duquesne the cadre strength of the 44th and 48th had been dangerously weakened, with each containing nearly a third of inexperienced colonial recruits as well as a large number of misfits and difficult men from other British regiments. It was a formula for disaster and reflected the view that second-rate troops would be good enough to overcome French colonials and their Indian allies.

Before Braddock left England he was given clear instructions by the Commander-in-Chief, the Duke of Cumberland, known far from affectionately as 'Butcher' for his treatment of the Scots at Culloden in 1746, and afterwards. Dealing with a martinet like Braddock one might have felt that Cumberland's strictures about discipline were hardly needed, yet the Duke was wise enough to warn him about the panic that Indians might cause among green and undisciplined troops, particularly in North American conditions. It might have been wiser on Cumberland's part to ensure that Braddock's army did not contain such troops, notably the 400 or so colonials, many of whom would break and run at the first shot, or the 300 or more British 'undesirables' who would serve only to lower the morale of the rest of the redcoats. It was asking too much of Braddock and his officers to turn such poor material into an efficient fighting force in a matter of months. And nowhere would this deficiency be more apparent than in the quality of their fire discipline, rendering the likelihood of substantial friendly casualties a near certainty.

Braddock left Fort Cumberland on 10 June 1755, to begin his march to Fort Duquesne. Progress was slow – just 30 miles in eight days – and the 'gloomy, interminable forest' exercised a malign influence on the minds of the simple Irish lads who comprised much of the British infantry. Nor were the American recruits any happier. Most had been accustomed to life on the eastern seaboard and they had no experience of the wild country of the Ohio. At each stage of the march Braddock had maintained the tightest possible discipline, aware that there was always the chance of being ambushed by Indians. On 8 July he successfully crossed the Monongahela River at Turtle

Creek and concluded that the greatest danger was past. Only a few miles separated the British force from the French in Fort Duquesne. But with the hardest part already behind him Braddock seems to have relaxed his precautions against ambush at the very moment that the French and their Indian allies were about to strike. The British advance guard, commanded by Lieutenant-Colonel Gage, was surprised by a group of Indians, led by a French officer, who rushed down the path towards them and then fanned out into the trees on either flank. As Gage formed up his men with great precision, aligning them to the front, the Indians opened up a galling fire from behind cover. Gage replied with a series of well-ordered volleys against a virtually invisible enemy. By chance one British ball killed the French commander, Captain Beaujeu, but that was almost the last success of the day for the British redcoats. While Gage's men stood, facing the front, the Indians ran from tree to tree, working their way down both British flanks, giving the stationary redcoats the unpleasant feeling that they were being surrounded. Gage now fired his two cannons into the trees, splintering wood, bringing down branches and showers of leaves. The Indians, meanwhile, stayed behind cover and picked off the redcoats with ease. It was like no battle that the British officers and their men had ever seen or heard of. Discipline cracked and soon the redcoats took to their heels, rushing in panic back to the main part of the column. To make matters worse, the flank guards abandoned their positions and joined the scramble into the centre, allowing the Indians to enclose the British column on three sides.

The British position was very dangerous but not hopeless. Everything depended on how Braddock brought his main force into action. Gage had already made things difficult by losing control of the advance guard and allowing it to run pell-mell into the main body, spreading despondency and disorder. As one observer commented on the chaos of the British troops, 'men without any form of order but that of a parcel of school boys coming out of school'. The problem for Braddock was that his regular soldiers had been marching on either side of a long line of wagons. In order to reach the firing lines the men had to march under fire and in the chaos of battle up the side of these obstructions until they could form up at the head of the column. With Gage's men rushing back towards them, confusion and panic were almost inevitable. Moreover, the Indians had picked off many of the officers, notable by their uniforms and gorgets, so that there was no one to give orders and the men were not trained to act on their own initiative. No European army could be expected to act effectively in the event of an ambush and so, thrown back on their own resources the common soldiers tried to do two basic things: fire as soon as they could reload and find cover, both things that were absolutely anathema to the eighteenth-century method of warfare. The result of the former was that with masses of soldiers, in improvised ranks twelve deep firing anywhere, the majority of casualties would be friendly ones. With an enemy concealed behind trees the only targets were British ones and hundreds of men fell, shot in the back by their terrified colleagues. Deprived of the certainty that fire drill had given them and deaf to the entreaties of the few officers left standing, the British soldier could think of nothing but to keep firing his musket in an attempt to ward off a fearsome enemy he could not even see. As an eyewitness commented later, 'The confusion and destruction was so great, that the men fired irregularly, one behind another, and by this way of proceeding many more of our men were killed by their own party than by the enemy, as appeared afterwards by the bullets that the surgeons extracted from the wounded, they being distinguished from the French and Indian bullets by their size.'

Given the conditions and the fact that the enemy was already using cover to very good purpose, it might be supposed that the British soldiers would themselves find cover behind trees. But the idea of breaking formation was unacceptable to men drilled in the traditions of the Prussian system of Frederick the Great and his father, the 'Sergeant-Major King', Frederick William I. Braddock went purple with rage when he saw redcoats hiding behind trees, beating them black and blue with the flat of his sword, forcing them back into the open and calling them cowards. But as one of the men stoutly replied, 'We would fight if we could see anybody to fight with.' One Virginia captain ordered his company of colonials to take cover behind a fallen tree trunk only for them to be fired on by British regulars who mistook them for the French. When George Washington, one of the few officers – American or British – to survive the massacre, asked Braddock's permission to scatter 300 men among the trees and fight the enemy Indian-style, the general lost all control and threatened to run him through with his sword. Just before Braddock was himself shot and mortally wounded, presumably by an enemy ball, he is reputed to have shouted, 'We'll sup tonight in Fort Duquesne or else in hell!' Nobody could doubt Braddock's courage but even by the standards of the British army of the time his performance under extreme pressure left much to be desired. His inflexibility was to be both his own undoing and that of his entire command. Discipline was one thing but a closed mind was no adequate response to a crisis. Washington's suggestion, or indeed the advice of the Indian scout Scaroudy, that an immediate retreat was a good idea, could have saved many lives and enabled the expedition to be reorganized for a second attempt on the fort. The very worst response was simply to stand still in a clearing between the trees and allow skilled woodsmen to snipe officers and men alike at their leisure. Nor should the massing of men together, firing their muskets into the backs of their fellows, be confused with the kind of fire discipline expected of good European officers. Braddock had allowed himself to be ambushed in the first place but what was worse was that the arrangement of his column – with too little distance between the various parts and with the main infantry body divided in half by the wagons and cannons – ensured that if he were surprised he would not have any time to form his men into drill lines, after which they would simply dissolve into a frightened rabble doing far more damage to themselves than to an unseen enemy. In such a case the incidence of friendly fire would prove far heavier than on a modern battlefield where each soldier fights as an individual as well as part of a larger unit. Ironically for the young Washington, some 36 years later – as President – he ordered an American army under General St Clair into the forests against Indian opponents and suffered a similar disaster on the Wabash River. Both American regulars and militiamen succumbed to the fire of concealed Indian snipers and in return inflicted dozens of casualties on their own men. Few of the new recruits knew how to use their muskets properly and, according to one survivor, did much slaughter on the 'twigs and leaves of distant trees' as well as their fellow Americans. Like Gage's cannons, St Clair's proved impotent, defoliating the forests but inflicting no harm on the Indians. The parallel between Braddock's and St Clair's disasters was not lost on contemporaries, yet in the latter case fewer of the wounded survived long enough to have their wounds dressed and the offending bullets examined.

A combination of low morale, poor discipline and a night march put paid to the Austrian army of the Emperor Joseph II, near the village of Karansebes in Transylvania, in 1788. In almost certainly the most remarkable example of amicide in all military history, the Austrian army disintegrated and fought itself, inflicting thousands of casualties in a series of panicky fire-fights in the darkness. And at no point during this grim and unnecessary slaughter did an enemy soldier come within miles of the battlefield.

The fiasco at Karansebes was, in a sense, a natural outcome of the fracturing of the tight discipline that was the most important part of eighteenth-century European warfare. Like their counterparts in Prussia, Russia, France and England, the Austrian infantry were drilled to a point where individual thought was unnecessary and initiative impossible. If the normal conditions of engagement were to change, as for example in a night action where the drill sergeants were unable to form the soldiers up in parade-ground order, or where an enemy exploited the conditions by hiding behind trees and refusing to form up in ranks to be shot down by well-ordered musket fire, soldiers were robbed of the certainty that drill had given them and thrown back on their own abilities, which had been beaten out of them in the interests of conformity.

In the case of the Austrian troops, they were also suffering from low morale brought on by a series of unexpected setbacks at the hands of the despised Turks, as well as poor health resulting from the Emperor's absurd decision to camp in a malarial area near Belgrade. In the space of six months 172,000 of his troops had fallen ill with malaria, of whom 33,000 had died. Nevertheless, in spite of the fact that morale was low and the condition of even the supposedly fit men was questionable, when news was received that a Turkish army, under the Grand Vizier, was approaching, the Emperor marched off with just half of his army to force a battle.

The massed Austrian columns reached the town of Karansebes in good order, flanked on the march by regiments of hussars. As night fell the army crossed a bridge, watched by crowds of Wallachian peasants. Apparently some of the hussars then stopped to buy liquor from the pedlars. However, when some of the infantry, tired from a day of footslogging, left their ranks to buy some wine as well, they were driven away by the hussars. This was a job for subaltern officers, but the indiscipline was not stamped out and the disorder grew. The infantry, enraged at the arrogance of the cavalrymen, fired some shots in the air and tried to frighten them by yelling '*Turci! Turci!*' pretending they were about to be attacked. Joining in what seemed to be a bit of fun, the now drunken hussars also shouted '*Turci!*' and let off some shots as well.

What had started as a minor scuffle suddenly flared up into a major incident. The rear columns of the army were still approaching the bridge and, hearing firing and shouts, and in the darkness perhaps expecting the worst, assumed they had been ambushed and began to panic. Men began firing at each other in the darkness. But when officers started to rush up and down the columns shouting 'Halt!', the panic-stricken soldiers thought they were shouting 'Allah!' It seemed that the whole

Turkish army had fallen upon them in the darkness. Clearly something disastrous had happened. Why else was there so much firing and why were the officers shouting so desperately? Ahead they could see the flashes of gunfire and all the turmoil of battle, with horsemen riding this way and that without any kind of order. The baggage handlers and transport workers at the rear of the army, afraid of being cut off by the ambush and slaughtered by the Turks, panicked and drove their wagons through the massed troops ahead, knocking soldiers in all directions and spilling many into the waters of the river. A great roar of terror was heard and thousands of men began to stampede in the darkness.

The Emperor, himself sick, was travelling in an open carriage. The first he knew of the disaster was when he heard a sudden outburst of shouting as a flood of men, horses and wagons swept by him, throwing his carriage off the road and tipping him into the river. Although he mounted his horse and with his staff officers tried to bring order to the chaos, nobody could have rallied such broken troops. Soon, heavy fighting had broken out on both sides of the bridge. Everywhere the cry went up 'The Turks are here; all is lost; save yourselves.' Meanwhile, junior officers were actually bringing their units into action against the unseen foe. Volley fire broke out across the river, cannons fired into the inky void, while swarms of cavalry raced up and down the long columns of infantry, hacking and slashing at imaginary Turks. By the time order was restored with the morning light, it was found that the Austrian army – victim of mass hysteria – had suffered thousands of self-inflicted casualties.

3

The Nineteenth Century

During the Napoleonic Wars, with the enormous increase in the size of armies and the consequently larger battles – the battle of Leipzig in 1813 was not to be exceeded in numbers engaged until the First World War – there were inevitably many examples of accidents leading to friendly casualties in the armies of all the combatant nations. Armies were still the products of eighteenth-century drill practices and the problems of that system still lay heavily on the armies of England, Austria, Russia and Prussia, though the French were introducing more flexible methods.

Carelessness was at the root of numerous accidents causing friendly casualties or self-inflicted wounds. Peninsular War veteran John Green describes one sort of mishap that could occur as easily in battle as on the parade ground:

About three weeks before the half-yearly inspection, we began to prepare for it by going through our evolutions and manoeuvres in the large barrack-yard: towards the latter end of the time, in order that the regiment might learn to be steady, we fired with blank cartridge. A man called Malfrey, about five men from myself to the right, of Captain Gough's company, had loaded his piece five times, it missing every time. The sergeant in the rear told him he dare not fire it off; the man declared if it was full of devils he would; he did so in the next volley and the consequences were dreadful; for his musket burst into several pieces, carrying away part of his hand, and wounding or burning several men who were near him, so that this part of our line was thrown into confusion. I saw a dog run away with one of his fingers.[6]

Captain Alexander Gordon of the 15th Hussars recorded another curious accident. Engaging the French near Sahagun, in Spain, just as night was falling, Gordon heard an explosion behind him and turning back he was in time to witness one of his own troopers tumbling from his horse. Everyone around burst into laughter, in spite of the seriousness of the situation, because the trooper in aiming at a French dragoon had managed to shoot his own horse by mistake. Later, in the growing dusk, Gordon had less reason for merriment when he was attacked and almost killed by members of his own troop who recognized him only at the last moment before their swords descended upon his head.

Careless practice by the gunners was usually fatal, though not in this bizarre example related by Private Alexander Alexander in 1811:

One occurrence I witnessed here was almost incredible: a Portuguese governor touched at Colombo [Ceylon; now Sri Lanka] early in the year 1811; on the firing of the salute, Gunner Richard Clark was blown from the mouth of his gun right into the air, and alighted upon a rock at a considerable distance in the harbour, yet escaped without a bone being broken, almost unhurt. It was the most miraculous escape I ever witnessed; he was but an awkward soldier at the best; the gun of which he was No.1, went off by accident, but not just at the time of loading, otherwise the left arm, or perhaps both arms, of No.2 had been blown off, as No.2 loads and rams home, along with No.1. The gun was just loaded when she went off, through the negligence of Clark, in not spunging properly. He was not at his proper distance, like the other man, nor yet near enough to receive the whole flash. To the astonishment of everyone, he was seen in the air, the spunge-staff grasped in his right hand, the rammerhead downwards, which first struck the rock as he alighted on his breech. The rock was very thickly covered with sea weed. A party was sent down to bring up the body, as all concluded him killed upon the spot; he was brought up only stunned and slightly singed, and was at his duty again in a few days . . .[7]

Captain Cavalié Mercer, whose experience of friendly fire with the Prussians is told below, witnessed a tragic accident at the battle of Waterloo caused by the carelessness of one of his gunners. The man stumbled after loading his gun at the very moment of firing: 'As a man naturally does when falling, he threw out both his arms before him, and they were blown off at the elbows.' The man later bled to death before he could get medical attention.

If the British had their problems with training, the recruits of Napoleon's *Grande Armée* were not exempt, particularly in the early stages of their military career. In 1804, at Leghorn, a French soldier forgot to remove his ramrod during practice firing. When he fired his musket the ramrod shot out like an arrow, killing a spectator who, ironically, turned out to be a criminal wanted by the local police. Thus the incompetent recruit was rewarded rather than punished for his extraordinary example of friendly fire. An even worse incident of the same kind occurred at Valladolid, in Spain, four years later. Again blood was spilled on the parade ground while General Jean Malher was drilling a unit of raw recruits. He made the cardinal mistake of walking in front of the men when they fired their blanks. Unfortunately for Malher, no less than 18 of the recruits failed to remove their ramrods and one of them impaled him through the chest.

On the Napoleonic battlefield itself, the fog of war was all too real. Rifleman Harris, in his *Recollections,* describes the limited perspectives of a soldier of the period, with all the consequent chances of accidents or friendly fire. Harris was at the battle of Vimeiro in 1808:

> I myself was very soon hotly engaged, loading and firing away, enveloped in the smoke I created, and the cloud which hung about me from the continued fire of my comrades, that I could see nothing for a few minutes but the red flash of my own piece amongst the white vapour clinging to my very clothes. This has often seemed to me to be the greatest drawback upon our present system of fighting; for whilst in such a state, on a calm day, until some friendly breeze of wind clears the space around, a soldier knows no more of his position and what is about to happen in his front, or what has happened (even amongst his own companions) than the very dead lying around. Often I was obliged to stop firing . . . and try in vain to get a sight of what was going on.[8]

In the smoky chaos that Harris describes, accidental wounding of comrades and allies must have been widespread. In the great Napoleonic setpieces, notably those like Waterloo where infantry squares were formed to repel cavalry attacks, it was inevitable that front-rank soldiers would be raked by stray bullets from neighbouring units. Richard Holmes has cited an example from the Franco-Prussian War in 1870 where, at the battle of Rezonville, Lieutenant Devauriex of the 66th Regiment commented that his men were firing as if 'they were drunk on rifle fire during the gripping crisis.' His men were eventually reproached by the brigadier of a neighbouring regiment who gently called out to them, '*Mes enfants,* you probably do not realize it, but you are firing on my brigade.'

At the battle of Talavera in 1809, during the Peninsular War, the Spanish forces of General Cuesta, allied to Wellington's British army, were facing the French. Although the enemy were obviously well out of range, Cuesta's infantry insisted on firing a tremendous volley at them and then, apparently frightened by their own fire, panicked and fled. Before quitting the field, however, they took the opportunity to plunder the British camp, wiping out the various camp followers who were at that stage in possession of the wagons. One feels that to use the term 'amicide' in such a situation is to stretch the definition beyond reason. It is as well to add that the seriously depleted British, now outnumbered two to one after the Spanish flight, still managed to defeat the French.

Friendly casualties formed a high proportion of losses in Napoleon's battles, often as a result of the close nature of the infantry engagements. In the late evening of the first day (7 February 1807) of the battle of Eylau, the fighting between the French and Russians became so confused that both sides were guilty of firing on their own colleagues. The struggle at Eylau began as an encounter battle, with neither side intending at the outset to commit their full strength. Apparently it really began when Napoleon's baggage and his personal attendants arrived in Eylau by mistake, having not been informed that the Emperor was intending to spend the night some distance away at Ziegelhof. As the servants began unpacking what David Chandler refers to as the 'Imperial comforts', they were attacked by a Russian patrol and would have been captured or worse had not the detachment of the guards that always accompanied Napoleon's effects charged to their aid. At the sound of firing, both sides rushed up reinforcements. Marshal Soult in person descended on the Russians, who were already trying to pillage the baggage wagons, while the Russian generals, assuming that the French were occupying Eylau in force brought up more troops. Soon a fierce struggle was taking place in the streets of the town, and notably in the cemetery. Even after darkness fell the fighting continued, with many friendly casualties. Each side lost as many as 4,000 men in this part of the engagement, until the Russian General Bennigsen called his men back out of the town to occupy a nearby ridge. Further fighting flared up occasionally and throughout the night mistakes were so frequent that both sides had the greatest difficulty stopping their own men firing on each other. During the dreadful fighting in the blizzards the following day there were many further incidents of friendly fire, most significant of which was when Marshal Augureau's division was hit by a barrage fired by the French artillery, which had been blinded by the snow.

During the great battle of Wagram in 1809, French troops opened fired on their Saxon allies, whose grey uniforms were misidentified by the French as the white coats of their Austrian enemies, while in the opening stages of the battle of Busaco in Spain in 1810, Wellington's relatively inexperienced Portuguese troops – notably the 8th Infantry Regiment and a battalion of militia – fired several volleys by mistake into the ranks of their British allies. In fact, the Peninsular War was the scene of many such friendly-fire incidents. At the battle of Albuera the following year, the British 29th Foot inflicted heavy casualties on their Spanish allies. Having marched to the rescue of General Beresford and his staff, the 29th then opened a heavy fire on the dispersed French lancers. Unfortunately, their fire was wayward, and instead of hitting the French cavalry, they shattered the Spanish troops of General Zayas instead. During the bloody siege of Badajoz in 1812, there was so much confusion that the British redcoats fought a lengthy fire-fight amongst themselves. On the St Vicente bastion, members of the 5th Division first cleared away French resistance only to find themselves under fire from the British 3rd Division, which had entered the city from the other side. In the darkness, men of General Walker's brigade kept up an exchange of shots with General Picton's redcoats, until dawn revealed the true identity of their assailants.

In the opinion of the French marshal, Gouvion St Cyr, a quarter of all French soldiers who died during the Napoleonic period were killed in battle by their own artillery and musket fire rather than by those of the enemy. Exaggerated though this view may be, it is interesting to hear it repeated on the field of Waterloo by the colonel of the British 23rd Light Dragoons: 'It's always the case, we always lose more men by our own people than we do by the enemy.' We can excuse the colonel's frustration – he had just had his horse killed under him by one of the British redcoats. Nevertheless, a study of the fighting at Waterloo on 18 June 1815, enables us to tell just how widespread was the problem of friendly fire. Through the efforts of Captain William Siborne, who circularized all the British officers who had survived the battle, we are able to penetrate the fog of war and construct a view of the battle as seen from the British side. The picture thus created is one of considerable confusion and numerous accidents.

The arrival of the Prussian vanguard in the late afternoon of 18 June posed almost as much of a problem to the Duke of Wellington as to Napoleon himself. Both the Prussian artillery and the cavalry immediately joined battle with sections of Wellington's command. Captain Mercer, commanding a British horse artillery battery, recounts in his journal one of the most famous – and most amusing – examples of friendly fire ever recorded.

Mercer and his men had just helped to repulse the massive French cavalry charges on the British infantry squares ordered by Marshal Ney and were, no doubt, reflecting on a job well done, when suddenly they came under heavy fire from a most unexpected quarter. A Prussian artillery battery, wrongly identifying Mercer's guns as French, had opened fire without warning and was soon inflicting heavy damage on the British guns. As Mercer wryly commented: 'The whole livelong day had cost us nothing like this.' Exhausted as were all of the British gunners by the titanic struggle against the French, it would have been a perverse chance to succumb to one's supposed allies rather than the enemy, and Mercer soon decided to fight back, turning his guns to fire at the new 'enemy'. Hardly had he done so than a rider, dressed in the black uniform of Brunswick, rode up to his battery calling at the top of his voice, 'Ah! *mine Gott! mine Gott!* Vot is it you doos, sare? Dat is your friends de Proosiens; an you kills dem! Ah *mine Gott! mine Gott!* Vill you no stop, sare? Vill you no stop? Vat for is dis? De Inglish kills dere friends de Proosiens! Vere is de Dook von Vellington?' Mercer, with appropriate

British understatement, observed that the officer was 'raving like one demented'. He then suggested to the Brunswicker, 'that if these were our friends the Prussians they were treating us very uncivilly; and that it was not without sufficient provocation we had turned our guns on them.' Mercer agreed to stop firing for a while to see if the Prussians would recognize their error and also stop firing. However, with the German officer standing beside him, Mercer was forced to dive for cover as more Prussian shells arrived. He now prevailed on the German in no uncertain terms to ride back and tell his friends that the British would stop firing when they did – and not before. The bemused German returned to his horse, muttering, 'Oh, dis is terreeble to see de Proosien and de Inglish kill vonanoder!' Mercer relates that his problem was solved for him not by the German officer's mediation but by a further bizarre intervention. A battery of guns manned by Belgian troops whom Mercer describes as 'beastly drunk and . . . not at all particular as to which way they fired' mistook the Prussian gunners who were firing at Mercer for Frenchmen and promptly shattered them with shot and canister. As Mercer reflected, 'The Belgians . . . would have fired on us too, had we not taken pains to put them straight.'

While the above farce was taking place, on another part of the field an even more costly friendly engagement was taking place. As the first Prussian troops came up in support of Wellington's left flank, they encountered Nassauers, commanded by the Duke of Saxe-Weimar, wearing the same uniforms that they had worn only twelve months before when they had fought the Prussians as allies of Napoleon. To compound the mistake, the Duke of Saxe-Weimar, assuming that the newcomers were men from the French Marshal Grouchy's detached corps, opened fire on them and a savage fight ensued. The Nassauers who had held their defensive positions all day were now driven from the line by the Prussians, with heavy losses on both sides. Even though the tragic error was eventually pointed out the Nassau troops were too exhausted to return to their positions and took no further part in the battle.

While the Prussians were engaged in fighting both friend and foe alike, various revealing but otherwise less significant 'encounters' were taking place in other parts of the field. Siborne's research has thrown up a number of incidents which must have been replicated on battlefields throughout the eighteenth and nineteenth centuries, wherever troops fought in the open armed with muskets, bayonets, swords and lances. In the congested battlefield of Waterloo – one of the smallest in area of all Napoleonic battles, consequently producing one of the bloodiest of all such engagements – thousands of men must have fallen on both sides to friendly fire. Only discipline, in the shape of a mind-numbing regime of drill and more drill, kept soldiers of this period from cutting swaths through their own ranks before ever coming to grips with the enemy. And in such a hard-fought battle as Waterloo and with so many different nationalities present in Wellington's army – British, Portuguese, Belgian, Dutch and men from Hanover, Brunswick and other principalities – it is hardly surprising that discipline faltered and accidents occurred.

With the help of Siborne we know that, in the last stages of the battle with discipline stretched beyond its limits and the French army disintegrating, many accidental assaults took place in the growing darkness. Colonel Hay of the 16th Light Dragoons was shot by British infantry, while the 10th Hussars were fired on by British artillery who had been firing at the same French cavalry that the hussars were pursuing. The 12th Light Dragoons clashed briefly and – fortunately at the cost of a single injury – with the 1st Hussars of the King's German Legion. In the confusion of a stricken field, the 16th Light Dragoons only narrowly averted clashing with the same body of German hussars in the growing darkness. A little earlier – though still late in the day – the 18th Hussars of Vivian's brigade clashed with Prussian cavalry near La Belle Alliance and some of the latter were sadly cut down in the confusion. Nor were the infantry guiltless. As the 52nd Regiment – part of Adam's Infantry Brigade – was advancing at the end of the battle, it encountered two or three squadrons of the 23rd Light

Dragoons and, supposing them to be French, fired into them, unhorsing Lieutenant-General Lord Seaton, who came out of the incident unscathed and wrote amiably of it to Siborne in 1843. In the clashes between British and French horsemen, many accidental woundings took place. The crowding together and intermingling of enemy and friendly horsemen, combined with the nature of the weapons employed, heavy sabres or lances, both of which required space to be employed successfully, made friendly casualties inevitable. As Trooper Tomkinson of the 16th Light Dragoons recorded, 'Lieutenant Beckwith . . . stood still and attempted to catch this man on his sword; he missed him and nearly ran me through the body. I was following the man at a hard gallop.'

Hardly a generation after the Napoleonic Wars, the problems of controlling troops in a night operation were well illustrated in an incident during the French invasion of Algeria. The French had landed at Sidi Feruch and had established a camp on the beaches. However, at two o'clock in the morning, the sound of a loose horse running in front of the line alerted a sentry who fired wildly into the darkness and sounded the alarm. Soon hundreds of men were awake and rushing to get their muskets. In a matter of moments there was a blaze of musketry all along the beach that lasted for more than fifteen minutes. In the confusion four men were killed and ten others wounded, although there was no sign of any enemy troops. It had been a panic about nothing.

During the First Afghan War of 1838–42, Colour-Sergeant John Clarke of the 17th Foot remembers an accident that occurred on the march to Kabul:

> About the fifth day's march (we were on the advance guard) our artillery came galloping up to us about daylight.
>
> We halted to let them pass, and they told us there was a battery on the plain and they were to take it. They went through a little pass to Paradise Valley. When we got to

the pass we heard a loud report and thought they were engaged, but when we got through nobody was in sight but our own artillery. We hastened up to them and found a beautiful half-moon battery formed round the pass.

The report we had heard was caused by one of our artillerymen, who had got on the ammunition-box and was lighting his pipe when a spark had got into some loose powder. This had exploded and blown him away.[9]

The incidence of friendly casualties was notably high during the American Civil War. Large numbers of eager civilian recruits needed to be taught the rudiments of the military profession quickly and this resulted in alarming gaps in some men's knowledge. Benjamin Andrews of the 4th Connecticut Infantry remembers how little training the average Union soldier had before facing the dreadful person of General 'Stonewall' Jackson and his Confederates:

At last we had formed line, and the Colonel, probably on the grounds that more battles are won by marching than by fighting, started us, raw levies, with six long miles and probably a battle before us, off on a double quick. We ran a mile, puffing, sweating, straining our eyes to see that foe we so longed to annihilate. 'Halt!' What for? Why, the line officers have held a council of war while trotting along on their horses, and have concluded that if we are to fight it maybe well to have our muskets loaded. No one had thought of it before. We had supposed that our brave Colonel, in whose skill as a tactician we had the most unhesitating confidence, intended on meeting Jackson, to charge with the bayonet. We concluded that he now alters his mind. At all events he commands to 'load'. But we have no instructions in loading. Which end of the cartridge shall go downwards? About a third of the men, reasoning *a priori* that the bullet was the main thing, put it in first. A good number of those who did not do this failed to tear the cartridge paper. Several put two or three

cartridges in; some even more. It was the work of a week
to empty these muskets. Having loaded and breathed we
began to race again.[10]

Even as late as the battle of Gettysburg in 1863, faulty
loading was a feature of the fire discipline. After the fighting
had ended Union troops tried to clear the battlefield, finding
there an incredible 27,574 abandoned muskets and rifles, of
which 24,000 were loaded, 12,000 loaded twice, 6,000 loaded
between three and ten times and one boasted 23 charges and
no balls, little less than a bomb rather than a firearm. Every
kind of curious combination of ball and powder charge had
been attempted, including one musket loaded with 22 balls and
66 buckshot. Many had the ball behind the charge and could
not have fired whatever the soldier did. Paddy Griffith in his
book *Rally Once Again* has concluded that some 9 per cent of
all muskets were misloaded. According to Griffith, 'a very high
proportion of infantry weapons must indeed have become
inoperative in combat due to faulty handling.' And a
consequence of this was that many friendly casualties were
suffered when these muskets exploded or misfired, as so many
of them obviously did in the heat of battle.

The real problem with Civil War infantry fire always lay
in the most rudimentary aspects of maintaining the men's
concentration on their job. In combat, fire would usually
be delivered from a line two ranks deep, with the soldiers
in each rank almost touching each other's elbows. They
would naturally jostle and shove each other as they drew
their ramrods and pushed home their cartridges. Anyone
in the second rank would have to lean forward to fire
through the space between two men in the front rank, who
would receive a flash and a cloud of smoke in their eyes
and a numbing explosion at the level of their ears.[11]

At the first battle of Bull Run (First Manassas) in 1861 the
new recruits on both sides found it immensely difficult to

maintain tight discipline. One Union soldier remarked, 'The men were a good deal excited. Our rear rank had singed the hair of the front rank, who were more afraid of them than of the Rebels.' A Confederate soldier sees things in very much the same way:

> A battle is entered into mostly in as good order and with as close a drill front as the nature of the ground will permit, but at the first 'pop! pop!' of the rifles there comes a sudden loosening of the ranks, a freeing of selves from the impediment of contact, and every man goes to fighting on his own hook; firing as and when he likes, and reloading as fast as he fires . . . A battle is too busy a time, and too absorbing, to admit of a good deal of talk. Still you will hear such remarks as 'Looky here, Butler, mind how you shoot; that ball didn't miss my head two inches . . .'[12]

General Sherman noted that during the Civil War perfect fire discipline in battle was hardly ever attainable:

> Very few of the battles in which I have participated were fought as described in European text-books, viz., in great masses, in perfect order, manoeuvring by corps, divisions, and brigades. We were generally in wooded country, and, though our lines were deployed according to tactics, the men generally fought.[13]

During the battle of Seven Pines in 1862 the woodland setting contributed to much confusion on both sides. Units would appear from thick foliage and encounter 'enemies' at close range. This being the case it was rarely possible to make an early identification of the opposition and it was often impossible to separate two friendly units before blood had been spilled.

The 24th Michigan Regiment, formed in July 1862, was rushed into action before it had received proper training. On the only occasion it was allowed a target practice, three men were wounded in 'accidents' and one died of a heart attack. In

Paddy Griffith's opinion, 'Live fire was almost as dangerous to the men who were delivering it as it was to the enemy.' If this standard of fire discipline is to be considered as typical of the hastily raised Union forces, it is not difficult to imagine why friendly-fire casualties were so heavy in the often confused fighting that typified the Civil War period. As Griffith has demonstrated, 'An almost total lack of target practice meant than many rifles were misloaded in combat and that the finer points of long-range accuracy were neglected or ignored. The close-order drill of the day also meant that the soldier in battle was subjected to a barrage of sights, sounds and emotions which must have distracted him powerfully from his task.' It was not possible – either in the United States or in Europe – to transform an essentially civilian population into a military one without a prolonged period of training. The United States, like Great Britain, had a fear of standing armies and preferred to raise her military forces when the need arose. Thus the number of well-trained regulars available in the USA or in Britain was tiny when compared with the conscripted mass armies available in France and Germany. The transformation of American civilians in 1861–2 into soldiers resembles the creation of Britain's first civilian army by Lord Kitchener in 1914–15. The raw material was good but the process of metamorphosis was often a long one, and was not achieved without numerous hiccups, in terms of friendly fire and camp 'accidents'.

John Pullen's *The Twentieth Maine* describes several of these camp accidents, even late in the war, when one might have assumed that the regiment had overcome such teething troubles. During the winter of 1864 Pullen describes a lowering of discipline through inactivity. Scuffles were taking place over slight or imagined insults, drunkenness was more common and there was a general air of restlessness. In this atmosphere soldiers become careless. One private soldier, we are told, was shot through the head by his tentmate, who aimed what he believed to be an empty rifle at him and pulled the trigger. In the last few days of the war a careless wagoner accidentally 'discharged a carbine'. The bullet apparently passed through several tents before killing Lieutenant George Wood, a brave officer who had fought with the regiment all the way through the war.

At First Bull Run Confederate Brigadier-General John Imboden nearly paid with his life for his carelessness. As he wrote:

> Lieutenant Harman and I had amused ourselves training one of the guns on a heavy column of the enemy, who were advancing towards us, in the direction of the Chinn house, but were still 1,200 to 1,500 yards away. While we were thus engaged, General Jackson rode up and said that three or four batteries were approaching rapidly, and that we might soon retire. I asked permission to fire the three rounds of shrapnel left to us, and he said, 'Go ahead.' I picked up a charge (the fuse was cut and ready) and rammed it home myself, remarking to Harman, 'Tom, put in the primer and pull her off.' I forgot to step back far enough from the muzzle, and, as I wanted to see the shell strike, I squatted to be under the smoke, and gave the word 'Fire'. Heavens! what a report. Finding myself full twenty feet away, I thought the gun had burst. But it was only the pent-up gas, that, escaping sideways as the shot cleared the muzzle, had struck my side and head with great violence. I recovered in time to see the shell explode in the enemy's ranks. The blood gushed out of my left ear, and from that day to this it has been totally deaf.[14]

The unintentional killing of officers, as against the deliberate 'fragging' (see pp. 259–265), has always been a feature of large-scale military engagements. With the advent of musketry and long-range cannon the commander, whatever protection he might have from bodyguards or aides, became as vulnerable as any other man on the field. By his uniform or by the elevated position he occupied to get a better view of the fighting, he might even be more noticeable to the enemy. Yet it has been in the metaphorical 'fog of war' that commanders have succumbed to the fire of their own, sometimes disorientated, troopers. During the American Civil War several prominent officers were shot by their own side, by far the most famous of whom – an irreplaceable loss to the Confederacy – was General Thomas 'Stonewall' Jackson, the most renowned of Robert E Lee's lieutenants. Lee always claimed that it was Jackson – his 'strong right arm' – who contributed most to his greatest victories. Certainly with the death of Jackson, Lee seemed to lose his capacity to virtually hypnotize Union commanders. In 1863, at the battle of Chancellorsville, Jackson had literally run rings round the Union commander 'Fighting Joe' Hooker and had laid the foundation for Lee's most perfect victory. Yet for Lee, Chancellorsville was a Pyrrhic victory when news reached him that Jackson had been mortally wounded by his own men.

One of Jackson's ADCs, the Reverend James Power Smith, was with him when he suffered his fatal accident and wrote a full account of what happened. About a mile to the west of Chancellorsville, Jackson found his front-line troops little more than half a mile from the Federals. It was dusk and in the poor light, made even worse by the dense thickets of under-growth, Jackson was finding it difficult to align correctly the troops of General A P Hill's division. With just two or three of his staff and a small group of couriers and signallers, Jackson rode down the turnpike in the direction of the Federal lines before encountering their pickets and turning back towards his own lines. It was this turn backwards that was to prove fatal. In the growing darkness all the Confederate troops could identify was a body of horsemen riding towards them from the direction of the Federal lines. Some of the Confederate troopers opened a ragged fire at Jackson and his band and two of the riders, an engineer officer, Captain Boswell and a signaller, Sergeant Cunliffe, were shot dead as they approached. Jackson and the survivors veered away only to be hit by a second volley of fire from a company of General Pender's North Carolina Brigade. Jackson was hit by three separate balls, one through the palm of his hand, another through his left wrist and the third through his left upper arm, splintering the bone from shoulder to elbow. His horse turned away from the fire and rushed off, dragging the wounded general into thick bushes.

Before Jackson could fall from his horse he was caught by a signals officer, Captain Wilbourn, and gently lowered to the ground. Almost at once General Hill rode up with his staff and dismounted at his prone leader's side. The Reverend Smith staunched the flow of blood from the wound in the upper arm but it was very difficult to move Jackson from such a forward position to an ambulance. Federal guns were sweeping the whole area with canister shell and it was impossible for the litter bearers to carry the general out of danger. Even in his desperate state Jackson did not forget his responsibilities. When General Pender remarked that he would have to withdraw his troops to re-form them, the injured commander replied, 'You must hold your ground, General Pender; you must hold your ground, sir.' As the Reverend Smith observed, it was his last command on a battlefield and it was in keeping with his nickname of 'Stonewall'. Once Jackson reached an ambulance he was taken back to a field hospital where his good friend, Dr Hunter McGuire, amputated his left arm, just below the shoulder. At first it appeared that the general would make a complete recovery and a dispatch was sent to the Confederate Commander-in-Chief Robert E Lee, informing him that his 'strong right arm' was wounded. Lee apparently received the news 'with profound grief' and replied, 'Could I have directed events, I should have chosen, for the good of the country, to have been disabled in your stead. I congratulate you upon the victory which is due to your skill and energy.' Typically, Jackson preferred to attribute the victory to God's work rather than man's.

At first the doctors were hopeful of Jackson making a complete recovery, but in spite of every effort pneumonia set in and, on 10 May 1863, the great Stonewall Jackson died. His last words, apparently, were 'Let us pass over the river, and rest under the shade of the trees . . .'

The death of Jackson was a blow to the whole Confederacy. Had he been at Lee's side at the battle of Gettysburg, a

Confederate victory would have been probable on the first or second day of fighting. But for Jackson's untimely end the whole history of the United States might well have taken a different course. Nor was Jackson the only Confederate general to suffer at the hands of trigger-happy Confederate troops. During the Wilderness fighting, on 6 May 1864, General 'Old Pete' Longstreet – another of Lee's most able lieutenants – was severely wounded by friendly fire. Longstreet was riding with Brigadier-General Micah Jenkins at the head of his brigade, when they encountered units from Major-General William Mahone's division. Failing to identify each other as friends a ragged exchange of fire took place between Jenkins's men and Mahone's, during which General Jenkins was killed and General Longstreet seriously wounded.

The 20th Maine were also plagued by that bane of all modern infantry – 'short' firing by friendly artillery. At the battle of Ball's Bluff, one of the soldiers, Private William Livermore, wrote, 'The shells from our batteries would go so near our heads it seemed as though it would take the hair off from my head, and the air was full of shells and some of our own burst overhead and wounded some of our own men.' But Livermore seems to have taken this friendly fire in his stride and expresses no criticism of the Union gunners. Yet at this stage many of the artillerymen deserved more than just verbal criticism. A few days later the 20th Maine was again the victim of short firing. During a bombardment of Confederate positions, one artillery battery had set its fuses so badly that its shells were bursting after completing only 50 per cent of their flight. The result was that they were bursting as they passed over the men from Maine and many of them were wounded by a shower of metal. Eventually, a delegation was sent back to reason with these gunners and, in the words of John Pullen, the guns 'fell silent with dramatic suddenness.'

The problem of undisciplined artillery fire was a feature of the land fighting during the war between the United States and Spain in 1898. The high number of friendly-fire incidents that occurred was a reflection of the chaotic nature of the conflict and the poor training of the troops on both sides. The main land campaign took place in Cuba between the numerous but poorly motivated Spanish troops and the exuberant but undisciplined Americans. As a result it was remarkable for some of the grossest inefficiency ever witnessed in the history of the American army.

The Spanish capital on Cuba, Santiago, was protected by strong entrenchments on San Juan Hill, which the approaching US troops would need to assault before they could advance on the city. On 1 July, two divisions under Generals Sumner and Kent moved through thick jungle towards the base of San Juan Hill. On a hill near El Pozo Captain Grimes, commanding the US artillery, established his batteries to support the infantry assault. As he did so he attracted a large crowd of tourists and onlookers. Grimes, an incompetent gunner to say the least, was still using black powder and his guns produced so much smoke that the Spanish counter batteries were able to locate him easily and force him to stop firing. As Walter Millis wrote,

> Congress had neglected to provide our artillery with the modern smokeless powder, and as the first great clouds of white smoke billowed forth from El Pozo, the Spaniards very naturally took them as a target for their own artillery. The cameras recording the first 'shot' were still clicking and an interested crowd of people from the regiments below was just gathering upon the hill to see what was going on, when the first answering shell sang over the battery and burst on the slope behind it, extinguishing a number of Cubans and wounding several Rough Riders who were in the farmyard below.[15]

For a while the American infantry advanced peacefully through the jungle but when they reached the bottom of San Juan Hill, they faced a daunting prospect of having to attack a heavily entrenched enemy without artillery support. Fortunately, a battery of Gatling guns (a hopper-fed multiple-barreled machine-gun operated by turning a crank which in turn caused the barrels to rotate, each firing as it came into position) commanded by Lieutenant Parker opened fire on the Spanish positions, causing many of the defenders to fling down their weapons and take to their heels. Seeing this the American infantry now stormed up the slopes of San Juan Hill. The scene was set for Captain Grimes to make a serious contribution to the American victory. From El Pozo he had been unable to follow the fighting very well and so was unable to identify the figures who began to appear on the green slopes of the hillside as blue dots. Wrongly assuming them to be Spaniards, he decided to join the battle. His guns were trained on the slopes of San Juan Hill and opened fire with farcical consequences. As Captain Allen of the 16th Infantry wrote:

> The advance continued steadily and without a pause until we were on the steep slope near the crest, two-thirds of the way up, when our artillery fire coming from our rear became dangerous . . . Some shells struck the slope between me and the crest . . . there arose at the foot of the slope and in the field behind us a great cry of 'Come back! Come back!' The trumpets there sounded 'Cease-firing', 'Recall' and 'Assembly'. The men hesitated, stopped, and began drifting down the steep slope . . .[16]

One officer had the initiative to wave his hat at the gunners, whereupon they fired and wounded him. It took some time before the artillery could be silenced so that the advance could continue. What would have happened had the Spaniards counter-attacked at this moment and recaptured the hill it is perhaps futile to ask. But Captain Grimes and his guns had contributed not only to friendly casualties – light as these were – but to repulsing a major attack by his own troops on a vital enemy target.

One of the most remarkable incidents of friendly fire in naval history occurred on 22 June 1893, when Admiral Sir George

Tryon, commander of the British Mediterranean Fleet, was cruising off the coast of Lebanon. Out of the blue – almost literally – Tryon ordered the fleet to undergo a manoeuvre which resulted in the sinking of his own flagship, HMS *Victoria*, by the ram of HMS *Camperdown*, commanded by his second-in-command, Rear-Admiral Sir Albert Markham. This famous incident, which revolved around the personalities of commanders and their deputies, contained elements that are central to an understanding of many friendly-fire incidents. It confirmed that human errors are at the root of most military disasters which might otherwise be explained away in terms of technological failures.

Vice-Admiral Sir George Tryon, was a tall, massive-chested, black-bearded, colossus of a man, who had a mind that was constantly at work trying to find ways to perfect the performance of the ships and men of Her Majesty's Mediterranean Fleet. Tryon conducted his work so skilfully as to prove every admiral arrayed against him his inferior. He had performed brilliantly in the 1888 annual manoeuvres, when he had made complete fools of the main Channel Fleet and the admirals leading it and that really got him the Mediterranean Command. He was immensely popular with the British public because many amateur strategists had followed the 1888 manoeuvres in the newspapers in great detail. As a result he was a national hero. Adopting the part of commander of the 'French' fleet, Tryon was supposed to be overwhelmed by his seniors commanding the British Channel Fleet. Instead he had shown the 'Nelson touch', escaped from his pursuers and pretended to attack towns and cities around Britain, inviting the mayors to dinner instead of having their cities levelled. It was all very gentlemanly but he was making a point about Britain's vulnerability to the French and the result was incorporated into the 1889 Naval Defence Act.

The people who served with Tryon absolutely idolized him but he was not a man to be crossed and people found it difficult to get on to his intellectual wavelength. He was something of a butterfly, jumping from subject to subject as a lot of brilliant thoughts came flying out and it was the job of his staff to try to interpret and implement these great bursts of vision. He was a very tall man and when he was angry his eyes would knot together: he was known as Cyclops because of this great eye and he had a temper when things did not go his way; he also had no truck with subordinates who could not keep up with his intellectual capabilities and his operational demands.

Tryon's second-in-command, Rear-Admiral Markham, was an example of somebody whose peacetime attributes were exceptional. He was a very strict officer – punctilious, correct, always good at looking after his men, good at polishing and painting and supervising ship's performance. Yet he had an inferiority complex. Markham had been one of the admirals whom Tryon had made a fool of in the 1888 manoeuvres. Having been a victim of George Tryon once already he was afraid to cross his chief again. In 1891, nobody in the Royal Navy, however senior they might be, dared to question the orders of a man like Tryon. To do so would be to risk public humiliation.

Admiral Tryon had not needed wealth or family connections to start his career as did so many senior officers in both the army and navy in Victorian Britain. He had risen to the top through sheer ability. His intellect allowed him to dominate everyone around him and, as another officer wrote, 'Most people felt no use arguing with George Tryon, and that it was better to acquiesce quietly.' But this very quality was to bring ruin on him. Tryon did not want obsequious subordinates; he was looking for men to show drive and initiative in the way that he always had. Instead he found the majority of officers in the navy were afraid of his reputation, so that none dared to stand up to him or ever suggest that he could be wrong. Most of the officers who served with him simply wanted him to tell them what to do. So while Tryon tried to test them and develop their skills, they were afraid to show how inadequate they were. Tryon's greatest problem, of which he was only partly aware, was that the officer who most felt this way was none other than his second-in-command, Markham, a man who has been described as 'anxious, conforming, hidebound, conventionalist, dedicated to staying out of trouble and not displeasing his superiors'. In a war, this situation would probably have proved fatal to one or the other, but during peacetime it should have been possible for the unhealthy relationship to continue until one or other of the senior men was put out to pasture. But Tryon was not content to live peacefully in peacetime. For him, periods of peace were merely rests between wars, and should be used to hone to perfection the mighty weapon that their Lordships of the Admiralty had left in his charge.

On taking up command of the Mediterranean Fleet – the strongest naval weapon in the world in 1891 – Admiral Tryon set about introducing new ideas and challenging existing systems. Inevitably, he met not opposition but inertia. Accepted methods had been comfortable; Tryon was never comfortable. Sir Geoffrey Phipps Hornby observed that under Tryon, there was none of the friendly banter than used to characterize the Mediterranean Fleet in years gone by. Part of the problem was that Tryon was attempting to improve the speed and efficiency with which his ships manoeuvred, obviating the need for cumbersome flag signals. His own 'TA' method involved less a system for signalling than of simply 'follow my leader'. As Tryon wrote that he had long been impressed with the importance of exercising a fleet from the point where the drill books leave off. He believed that a fleet could be manoeuvred without having to wait for a series of signals. But this was deeply worrying for his subordinates, who would now have to manoeuvre their ships without signals from the flagship. All Admiral Tryon would do would be to raise the signal 'TA' and the rest of the fleet would then conform with the movement of the flagship. What would happen if, in action, the flagship was disabled, Tryon does not seem to have considered. Conservatives at the Admiralty were outraged and *The Times* declared that the new system was 'unsound in theory and perilous in practice'. But, although they sniped at him from a distance, nobody dared to tell Tryon that he was wrong. Prominent among Tryon's secret critics was Rear-Admiral Markham, who lacked the courage to admit as much to his face. In fact, Markham's thirteen months serving with Tryon had been little less than a nightmare. On manoeuvres

Markham simply could not deal with the constant tests set by
Tryon to keep the fleet on its toes. And if Markham refused to
express doubts to his superior, Tryon was quick to criticize his
second-in-command in public. Tryon was not a man to suffer
fools gladly, and in his view Markham was a fool.

On 22 June 1893, the eleven iron-clad battleships of the
Mediterranean Fleet left harbour at Beirut and put to sea on
manoeuvres. The sea was as calm as a millpond and the heat
was oppressive. Tryon was feeling lethargic after a heavy lunch
and the officers and men aboard the flagship *Victoria* went
about their duties as if the five days' leave they had spent in the
souks of Beirut needed to be cleared from their systems by a
short, sharp shock. The *Victoria* was a brand new battleship,
just three months old. Her massive guns – which supposedly
made her the most powerful ship afloat – were feared more by
her own crew than the enemy. When they fired her main
armament the blast often buckled the deck and damaged the
bridge, as well as playing havoc with the paintwork. In many
respects the *Victoria* and her sister, the *Sans Pareil*, were
unloved, especially by their own crews.

It is safe to surmise that none of this was passing through
Admiral Tryon's mind that warm summer's afternoon off
Beirut. Instead he was thinking of setting the captains and
crews of his fleet a really difficult test. He told Staff
Commander Thomas Hawkins-Smith that he would form the
fleet into columns of two divisions, six cables apart, and
reverse the course by turning inwards. Hawkins-Smith
immediately felt uneasy: six cables was just 1,200 yards, and if
the two columns were to turn inwards that would surely be too
close for comfort. Was this a deliberate mistake to see if he was
paying attention? He plucked up courage to say that this would
require at least eight cables. Tryon thought for a moment and
then agreed. After a few moments Tryon's flag-lieutenant,
Lord Gillford, came into his cabin and Tryon told him to make
the signal. 'Form columns of divisions line ahead, columns
disposed abeam to port. And make the columns six cables
apart.' To confirm the signal he handed Gillford a scrap of

paper on which he had scribbled the single figure 'six'. The flag-lieutenant left without questioning the order and set about preparing the signal. Within minutes the flags were fluttering and had been acknowledged by the other battleships of the fleet. Looking up from his work in the fore-bridge Hawkins-Smith experienced a moment's uncertainty – that was the wrong signal. He hurried over the Gillford to check if there was a mistake, as the admiral had said the columns were to be eight cables. But Gillford showed him the scribbled figure on the paper to confirm that Tryon had specifically ordered six cables. Hawkins-Smith was in a quandary. On the strength of his earlier conversation with the admiral he sent Gillford back to ask Tryon to confirm 'six cables'. Tryon was not pleased to be cross-examined by a subordinate and told Gillford brusquely to leave it at six cables.

Gillford was now thoroughly alarmed himself. A simple calculation told him that the combined turning circles of ships like the *Victoria* and the *Camperdown* – the flagship of Rear-Admiral Markham, leading the other column – was eight cables or 1,600 yards. The only answer must be the unthinkable – Tryon must have made a mistake, confusing the radius of the turning circle with its diameter. The manoeuvre he had ordered was impossible. Captain Archibald Maurice Bourke, the *Victoria*'s commander, saw immediately that the signal was wrong. As the ship's captain, its safety was his concern rather than Admiral Tryon's. Yet, as Bourke later commented, 'open criticism of one's superior is not consonant with true discipline,' and so he chose to do nothing but to grit his teeth and pray. Two of the most powerful battleships afloat, armed with ship-killing rams, had just been ordered to turn towards each other in such a way that a collision was inevitable. At least three men on the *Victoria* were quite aware of this, along with others presumably on board the *Camperdown* at the head of the parallel column of ships. In a military sense each commander was holding a loaded pistol to the head of the other and both were content to fire rather than admit that a mistake had been made. It was an extraordinary situation – amicide in slow motion and by common consent.

The great fleet was now travelling at about nine knots towards the coast of Syria and a turn of some kind would have to take place soon before the battleships ran aground. Tryon was growing angry; why had the *Camperdown* not begun to turn yet? Markham was holding up the entire manoeuvre. Tryon ordered a signal to be made to *Camperdown*, 'What are you waiting for?' It was a public rebuke and Markham would have to obey whatever the consequences. Markham was puzzled but clearly presumed that Tryon intended his column to turn first. But he was wrong and as the *Camperdown* began to turn so did the *Victoria*. Trying to conceal his anxiety Bourke remarked to the admiral that they had better do something, or they would be too close to the *Camperdown*. Tryon ignored him, absorbed in the awesome potential of his own flawed geometry. Bourke's voice began to rise slightly, reminding him of the danger and asking to go astern. Tryon's voice was no more than a whisper, 'Yes, go astern.' 'Full speed astern both screws,' bellowed Bourke, but he knew that it was far too late now – a collision was inevitable.

All Bourke could do now was to try to lessen the impact of the collision by ordering the watertight doors to be closed. It might do something to save the ship. As the *Camperdown* headed towards the *Victoria*, for a few seconds Tryon and Markham were within hailing distance and Tryon shouted through cupped hands 'Go astern, go astern.' He should have saved his breath, for at that moment the *Camperdown*'s huge ram ripped nine feet into the *Victoria*'s side, forcing her 70 feet sideways and wounding her fatally.

As the two battleships staggered under the impact, a yeoman passed a message to Tryon from the *Camperdown*. It was Markham's reply to his signal demanding to know why *Camperdown* had not begun her turn. It was simple: 'Because I did not quite understand your signal.' Less than fifty yards away Markham and his bridge officers were gazing in fascinated horror at the damage they had just inflicted on the fleet flagship. Tryon bellowed across, 'Go astern, go astern. Why didn't you . . .?' there was really nothing more to say but they were not quite Tryon's last words. 'It is all my fault,' he was later heard to mutter.

While time seemed to stand still on the flagship, the other battleships of the fleet had begun lowering boats to rescue Tryon's crew but the admiral would not give up his ship and angrily he sent the boats back. It was his second mistake of the day. He believed that the *Victoria* had not been struck in a vital spot: he was wrong. The flagship's low forecastle was already under water and the sea was pouring into the ship through every open porthole and door. The *Victoria* keeled to starboard and water poured in through the turret apertures. Within five minutes of impact the bows had sunk some fifteen feet. Everything was happening too quickly and many of his men were going to die because he had rejected the offers of help. In just four more minutes the *Victoria* began to slip beneath the waves. The men in the boiler rooms, receiving no orders to abandon their stations or even stop the engines, were drowned to a man. One lucky survivor was John Jellicoe – then a lieutenant but later Commander-in-Chief of the Grand Fleet in the First World War – who had been in the sick bay on the *Victoria* with Malta fever and had escaped in his pyjamas.

Admiral Tryon made no attempt to save himself. We can only guess what he was thinking as his flagship sank and his whole world came crashing down about his ears. He must have realized that the fault was his alone and he had no wish to outlive the disgrace. Hawkins-Smith was one of the last men to see him, standing 'perfectly calm and collected to the last' and dying 'as he had lived, a brave man'.

With Admiral Tryon, 357 officers and men died as the result of an inexplicable disaster on a sea as calm as glass and in perfect visibility. Yet the disaster was not really inexplicable: it was the result of a simple error in calculation made by a man who considered himself incapable of error. What is more difficult to understand is why Tryon seemed unprepared to admit his mistake and correct it, thereby preventing a disaster and the deaths of so many of his men. The exchanges with his officers over the figures 'six' and 'eight' indicate that Tryon did not enjoy being reminded of this first mistake and preferred to risk the consequences of it, whatever those might be, rather than admit to younger and more junior men, that their commander was not perfect. The only conclusion that can be drawn is that Tryon suffered from an ego of such staggering proportions that it could not admit even a semblance of doubt. There was a perpetual risk that the collapse of such a brittle persona, built on a platform of other men's fears and adulation, would be accompanied by disaster. That the disaster was of such proportions was both a misfortune and a disgrace. Modern psychiatric selection procedures might have warned against allowing a man of Tryon's character to control a powerful fleet, the lives of hundreds of men and the destiny of an entire empire.

After holding a sombre funeral ceremony at sea, Markham ordered the fleet to return to Malta. The court martial – inevitable in such a case – reached the decision that Sir George Tryon had been responsible for the disaster but also regretted that Markham had not questioned the fatal order more effectively before beginning the turn which led to the collision. This did not go down well in military circles. The Army Commander-in-Chief, the Duke of Cambridge, complained that, 'A good deal has been said of late as to freedom being given to inferiors to question and disobey the orders of a superior officer. Discipline must be the law, and must prevail. It is better to go wrong according to orders than to go wrong in opposition to orders.' Markham never held another important command and the Admiralty made it clear that they felt the *Camperdown* had been ineptly handled during the crisis. But none of this helped to restore the reputation of Sir George Tryon. His one mistake had been enough to destroy a career of unparalleled achievement. Command is a lonely business and nobody will ever know what was in Tryon's mind when he gave the order for the manoeuvre that killed him. We can only agree with a comment made by Admiral Kerr at the time: 'Sir George Tryon was not a person who was agreeable on being asked questions or cross examined.' The result of Tryon's unapproachability was one of history's most extraordinary naval blue-on-blues.

4

The First World War

In the history of modern warfare there can be little doubt that artillery has made the most devastating contribution to friendly-fire casualties. In the First World War the gunners of all armies were often hated by the front-line troops who suffered so terribly from the 'shorts' that fell regularly onto their positions from their own guns. Relations were sometimes so bad between the gunners and the 'poor bloody infantry' that fights broke out behind the lines and in *estaminets* in rear areas. The attitude of the PBI can be well understood. Their fate was hard enough, facing the shells and machine-guns of a vigilant enemy without having to fear for their backs. Yet the gunners were themselves victims of a new kind of warfare, both in scale and technique, and the degree of precision required for close co-operation with ground troops was beyond anything that had ever been asked of artillerists before. So if there were friendly casualties aplenty through human error, they were often a product of technology moving beyond the capacity of human beings to control it.

The demands on artillery in the twentieth century have indeed been far greater than ever before. Gunners, who in Napoleonic times were as much battlefield troops as the infantry and took their chance amongst the bayonets and sabres of the enemy like anyone else, were pushed far back from the front lines by the increasing ranges of their own guns and became indirect rather than direct participants on the battlefield. The infantry never saw their struggles, thousands of yards or even several miles behind the front lines, against an unseen enemy who sought their lives as eagerly as those of the men in the trenches. And fighting an unseen enemy was always fraught with difficulties. Indirect rather than direct fire was bound to increase the number of mistakes by which friendly forces might be engaged through errors of map-reading or even as a result of a rapidly changing tactical situation. The advent of aircraft which could report back the fall of shot to the gunners was an advance but was still too slow to guarantee that targeting of the guns was efficient. A published report of the performance of the French artillery from 1914–18 offered a sharp warning against complacency. Statistics for British friendly-fire casualties simply do not exist but there are numerous examples of artillery amicide by British gunners recorded in First World War diaries and military memoirs, some so dreadful that their details have been expunged as far as possible from any official records.

In 1921, an artillery expert and critic of the French high command, General Percin, published the first and most comprehensive account of friendly fire in military literature. He entitled his book *Le massacre de notre infanterie, 1914–1918* and in it claimed that as many as 75,000 French casualties had been caused in friendly-fire incidents involving the French artillery. It was an astonishing claim, yet he was supported by evidence from hundreds of correspondents, reporting from all periods of the war and from all parts of the French lines on the Western Front. There seems little doubt that a British or a German book of like kind could have been produced had an Anglo–Saxon or Teutonic Percin set his mind to it. That they did not is our loss, yet as I attempt to show below, numerous examples of friendly fire on the Anglo–German front on the Somme and in Flanders can be assembled by a close study of the huge literature of military memoirs and personal accounts by officers and men alike. Understandably, perhaps, the official histories – with the exception of C E W

Bean's Australian history – are less forthcoming about friendly casualties. When they were written the idea of heavy losses caused by human error and equipment malfunction was still far from an acceptable one. Nevertheless, it would not be stretching the bounds of credulity to assert that the static warfare in France and Belgium from 1915 to 1918 and the pre-eminent role of the big guns provided opportunities for mistakes on an unparalleled scale. The degree of precision required of both the guns and their gunners was frequently missing before technological and professional skills reached their height in 1918. Thus the massive British artillery bombardments on the Somme in June–July 1916 and prior to the third battle of Ypres in 1917 produced both a tragic and yet understandable quota of friendly-fire incidents.

There is a sameness about many of the French incidents Percin relates that must infuriate the sensitive reader, aware that the cost was being paid in human lives and suffering, because so little seems to change between his first example on 15 August 1914, and his last, on 1 November 1918, just ten days before the armistice. It seems that nothing was learned from the massacre of the French infantry and that the kind of errors responsible for decimating the exuberant *poilus* in their *pantalons rouges* in the first few days of the war were those that scythed down the grim-faced, cynical and mutinous veterans 51 months later.

On 22 August 1914, Percin tells us, the 1st Regiment of Colonial Infantry, led by Colonel Guérin, was moving towards the town of Neufchâteau in Belgium. Their path took them through dense forest near Rossignol. Information from the local people told Guérin that there were German troops in the forest yet, undeterred, the colonel marched in only to find himself confronted by three regiments of German soldiers, well dug-in. A bloody and confused fight took place that raged for hours. A battery of artillery that had accompanied Guérin's regiment set up its guns 400 metres from the forest and, lacking orders of any kind, fired blindly into the trees in apparent support of its infantry. But the gunners had no way of knowing where the French troops were at any one time and the battle became a lottery. By the end of the day, out of 3,250 *poilus* who had entered the forest, 2,000 were dead and a further 1,000 wounded or taken prisoner by the Germans. In the words of one of the survivors, 'Our artillery went mad'. It is estimated that more than a third of all the French casualties were caused by their own guns, including nearly 700 men killed. It had been a shocking example of the breakdown in liaison between different elements of an army. How had it been possible for the gunners to continue firing when they had no orders from a senior officer either to open fire in the first place or to continue firing without precise directions? This question remains unanswered both in this case and in the majority of examples given in Percin's book.

On 20 December 1914, French 75mm guns, situated 500 metres behind the front lines, shattered an attack by the 38th Regiment of Colonial Infantry in the appropriately named district of Calvary near Beauséjour, on the Marne. Throughout the day the *poilus*, reinforced later by the 33rd Regiment, clung to a toehold in the German lines, while they were alternately bombarded by the German heavy guns and raked by their own artillery. It is estimated that 35 per cent of their casualties were a direct result of friendly fire by their own gunners, who showed no thought for their plight but continued firing throughout the day, in Percin's words, 'without orders, without signals and without an officer present'.

Short shelling by the French gunners, caused by damp ammunition, worn gun barrels, unfavourable wind conditions and any number of other reasons – even including bad blood between officers of rival regiments – was not something the French kept entirely to themselves. Occasionally, the French gunners fired on British troops holding adjoining positions. The writer Jean Giraudoux once boasted to Paul Morand, 'I belong to the French regiment that has killed the most English.' It would be surprising if some British gunner was not able to boast as much of the French he had killed.

For France the tragedy at the village of Samogneux has come

to symbolize the true horror of friendly fire. On 21 February 1916, the Germans began their assault on the French fortress of Verdun. At Samogneux the 351st Regiment of the 72nd Division, commanded by Lieutenant-Colonel Bernard, heroically held up the German advance for two days. Hemmed in on all sides by Germans, Colonel Bernard found it increasingly difficult to communicate with his headquarters. As he wrote in the last message he managed to get through, 'All the horses have been killed, bicycles smashed, runners wounded or scattered along the routes. I shall be doing the impossible if I keep you informed of events.' After this, divisional headquarters received no further word from Bernard. The only evidence of what was happening at Samogneux was gleaned by Major Becker from the words of a courier, who rode past him at full gallop shouting, 'The Boche is at Samogneux'. Becker was unable to question the man further and so assumed that the worst had happened and that Bernard's resistance was ended. It was, after all, very likely that the Germans had in fact taken Samogneux. When this news was passed to General Herr in Verdun he ordered the village to be recaptured immediately. Before an assault could be launched, however, it would be necessary for the French heavy artillery – 155mm guns – to saturate the area and destroy the advanced German positions. On the night of 23 February, a massive artillery barrage rained down on Samogneux. Unfortunately, at the very moment that the first French shells began to land, Colonel Bernard had at last found a way of sending a message to tell HQ that he was still holding on. It was too late. In spite of the fact that Bernard's men fired green ceasefire rockets to try to stop their gunners it was to no avail. For once the French gunners showed unerring accuracy and the French defenders were massacred. Unknown to the gunners, they were making matters easy for the Germans who were able to walk into the village unchallenged. The sight that met their eyes was astonishing. The entire French garrison had been wiped out by their own artillery, except for one man. As they stepped over the rubble the Germans heard a weak voice saying, '*Pour mes enfants, sauvez-moi!*' By an incredible chance Colonel Bernard alone had survived the inferno. He was rescued and brought before the Kaiser himself. When questioned by the German Emperor, he defiantly replied, 'You will never enter Verdun'. And he was right. Yet the defence of Samogneux had shattered the 351st Regiment of Infantry, which suffered 80 per cent casualties. How many men died in the ruins of the village from General Herr's guns we will never know. But the effect of friendly fire had not only cost France hundreds of lives; it also presented to the Germans a strategic position vital to their efforts to capture Verdun.

In case one should suspect that the efficient German artillery never committed such errors as their French counterparts, it is as well to point out that there was much short shooting by the German guns throughout the entire war. More skilled in the use of creeping barrages than either the French or the British, the Germans still had one unit – the 49th Regiment of Artillery – that was dubbed the 48½th by the front-line soldiers because of its shorts. In addition, the first firing of one of the great German railway guns killed 30 German soldiers standing nearby with its blast. It was eventually only possible to fire the gun by electricity from a French farmhouse situated a quarter of a mile away.

While the massive French and German armies fought the great battle of the Frontiers in August 1914, things started on a more appropriate scale for the small, highly-professional British Expeditionary Force. In those early days of the war it is still hard to believe that British casualties could still be regarded as individual tragedies. The men who died still had names and identities; their deaths were tragic and significant events, not submerged by the sheer enormity of the carnage being inflicted on other fronts. But such feelings did not last long. They could not survive the revelation that rather than dying heroically, for some noble purpose, the first British soldiers of the BEF to die in France had been killed by their own side.

A battery of horse artillery, attached to the British 5th

Division, was moving towards the village of Le Cateau at nightfall, sending out riders to scout the road ahead. The local Civil Guard, which was composed mainly of untrained Belgian peasants, was guarding the road, and seeing the British riders approaching and hearing them speaking in a foreign language, they panicked and opened fire, spraying bullets in all directions. The British horsemen turned back and rode hard for the British lines. Unfortunately, British infantry picquets had seen them coming at the gallop and, presuming them to be hostile, opened fire down the road killing one man outright and mortally wounding another. To the British public it was incomprehensible: two men dead and 5th Division had not even seen a German yet.

On 27 September 1914, tragedy struck the little French village of Authuille, in the Somme region of France. A farmer named Boromée Vaquette had gone out early into his fields with his herd of cows. A little later a platoon of French soldiers, expecting to meet Germans, had emerged from nearby woods and had dimly picked out of the morning mist a grey-clad figure, hammering wood together and apparently building a barricade. As the troops had been expecting to meet Germans dressed in their *feldgrau,* they assumed the figure was a German soldier. Before investigating, the soldiers fired a volley at the figure in grey, who threw up his arms and fell dead. The soldiers then retreated into the woods. No more 'Germans' appeared and they ventured back to look at the body of farmer Boromée Vaquette. But before they could remove the body, a unit of real German troops was sighted, which advanced towards them and set up a defensive position only yards from where the farmer's body was lying. All the French soldiers could do was take the news to Madame Vaquette, the farmer's wife, and offer to retrieve her husband if and when the German invaders were driven away from the area. And so the body lay between the lines, hidden by grass, a victim of friendly fire.

The British attack at Neuve Chapelle in March 1915 contained several examples of artillery amicide which were pointers to what the British soldiers could expect from their grossly swollen artillery arm in 1916 and 1917. In the first case, the 2nd Scottish Rifles (Cameronians) were hit by shrapnel during the preliminary bombardment of the German trenches. Colonel Story remembered, 'The sickening fumes of lyddite blew back into the British trenches. Great masses of earth and huge jagged pieces of metal (shell fragments) hurtled through the air. In places, the waiting troops were covered with soil and dust.' The second-in-command of B Company, Captain Peter Kennedy, was killed by a piece of shrapnel from a British shell. Other men were wounded, but few severely. It would not have occurred to the British soldier at this period of the war that he would soon come to hate his own gunners more than he hated the enemy himself.

The Scottish Rifles advanced along with men from the Middlesex Regiment, but, as they approached an area marked 'Ruined House' on their maps, they came close to being shattered by the British artillery. The gunners were exceeding their own fire plan and were firing into an area that had not been designated theirs in the planning. This failure in co-ordination, as John Baynes points out, was at the root of many artillery blue-on-blues. Compared with the artillery disasters at Fromelles, Pozières, Poelcapelle and elsewhere in the years to come, this mistake seems trifling. Apparently only one officer, Major George Carter-Campbell, was wounded. But it was a mistake none the less, and if it were repeated on another day and on a larger scale the consequences could be tragic. One has only to think of the fate of the 66th Division at Passchendaele (see pp. 114–121).

On relatively few occasions in military history has an army employed weapons that are so intrinsically unreliable that they pose almost the same threat to the side using them as to the enemy. In such cases friendly casualties are almost inevitable. There have been few if any better examples of this process than the use of poison gas during the First World War. Subject to the vagaries of wind and weather, poison gas always posed a threat not only of blowing back onto the advancing formations of troops but also of gathering in thick clouds around the enemy trenches so that even if an initial attack was successful it was impossible for the attacking force to occupy enemy lines without falling victim to their own gas. The first gas used by British troops at the battle of Loos in September 1915 was a case in point. Of 50,000 casualties suffered by British forces during this disastrous battle, no less than 2,361 were poisoned by the first release of chlorine gas from the British lines prior to the infantry assault.

The use of poison gas by the Germans at the second battle of Ypres in April 1915 had come as a complete surprise to the British authorities and it was not long before the generals were pressing for a British response. The decision was therefore taken to prepare quantities of chlorine gas for use in the proposed offensive at Loos in September. However, although it was simple to produce the poison gas it was much harder to use it effectively in a war situation. There was simply not enough time to train men in this novel form of warfare. As was later to be the case with tanks, gas technology was misused through an inability to exploit it to its full potential.

The assault on Loos was to be carried out by Lieutenant-General Sir Henry Rawlinson's IV Corps of General Sir Douglas Haig's First Army. However, without adequate artillery to support the attack, Rawlinson was not optimistic about his chances. As he told Haig, 'I fear heavy losses and doubt if we will get through unless the gas turns up trumps which it may do, [though] we are not very good at these new improvisations.' In fact, with the French commander, Marshal Joffre, pressing the British to widen the range of the attack there was a danger that their gas supplies would be over-stretched. A month before the planned offensive, Rawlinson visited St Omer to attend a gas demonstration. He was far from impressed. But it was already too late to persuade Haig or Joffre that the Loos operation should be reconsidered. In view of the lack of artillery, and of shells for the guns, the British would be entirely dependent on the effectiveness of their gas attack.

At a conference on 6 September, General Haig explained to his corps commanders the role that the gas was expected to play in the attack planned for 25 September. Haig blithely spoke of the gas being carried on the wind 'in front of the assaulting divisions, and [creating] a panic in the German ranks, or at least [incapacitating] them for a prolonged period.' If the conditions were ideal, the British attack would proceed rapidly and capture both the first and second defensive lines of the Germans. But as Robin Prior and Trevor Wilson have pointed out, 'Haig's suggestion of a panic among the enemy when confronted with gas was little more than a chimera. It was known that opposing the British at Loos were seasoned troops equipped with respirators.' Under the circumstances there was no justification for expecting the Germans to panic. After all, even without gas masks the Canadians had held their lines against a German gas attack at Ypres earlier in the year. Too much was being expected of this most unreliable of weapons. Nevertheless, given ideal conditions the German defenders might be incapacitated for just long enough to allow the British troops to get across no man's land and seize their trenches. Moreover, if the German machine-gunners were troubled by gas or even if they suffered reduced visibility for a short period, it might be enough to allow an attack to succeed. The gas did not need to kill, or maim; it was enough if it reduced the combat efficiency of the defenders for even a matter of minutes.

The main problem in employing gas as a weapon was how to project it towards the enemy. Tests were made with gas grenades and gas shells but these were rejected in favour of gas cylinders. Grouped together in the forward trenches, the gas cylinders would be equipped with a nozzle and a pipe so that the gas could be forced under pressure towards the German lines. However, once it had left the cylinder the gas would be entirely dependent on the prevailing wind strength and direction. The next problem for the British planners was how much gas to use. The truth was that the British had limited stocks of chlorine gas and, once Haig was persuaded by

General Sir John French, the British Commander-in-Chief, and Marshal Joffre to widen the area under attack, the amount of gas needed to subdue the enemy exceeded Britain's capacity to produce it at that stage of the war. By the autumn of 1915 it was known that German respirators could protect a soldier for a maximum of 30 minutes, after which time he would succumb to the effects of the gas. It was therefore decided by the British experts that they would need to project gas on the German lines for a minimum period of 40 minutes. Only at this stage would it be safe to assume that the Germans – notably the machine-gunners – would be incapacitated and as a result be reasonably safe to launch the British attackers into no man's land. But there was not enough chlorine gas available for a 40-minute operation. The reason for this deficiency was threefold: in the first place, factory production had failed to keep up with demand. Secondly, under test conditions it had been found that the gas cylinders emptied in three minutes rather than the five minutes originally estimated. Finally, now that the area to be attacked had been extended, there would be fewer gas cylinders available for each yard of front. The lack of gas supplies mirrored the shells crisis of earlier in 1915. Haig and Rawlinson had to find some way of stretching the gas to fit the new conditions, and their solution – smoke – was imaginative if hardly innovative. It was eventually decided that the smoke – to be produced in three different ways: smoke candles, smoke bombs and phosphorus grenades – should supplement the gas, so that the enemy would never know whether harmless smoke or poison gas was billowing towards them at any given time. The enemy would therefore be unable to remove their respirators and by the time that their full 30-minute resistance was up, the British would be ready to give them a last ten minutes of gas. Even though the smoke would do them no lasting harm, it was surmised that the mere fact of having to wear the respirator for so long would reduce the combat efficiency of the German soldiers and make them vulnerable to an attack by fresh British troops. Furthermore, the smoke would help to conceal the progress of the infantry in crossing no man's land. However, smoke, like gas, was subject to the vagaries of the wind, and this was a factor quite beyond even the most careful military planning.

Dry weather had been prevalent in the middle fortnight of September but as the countdown to the attack began, wet and misty weather began to set in. Yet even the levels of precipitation were not as vital to the success of the attack as the direction of the wind. A gas attack was entirely dependent on a favourable wind direction and Haig had to face the awesome responsibility for deciding whether to release the gas at zero hour on 25 September or not. His meteorological adviser, Major Gold of the Royal Flying Corps, was in an equally invidious position, being responsible for advising the First Army commander whether to risk sending tens of thousands of British soldiers into the attack behind a drifting cloud of poison gas. If the wind was too strong the gas would be dispersed too quickly to affect the German defenders and protect the attackers; if too weak, it might hover in no man's land and provide a danger to the advancing British troops and, if it were to change direction at the wrong time, it could wreck the entire assault and gas thousands of British soldiers. Under these circumstances one would have expected Gold – and Haig – to approach the problem of whether to use the gas or not with extreme caution. In the event, Haig's own behaviour must be judged as extraordinarily rash.

On 18 September, under cover of darkness, the gas cylinders – called 'Oojahs' by the British tommies – began their journey to the front line, carried in the arms or on the backs of toiling soldiers. Yet, in spite of every difficulty, not one of the cylinders was broken or damaged in transit and by 21 September, 5,000 Oojahs – carrying 150 tons of chlorine gas – were in place. The artillery bombardment, which was to prepare the way for the infantry assault, began in a rather desultory way, convincing the Germans that it was merely a demonstration to distract their attention from the French lines, where the real attack would take place. In fact, it was the best the British could manage at that time.

While Haig was pondering the weather on 24 September, Sir John French arrived at First Army Headquarters to discuss with him the next day's attack. Sir John brought news that the French were due to attack at 1100 hours and asked if Haig could co-ordinate his own attack with theirs. Haig was unsure. He was a prisoner of the weather and explained that he hoped to be able to decide on zero hour later that evening. At 2120 hours Haig received the final weather report from Major Gold. It was essentially favourable: 'wind southerly changing to south-west or west, probably increasing to 20 miles per hour.' Armed with this, Haig sent out the order that the assault was to go ahead and the troops therefore moved into the forward trenches. But in the early hours of 25 September, it became obvious that the wind was not picking up as Gold had suggested it would. Haig demanded another forecast and was told that 'the wind would probably be stronger just after sunrise than later in the day'. This was an extremely vague piece of information on which to base a military action. Nevertheless, by his reliance on gas Haig had worked himself into a corner. The available British artillery was quite inadequate to support a full-scale assault and without the gas it would probably be necessary to call off the whole operation. This would have left the French attack high and dry without any British support on their flanks. In the final analysis, Haig had little choice but to order the release of the gas and hope for the best. He therefore ordered the gas attack to start at 0550, with the infantry to follow 40 minutes later.

But while Haig snatched a few hours' sleep the wind dropped to little more than a breeze, and from time to time it changed direction until it was blowing from the German lines towards the British. Major-General James Foulkes, who had the unenviable job of 'gas adviser' to Haig, was receiving hourly reports on wind speed and direction from all parts of the British line. The evidence that was coming in suggested that the wind would definitely be unfavourable in some parts of the line. To cover this eventuality Foulkes had given firm orders that under no circumstances were cylinders to be switched on if an unfavourable wind was blowing at zero hour. But the wind was fitful, and no amount of reporting could guarantee what would happen at 0550. The likeliest scenario was that the wind would be generally favourable but that gas would also be blown across the British lines and in a few places back into the British trenches. Towards dawn this was the actual situation. In many parts of the British lines individual officers responsible for releasing the gas faced the difficult decision as to whether to release the gas or not. The writer and poet Robert Graves has left us a description in his autobiography *Goodbye to All That,* of the extraordinary events in his sector. The Royal Engineers officer responsible for the gas phoned his divisional headquarters 20 minutes before the gas was to be released and reported: 'Dead calm. Impossible discharge accessory [code name for the gas].' To Graves's astonishment the reply was, 'Accessory to be discharged at all costs'. Hearing this one of his soldiers commented, 'such a decision seemed suicidal, and our officers were compelled to obey against all common sense.'

According to Foulkes's order, the incident Graves describes should not have occurred. To understand why this 'suicidal' order was given we need to find General Douglas Haig at 0500 hours, 'taking the morning air' and finding that the wind had almost completely dropped. With him was his cigarette-smoking ADC, Major Alan Fletcher, who was 'smoking furiously'. Haig, the non-smoker, was content to watch the young officer and note that his cigarette smoke 'drifted in puffs towards the north-east'. This was reassuring. Haig admitted to having had some doubts about giving the 'go-ahead' but apparently the cigarette smoke clinched his decision. At 0515, Haig announced that the attack would take place. He climbed a look-out tower and noted that the wind was coming gently from the south-west. As he later wrote in his diary: 'The leaves of the poplar trees gently rustled. This seemed satisfactory. But what a risk I must run of gas blowing back upon our own dense masses of troops.' If Haig had watched Fletcher's cigarette smoke more intently, as his own intelligence chief, General John Charteris, had been doing, he would have seen that the smoke was drifting towards the German lines but then stopping and, if anything, coming back.

At 0550, the big guns began to fire and the gas was released. In many places it billowed towards the German lines on a good breeze but generally it travelled no more than twenty or thirty yards and then slowed down, hanging like a curtain across no man's land. In some parts of the line individual officers had made their own decision, based on General Foulkes's order not to release the gas if there was a danger of it blowing back. Lieutenant White, RE, of the 2nd Division, telephoned brigade headquarters to say that he would not open the gas cylinders as conditions were not right. He was surprised to receive an outright order from his brigadier-general to carry on releasing the gas. Although the general was no happier than White about the situation, he himself had received orders from higher up to carry on. White later wrote:

At first the gas drifted slowly towards the German lines (it was plainly visible owing to the rain) but at one or two bends of the trench the gas drifted into it. In these cases I had it turned off at once. At about 6.20 a.m. the wind changed and quantities of the gas came back over our own parapet, so I ordered all gas to be turned off and only smoke candles to be used.

Punctually at 6.30 a.m. one company of the King's [(Liverpool) Regiment] advanced to the attack wearing smoke helmets. But there was a certain amount of confusion in the front trench owing to the presence of large quantities of gas . . . Nearly all my men suffered from the gas and four had to go to hospital. Three out of five [British] machine-guns on my front were put out of action by the gas.'[17]

The British troops, encumbered by their own gas masks, were suffering from the gas as heavily as the Germans. Hundreds of men were overcome as a cloud of gas rolled back in no man's land to engulf the King's Own Scottish Borderers.

Showing unbelievable courage the regimental piper, Piper Laidlaw, pulled off his gas mask, grasped his bagpipes and piped his men forward.

On another part of the front, Sergeant Packham of the Royal Sussex Regiment experienced the dreadful effects of the chlorine gas. Sent with a message to his platoon officer, Packham found the gas officer in the trench. 'He looked ghastly and all the buttons on his tunic were green as if they were mouldy. He was saying that the gas was blowing back into our troops' faces. The wind had turned round on us.'

The worst British casualties were suffered on the left wing of the attack by IV Corps, notably by the 1st and 2nd Brigades of 1st Division. On this front the British line ran towards the north-east and, with a wind blowing from south-south-west, it meant that here the troops were not only hit by their own gas but by that released by units to their right. Within a few minutes over 300 men of the 1st Brigade were down with gas poisoning. If it were possible, the 2nd Brigade was suffering even more. It was soon apparent that the British respirators were not working properly and many men were gassed even though they were wearing them. Ironically, while the British gas weapon was inflicting heavy friendly casualties, traditional blade and bullet were helping the British soldiers to achieve a considerable success on the first day of the battle. Gas had played no part in this success other than in its capacity to conceal the advance of the British troops across no man's land. Smoke alone would have done as well, and without poisoning large numbers of friendly troops in the process. Haig's decision to release the gas in the circumstances that prevailed on 25 September was unjustifiable and the heavy gas casualties of 2,361 men could have been avoided.

One of the main aims of the British Fourth Army's offensive on the Somme in July 1916 was to seize possession of the Pozières Ridge, which overlooked the British front lines. After the failure of the great 1 July assault, Douglas Haig (who had succeeded French as C-in-C in December 1915) made several other attempts to take the ridge, calling up the new Anzac divisions that had been brought to France after the collapse of the Gallipoli campaign. The Anzacs – Australians and New Zealanders – were outstanding troops and were eventually to form the main strike force of the British army in 1917 and 1918, but at this early stage they were relatively inexperienced in the techniques of trench warfare. Their initiation – at Fromelles and at Pozières – was to see them subjected to a series of appalling friendly-fire incidents as a result of poor co-ordination with their artillery.

At dawn on 19 July, the Australians and New Zealanders began their attack on Pozières after a period of two days' preliminary bombardment. However, the German artillery had not been silenced and the Anzacs found themselves under fire both from in front and behind as their own artillery was firing short. Many Australian troops fell in no man's land as a result of short shells. In some areas, aware of the danger of hitting their own troops, the British artillery simply ceased fire, allowing the German machine-gunners at the Sugar Loaf an opportunity to cut swaths through the attacking troops. As Brigadier-General 'Pompey' Elliott later explained, the gunners 'were really afraid, as we learnt later on, of aiming at the Sugar Loaf at all for fear of hitting our own lines.' The truth was much starker than this. It was not only a case of the gunners not being willing to risk hitting their own men, but rather that they knew that their equipment was obsolete and that their skill was insufficient. The guns supporting this Australian attack in their assault were of the poorest quality, many quite antiquated, with a tendency to inaccurate fire. The gunners simply could not provide the precise creeping barrage that the infantry needed, without spraying shells onto their own troops, as happened all too frequently at this stage of the war.

The officer commanding the artillery for the Anzac Corps, Brigadier-General Cunliffe-Owen, bore the brunt of General Haig's dissatisfaction with the Australian assault. Haig sacked him on the spot. Only later did the truth emerge that Cunliffe-Owen had planned one barrage so badly that had it been fired it would have achieved one of the most complete blue-on-blues in recorded history. The fact that it was not fired was entirely a matter of chance. General Brudenell White, concerned about the haphazard British planning, chose to look in at Corps Artillery Headquarters just as the gunners were being given their orders to fire. A quick calculation told him all he needed to know and that particular barrage was stopped. Nevertheless, many Australians did suffer from friendly fire and the Germans later reported that some of their Australian prisoners had endured not only fire from their own gunners but had also been fired at in error by British infantry.

As the British demonstrated by their use of gas at Loos in September 1915, some weapons could be as dangerous to friendly troops as they were to the enemy. A year later the British were to find that this held true for tanks as well as for gas. The appearance of the first tanks on the Somme battlefield in September 1916 signalled one of the most important advances in warfare since the discovery of gunpowder. Yet in his hurry to use them General Haig was willing to reveal this secret weapon before it was ready. Winston Churchill, for one, believed the tank should have been kept secret until Britain had enough ready to make a decisive breakthrough in the German lines. Lieutenant-Colonel E D Swinton, the man most associated with the development of the early tanks, agreed:

> Some of the machines were asked to force their way through a wood and knock down trees – tricks which they had not been designed to play and which were likely to damage them seriously. I protested against these 'stunts' and the frequent exhibitions, which were wearing out both machines and personnel. In addition to the almost continuous work of repairing, cleaning and tuning their tanks, the men barely had time to eat, sleep and tend to themselves. I speculated as to how many machines would be one hundred per cent fit to go into action when their day arrived; and wondered how the Royal Flying Corps would have fared if it had made its début during the War

with fifty aeroplanes of the first type produced, and had to submit to similar preliminaries before it went into action. As had been the case in England, it seemed impossible to establish a realization of the fact that the New Arm was a mass of complicated, and in some ways, delicate, machinery in an embryonic shape, and not the fool-proof product of long trial and experience.'[18]

But Haig was adamant – the tanks must lead the assault at whatever cost – and as usual it was the common soldier who suffered.

The first tanks were really just armoured machine-gun or light-artillery carriers, with the ability to resist anything less than a direct hit from an artillery shell and able to cross trenches, crush barbed wire and engage enemy pillboxes. In the context of the static fighting that had dominated the Western Front for two years the generals might be excused for seeing in them the answer to all their prayers. However, the tanks had severe limitations, some of which imposed crippling handicaps on the infantry that advanced alongside them. Frankly the Mark I tank was merely a prototype and should not have been committed to action so readily. In the first place, it was painfully slow, capable of just 55 yards per minute (about 2 miles an hour) and as such was far slower than the infantry. Secondly, the tanks were so prone to mechanical failure that two of the six demonstrated to General Rawlinson in the summer of 1916 broke down in ideal conditions and behind the lines. The sheer size of the tank and the fact that its slow speed made it an almost stationary target rendered it very vulnerable to artillery fire. Its weight also made it liable to bog down in heavy mud. But what was worse from the point of view of the long-suffering infantry was that with a poor range of vision from within the tanks, their generally inexperienced crews were sometimes unable to differentiate between friend and foe. As a result, tanks caused a number of friendly-fire incidents, two of which were especially costly on 15 September.

In spite of the tanks' limitations, the Fourth Army commander, Rawlinson, was 'on the whole . . . rather favourably impressed.' So much so that he welcomed the chance offered by Sir Douglas Haig to use the 49 tanks that were, at that stage, the only such weapons in existence. Rawlinson gave the tanks a key role in the attack on 15 September, planning – somewhat illogically – for the tanks to attack at night and move ahead of the British infantry to subdue the German strongpoints and wipe out the machine-gunners where possible. In his view the tanks would reduce the infantry casualties to a minimum, yet how he expected the tank crews to navigate by the light of the moon was not made clear. In the end the night option was cancelled and an attack at dawn substituted. Obviously Rawlinson was unaware of the tanks' real limitations, notably their slow speed and the poor visibility offered to the crew within. These two factors were soon to be the cause of heavy British losses.

The next major problem for General Rawlinson in planning his new offensive was how to co-ordinate the tanks with their artillery supports. The assumption was that the tanks would move ahead of the infantry and eliminate obstacles and German machine-gunners but, if this was to happen, it would clearly be impossible for the artillery to provide a creeping barrage for the infantry without hitting the tanks. So Rawlinson decided that the gunners would leave corridors in the barrage, within which the tanks could operate. Yet with corridors 100 yards wide there would be large sections – and the most formidable sections at that – of the German lines free of bombardment. Unless the tanks were able to subdue these sections then the infantry following them would simply be massacred. Rawlinson was expecting too much of the tanks, which could only engage German strongpoints from relatively close range, meaning that the British infantry would be exposed to German fire for much of their advance before the tanks could become really effective. And bearing in mind the snail-like speed of the tanks, as well as their vulnerability to gunfire, there was every chance that the infantry would overtake them and have to assault strong German defences without any artillery support whatsoever. In this way, the appearance of the tank on 15 September, rather than providing protection for the British infantry, actually contributed to even heavier casualties than would have been the case without them.

The pre-assault barrage of the German defences began on 12 September and for three days the great guns cratered and ploughed up the land, making it as unsuitable for tank warfare as can possibly be imagined. Combined with heavy rain the British artillery now turned that area of the Somme front into a morass. By 15 September when the attack began, the weather had improved but the ground was still difficult for the tanks and their top speed was reduced even more. It was soon found impossible for the infantry to stay behind the tanks and so they were forced to brave the German fire unprotected. In one area – the Quadrilateral near Bouleaux Wood – 13 of the 15 tanks allocated simply failed to turn up, getting lost on the way or breaking down. Here the British 6th Division, ordered to attack the Quadrilateral head-on, were massacred by the German machine-guns, while the 56th Brigade and the Guards Division were enfiladed by machine-gun fire. At one stage a group of men from the Worcesters were mistaken for Germans and shot down by a British Vickers machine-gun.

Few infantry commanders of the time understood the difficulties faced by tank crews. Inside the steel 'coffins', the tankmen had very limited vision and were constantly deafened by the unbearable noise of the 105-horsepower petrol engine. In addition, the heat and fumes were overpowering for the eight-man crew who had somehow to navigate the cumbersome machine through some of the most difficult terrain ever chosen as a battlefield, while suffering the discomfort of near-misses by German heavy artillery and the constant rattle of machine-gun bullets striking their armoured exterior. In such conditions it was hardly surprising that tanks frequently lost their way and inflicted friendly casualties. Even before reaching the start line on 15 September one tank had already fired its six-pounder main armament at the battalion headquarters of the Post Office

Rifles, while another nearly succeeded in destroying the headquarters of the Civil Service Rifles. Navigation was so difficult that tank commanders frequently stopped their tanks and got out to ask the infantry which way they were supposed to be going.

Incredibly, 15 September was not a day of total failure. Three divisions of XV Corps, attacking towards Delville Wood and Longueval, achieved the greatest success, taking the village of Flers and overrunning the second line of German trenches. Here four tanks were responsible for the breakthrough, with the Germans showing little fight and surrendering, many in terror of the new weapons. But elsewhere the tanks had played a more deadly part in the proceedings. Foolishly, General Pulteney, commanding III Corps, had widened his artillery corridor on the assumption that his tanks would quickly capture the German positions in High Wood and therefore his infantry would not need a creeping barrage. In fact, the tanks were quite unable to operate among the trees, with the result that the Germans were free to bring a heavy fire down on the infantry of the 47th Division. Four tanks gallantly tried to move through High Wood on Pulteney's orders but immediately lost their bearings in the confusion of tree stumps and German shells. Two of the tanks turned completely round without noticing it and emerged from the wood into British lines. One became bogged down in a shell hole but the other, commanded by Lieutenant Robinson, seeing trenches filled with troops, assumed that it had reached the German positions in High Wood and immediately raked the trenches with machine-gun fire. But the trench was a British one, known as Worcester Trench, and the men were from the London Regiment. In a storm of fire dozens of men were killed and wounded before the tank commander realized his mistake. The immediate blame for this blue-on-blue was his and yet the greater error was made by General Pulteney in ordering tanks to clear a wood without artillery support. Eventually, High Wood was taken, but only after a heavy mortar bombardment had cleared the way for an attack by New Zealand infantry.

There was great excitement at Fourth Army Headquarters when it was reported that two tanks had broken through the German lines to reach the village of Flers. General Haig even passed the news on to the waiting pressmen and it was relayed back to Britain. What was not reported was that another tank had wiped out nearly all the troops in a nearby trench – a British assembly trench. The 9th Norfolks had been in the trench, preparing to go over the top when a tank lumbered up, lost its bearings and confused their trench with the German front line. At once its machine-gun raked the trench, killing many of the helpless soldiers. An infantry officer, Captain Crosse, ran towards the tank, waving his arms and trying to make himself understood. Peering through a slit in the armoured side the machine-gunner at last understood and the tank stopped firing and swung away, having wrecked the British attack and leaving the German front line unharmed. When the remnants of the Norfolks attacked later that day they were cut down by the same German defenders who had been the tank's real target.

The first appearance of tanks in battle on 15 September 1916 had not been an unmixed blessing for General Rawlinson. It had been expected that the tanks would not only help in overrunning German trenches and capturing the target village of Flers, but would help to keep casualties to a minimum. In fact the tanks did the very opposite. In two serious cases of amicide they had killed many British soldiers, while in their failure to keep up with the advancing infantry they had contributed to the massacre of thousands of men by unhampered German machine-guns and strongpoints. 1 July 1916 is known to history as the black day of the British Army, during which nearly 60,000 casualties were suffered. What is less well known, however, is that on 15 September 1916, British Fourth Army casualties of 29,376 were suffered out of an attacking force only half the size of the one that attacked on 1 July. And yet, of course, both Haig and Rawlinson – and the British public – viewed the 15 September offensive as a success and the performance of the tanks as a triumph. This overlooked the fact that in 1916 the tank was a luxury weapon which through the high price it exacted in friendly casualties few armies could afford.

As the battle of the Somme continued into the autumn of 1916, the British struggle to capture and hold the strategically important High Wood was accompanied by a number of serious blue-on-blue incidents, mostly involving the artillery. During an operation by the Royal Engineers to tunnel under the German defensive redoubt, the Highland troops were hit by a series of short barrages from British guns which cost them three officers and 45 men dead and wounded. In the days just before the 18 August Anglo–French assault, the British field artillery worked to perfect their creeping barrage. Their aim was to lay down a curtain of fire some 100 yards in front of the advancing infantry. One minute later, during which time the gunners calculated the foot soldiers would have moved forward 50 yards, the barrage would be lifted a further 50 yards and so on every minute. This kind of precision, while possible in ideal conditions, was quite beyond gunners who were themselves subject to counter-battery fire and who were using artillery pieces that had grown worn and unreliable from heavy use. And while the gunners suffered such heavy casualties themselves, new and inexperienced crews were constantly being brought in who rarely survived long enough to perfect the techniques necessary to run an efficient creeping barrage. The result was that the gunners lost confidence in themselves and in their guns, while the infantry lost confidence in the gunners. As one gunner told an infantry officer, 'If we fire over you, God help you – we've only one trained gunner per gun left.' The gunner was prescient: the following day the 2nd Battalion of the Argyll and Sutherland Highlanders were caught by their own barrage near High Wood. The British shells 'walked through' the Argylls' positions, causing heavy casualties. To make matters worse, the Scotsmen had with them some new gadgets, known as pipe-pushers, which were designed to speed the entrenching process for assault troops. Unfortunately, when the Scots tried to use them they simply blew up, one blowing such a crater in their position that it exposed many of the Scottish troops to sniper fire.

One of the keenest critics of the British Army in the First World War was the Australian military correspondent and later official historian, C E W Bean. Bean would have been the first to admit his partiality when it came to discussing the performance of British generals, selected as most of them were from a system that favoured men who had attended certain privileged schools and which was above all a reflection of the rigid class structure he saw as typical of pre-1914 Britain. On the other hand, his honesty and independence allowed him to write about things that the British would rather have concealed. On the question of friendly fire, for example, the historian owes much to Bean's incisive pen, for he will seek in vain to find it given much coverage in British official histories. As Bean has made clear, throughout the conflict the British artillery all too often fired 'short' in support of the infantry and, from 1916, among those who suffered were his own beloved Australians.

It has been said with much justice that the First World War was an artillery war and it was the big guns that did most of the killing and the maiming – some estimates claiming that nearly three-quarters of all wounds were caused by artillery shells and shrapnel. But it was also the sheer violence of the guns that administered the 'shell shock' to so many soldiers. Yet the art of long-distance indirect artillery fire was still in its infancy and the precision needed to achieve a perfect creeping barrage to precede an infantry attack was a skill few gunners on the Allied side could boast even in 1917. And it was in trying to provide these creeping barrages that the British and French guns killed and wounded so many of their men. On the Western Front, the Germans had adopted a defensive posture since 1915 and it was not until the spring of 1918 that they returned to the offensive, strengthened by troops returning from the east, where Russia had been defeated. Thus for three years of the war, the Germans were free of much of the short firing that, according to Percin, cost the French so many casualties and which, it must be conceded, may well have cost the British almost as many. Without a Percin to provide figures, one can only rely on scattered reports in diaries and memoirs, or use the reports of a keen student of military tactics like Bean. The incidents are scattered across miles of battlefront and follow no sort of pattern. Yet they are not mere isolated examples. Almost every British soldier would have had a fund of friendly-fire stories and most of them would be at the expense of the gunners, the unseen killers who slew at a distance and never saw their victims.

The PBI were not always passive receivers of short firing by the artillery. During the second battle of Ypres in May 1915, Corporal A Wilson of the West Yorkshire Regiment was one man who intended to find out the truth about friendly fire. With his friend Walter Malthouse, Wilson was in the trenches near Fauquissart when a shell suddenly landed alongside them:

> I was stunned, of course, but when I got my wits together I could hardly believe it, I was covered in blood – saturated – and I really thought I'd bought it. But it was Walter's blood. I didn't have a scratch myself. Walter had taken the full blast and somehow or other it hadn't touched me. He was blown to bits. A terrible sight. I don't think there was a bit of his body bigger than a leg of lamb. I gathered up what I could, put him into a sandbag and later on when it got to dusk, a few of us got out of the trench and buried him . . . The worst of it was that from the direction of the shell we felt almost sure it was one of ours. Of course the authorities wouldn't have that! But I got a few of the men digging and it only took us half an hour to find the nose-cap. Sure enough it was marked 'WD' – War Department. It was from a naval shell fired by one of our long-distance guns mounted on an armoured train.[19]

During the later stages of the battle of Messines on 7 June 1917, the problem of artillery supporting advanced troop positions was starkly illustrated by a series of blue-on-blue incidents. Australian troops of the 47th and 37th Battalions were holding a position known as Hun's House, south-west of Messines. German and British troops were closely engaged and when a British aircraft flew over to spot for artillery support the Australians, fearful of revealing their positions to the Germans, refused to fire their identification flares. The result was that the gunners at the rear were unaware of the fact that the infantry had advanced so far. One Australian named Shang, situated some 400 yards behind the most advanced troops, managed to signal his position by a Lucas lamp, and this position was assumed to be that of the most advanced British troops. When, therefore, a German counter-attack was observed, the artillery prepared to intervene. Meanwhile, at Hun's House, the Australians, though heavily outnumbered, fought off the German attack, only to find themselves under a British bombardment. Assuming at first that the shells were German the Australians fought on, until suddenly they were hit by the full fury of the British barrage. As Bean writes, 'Their position was deluged with shell. Roots were torn from the hedge and tossed in the air, shrapnel began to crack overhead. A tree split and crashed. Fragments of steel swished along the ground and lay smoking.' A wounded officer checked an attempt to retire but eventually the men fell back to a line being established by New Zealand troops. Yet going back meant once again passing through the British barrage and more men were killed in the process. Eventually, with their men having retired, just two officers – Captain Williams of the 47th and Captain Allen of the 45th – stood facing the Germans together. As Williams later explained, his men 'would stand all the enemy fire you like to give them, but they would not put up with being shelled by their own guns.' Some of the Australians who had fallen back now took up positions at the Owl Trench on an earlier line at Oosttaverne, but the majority retreated all the way back to where the New Zealanders were still digging in.

The retreat of the Australians naturally came as a shock to

the New Zealanders, who were still consolidating their position. As a result, some of the New Zealand officers, assuming that there were no longer any Australian troops beyond their line and fearing a German attack, asked the gunners to shorten their barrage and bombard the Oosttaverne Line. This was done and soon the Australians who were grimly hanging on to Owl Trench were driven out once again by their own guns. Not surprisingly morale among the Australian troops was becoming very fragile. Part of the 37th Battalion, however, still held on to the line of Owl Trench but again, through faulty co-ordination, it was assumed by the gunners that all the Australians had withdrawn and so the barrage was once again shortened to prevent a German follow-up. This new barrage fell on the doughty members of the 37th who were still hanging on and they were in turn forced to retreat, through their own barrage. The entire day's fighting on this front was a fiasco. Bean later wrote, 'thus, owing to the action of its own artillery – for which defects in the maps, over-eagerness of the infantry, over-anxiety of some of the staffs and commanders, and a dangerous degree of inaccuracy in the barrage was responsible – the whole of the final objective between the Blauwepoortbeek valley and the double had by 9 p.m. been left open to the enemy.'

North of Hun's Walk, the Australians were encountering similar problems with British artillery. At 0805 hours on 7 June, word spread that the Germans were planning a major counter-attack and Captain Maxwell of the 52nd Battalion, Australian Infantry, called in artillery fire to break up a German advance. Unfortunately, the gunners were firing short and deluged British positions behind the front lines. In a rear strongpoint held by the Sherwood Foresters, a Royal Engineers officer was killed, while an entire unit of the 6th Border Regiment was driven back from Van Hove Farm. Maxwell, alarmed at the devastating effects of the friendly fire and failing to get it stopped by signal or messenger, set off himself to stop the gunners. At battalion headquarters he heard to his surprise commands being issued: 'Lord! Fire! See them on the right there!' As Bean writes, 'Rushing forward with a furious question as to what was going on, Maxwell found himself facing a British battalion commander, who said that the line had fallen back and that he was directing fire on the advancing enemy. The young Tasmanian offered to go down to this target himself to prove that the men seen were not German; immediately afterwards a flare revealed them, and a patrol found them to be a party of British machine-gunners searching behind the lines for a new position.' But so powerful were the effects of the rumours that were rife that day of a major German counter-attack that the gunners were firing at anything coming from the direction of the German lines, even their own troops falling back.

The third battle of Ypres – popularly known as the battle of Passchendaele – has a very fair claim to be considered the most terrible battle ever fought. It is difficult to accept the idea of man as an intelligent animal when one considers this grimmest of slaughters, conducted in what historians were quick to describe in terms of John Bunyan's 'Slough of Despond'. Yet the battle's architects, Haig and Lieutenant-General Sir Hubert Gough, never lost faith and in spite of enormous losses in man-power, equipment and most of all, in morale, they continued to believe that something worthwhile could be snatched from the Germans to justify all the bloodletting. And so the British kept the battle going, from July into October and November 1917, with the aim of taking Passchendaele village itself. In order to do this Haig decided to use his best strike troops – I and II Anzac Corps. Their initial target was to take the village by 12 October, after which the Canadians and the British Cavalry Corps would push on to the railway junction at Roulers and cut the Germans off from the coast. It sounded easy but the condition of the ground made it simply impossible.

For what history records as the battle of Poelcapelle, two British divisions – the 49th and 66th – were earmarked to carry out preliminary attacks to pave the way for the Australians. The terrible fate of the 66th Division constitutes one of warfare's most horrible examples of blue-on-blue. In the first place, the choice of the 66th for so arduous a task was a particularly bad one. The division had no previous battle experience and had only been in France for a few months. In view of its inexperience and the apparent incompetence of many of its officers, it was assigned an area of attack where British intelligence reported that there was no barbed wire. They were mistaken. In addition, ground conditions were so appalling that it was decided to bring the men up to an assembly point just two and a half miles from their starting-tapes. They would therefore begin their march to the front line at 1900 and, assuming at worst a speed of half a mile an hour in the thick mud, they should arrive at the front line by midnight, allowing them at least four hours' rest before the 0520 attack. That was the general idea. But with 9,000 men trying to march forward in darkness across muddy and slippery duckboards, chaos was never far away. Lieutenant Patrick King of the East Lancashires reported his experiences:

> It was an absolute nightmare. Often we would have to stop and wait for up to half an hour, because all the time the duckboards were being blown up and men being blown off the track or simply slipping off, because we were all in full marching order with gas-masks and rifles, and some were carrying machine-guns and extra ammunition. We were all carrying equipment of some kind, and all had empty sandbags tucked down our backs.[20]

The movement of the heavy guns over ground already possessing the consistency of porridge made the forward progress of the troops almost imperceptible. Every step was a battle. Men fell off the boards and were at once swallowed up in flooded shell holes. Dozens drowned in the darkness, unable to get free even with the help of colleagues. To make matters worse, every man was loaded with 60 pounds of kit and weapons, ensuring that they drowned even in a few feet of water which, in the words of Leon Wolff, 'was foul with decaying equipment, excrement, and perhaps something dead;

or its surface might be covered with old, sour mustard gas. It was not uncommon for a man to vomit while being extracted from something like this.' In places the men of the 66th were trying to march through liquid mud more than three feet deep.

At midnight – by which time they should have reached the front-line trenches – few of the men had covered as much as a mile. Even the deadline of 0500 seemed impossible now, and the decision was taken to get as many men as possible forward, with the rest joining the attack as soon as they arrived. Incredibly, many men of the 66th – green troops that they were – kept marching in darkness, high winds and torrential rain and under a heavy German bombardment, reached the front after a ten-hour march, fixed their bayonets and marched straight out into no man's land. There they were shattered and slaughtered by their own guns. Lieutenant King was one of the men who arrived in time to help organize that attack:

> The Colonel had led the battalion up the track – Colonel Whitehead, a very terse man, a very brave man. And he said to me, 'Get them into the attack.' I passed it on to the NCOs, who gave the orders: 'Fix bayonets. Deploy. Extended order. Advance!' We went over into this morass, straight into a curtain of rain and mist and shells, for we were caught between the two barrages.[21]

King watched the attack disintegrate under the machine-gun fire from the Germans and short artillery fire from the British guns. With a handful of men he occupied a shell hole and sandbagged the rim. Here he had to remain for 24 hours in heavy rain and under constant shelling from both sides. He does not seem to have felt any bitterness towards the British gunners who, by this stage, had no real way of knowing where the British front line was. They seemed to be lobbing shells hopefully towards the Germans but most were falling amongst the wretched groups of the 66th Division, as they lay scattered in shell holes in no man's land. The other British division – the 49th – fared little better, having to cross the flooded Ravebeck river, a 50-yard wide steady stream of waist-deep liquid mud.

At dawn on 10 October Lieutenant King, in his shell holes, was surprised to hear voices behind him. 'Who the hell are you?' he called out to a group of unidentified solders. 'Well, come to that, who are you?' replied one of the men. 'I'm Lieutenant King of the 2/5th East Lancashire Regiment.' 'Well, we're the Aussies, chum,' was the reply, 'and we've come to relieve you.' At which, to King's astonishment, the Australians proceeded to occupy his shell hole, already half filled with putrid water. As King and men like him struggled back to the British lines, Charles Bean recorded the views of one of them, who had been injured in the attack:

> Ah doan' know what our brigade was doin' to put us in after a twelve hours' march – twelve hours from beginning to end. We had no duckboards like these – we plugged through the mud. We didn't know where the tapes were, and by the time we arrived there our barrage had gone on half an hour. The men were so done they could hardly stand oop an' hold a rifle. We didn't know where our starting position was, but we went on after the barrage. I'm sorry for the Australians, and it was our first stoont too. We're a new division, ye know.[22]

The truth was that the men of the 66th Division, who had attacked at dawn the previous day, had been so thoroughly exhausted that they had fallen far behind the creeping barrage that had been arranged for them. The divisional commander, Major-General the Hon. Sir Herbert Lawrence, therefore ordered the British gunners to bring back to the barrage which, without checking where the 66th had got to, the artillery did by simply shortening its fire. The result was that British shells cut the 66th Division to pieces in no man's land, inflicting heavy casualties. The massacre was witnessed by Australian troops, one of whom reported what he had seen to the Australian commander, General Birdwood. Birdwood at once complained to GHQ that he had just heard that British soldiers had been wiped out by their own gunners. But the commander of the 66th Division, embarrassed rather than concerned over the blue-on-blue, furiously critcized Birdwood for reporting this tragedy and demanded to know where he had got his information. Birdwood had, in fact, been informed by an Australian officer who had personally witnessed the carnage. Lawrence then insisted that Birdwood withdraw his charge of amicide and discipline his witness, or else he would personally block any promotions from within the Australian Corps. The matter was eventually hushed up, with Lawrence being promoted to the position of Sir Douglas Haig's Chief of Staff. It was obvious that the British were less willing to acknowledge the existence of friendly fire than their French allies.

Meanwhile, Haig, by now Field Marshal, was confident that the Australians could achieve their mission, which was to take Passchendaele village. 'The New Zealand and Australian 3rd Division are to put the Australian flag in the church there,' he told his wife. But there were no flags and no celebrations; the attack was a disaster, with the Australians suffering 60 per cent casualties. Even Haig was now forced to admit that the ground was 'quite impossible'.

But still the battle went on. Now it was the turn of the Canadians. On 16 October, Lieutenant-General Currie, commander of the Canadian Corps, declared that if the weather improved and enough artillery could be assembled in time, he was prepared to commit his troops to a new attack on the 26th, followed – if necessary – by further assaults on 29 October and 2 November. The important provisos should be noted: if the weather improved and if there were enough guns. In fact, for a while in the middle of October the weather did relent. But the Canadians discovered that fewer than half of the British guns that had been promised would be available; the rest were under water or clogged with mud or just 'missing'. They were also too far back and generally out of communication with each other. When the Canadian commander complained and demanded more guns he was told that he would have to send an indent to GHQ as there were no more available.

However, it is all too easy to criticize the much-maligned British gunners. With the rain incessant through October, one gunner reported that in his battery the water was as deep as the guns' breeches, which went under water every time the weapons fired. The gunners had tried to convince GHQ that if the battle went on there would be no heavy guns at all for use in 1918, as they would all be thoroughly worn out. Colonel Rawlins, artillery adviser to Haig, even had the temerity to make this view known to the great man. Haig went white and shouted, 'Colonel Rawlins, leave the room!' When Brigadier-General Edmonds tried to support Rawlins, Haig turned on him, 'You go too, Edmonds!'

Lieutenant-Colonel Alan Brooke, of Second World War distinction, but at that time attached to the Canadians as the chief artillery staff officer, attended on one of Haig's briefings for the Canadians and wrote later that he could hardly believe what he heard on that occasion. Haig spoke as if the attack was taking place in normal conditions against a weakening enemy, on the point of rout. Alan Brooke suggested that Haig could never have seen what it was like at the front. In fact, the British commander had closed his mind to all objections.

The Canadians began their attack at 0540 hours – in heavy rain. Nothing had really changed from when the Australians failed a fortnight before. Yet German resistance was weaker and by the end of the day the Canadians had made progress, occupying land to the west of Passchendaele itself. But to reach them with ammunition and supplies was almost impossible through the mud and hundreds of mules died by drowning after slipping, fully laden, from the greasy duckboards that were hastily brought up to bridge the morass. Two days passed and the Canadians tried again, inching closer to their goal. On 30 October, the Germans began to give way, but the advance was costing the Canadians up to 50 per cent casualties. Five German counter-attacks were repulsed. Now the Canadians had got a foothold on the high ground of the Passchendaele Ridge they were not going to allow themselves to be driven back into the muddy horror through which they had fought at such cost. On 6 November the village of Passchendaele, which Douglas Haig had valued at a third of a million British casualties, at last fell to the Canadians and a week later the battle was brought to a close. But the last dismal fortnight of the fighting, which had brought such success to the Canadians, had contained at least one serious blue-on-blue incident. During the assault of 6 November, and as a result of inaccurate orders, two companies of the Canadians had been positioned 100 yards ahead of instead of behind the artillery barrage. As the creeping barrage advanced both companies were blown to pieces by the British guns. The Canadian survivors, retreating from the slaughter, were then attacked in error by two British companies supposedly supporting them.

Denis Winter in his recent book, *Haig's Command*, has described the reaction of Canadian Prime Minister Sir Robert Borden to what the Canadians had had to endure. It so infuriated him that at one meeting of the Imperial War Cabinet he took British Prime Minister David Lloyd George by the lapels and shook him furiously.

For all the titanic efforts the British had made during the fall of 1917, Haig had merely demonstrated his – and Britain's – incapacity to win the war alone. Britain would now have to sit tight and wait for the Americans to redress the balance on the Western Front. The battle of Passchendaele, for all its secret political agenda, had been what everyone believed all along, a doomed offensive that should have been aborted as soon as its faint trickle of life began to fade, just days into the offensive.

Even during the victorious second battle of Villers–Brettoneux in August 1918 the Australians were still having trouble with the British gunners who were supposed to be supporting them. The Australian 53rd Brigade came under fire from British guns, presumably as a result of an aircraft reporting the wrong grid references back to the gunners. Sergeant Kahn of the 54th Brigade had been responsible for running the telephone lines out between the gunners and the brigade headquarters. Seeing the friendly fire developing he desperately tried to stop the guns firing, only to find that the telephone lines had been cut by

Somme 1916: 'Hey, Sarge, which are the friendly ones?'

Kosovo 1999: 'OK, so I missed again. But we're getting warmer...'

Gulf War 1991: 'Sure, it was one of ours — but did you see that sucker blow?!'

Afghanistan 2002: Smart Bomb; Stupid Bomber.

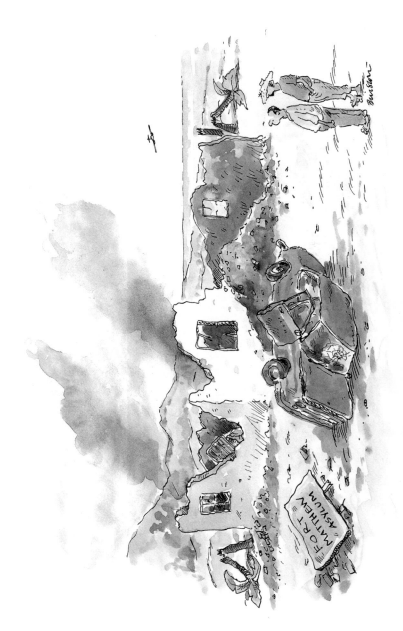

Grenada 1983: 'Have all the lunatics gone?' 'No, another one just flew over.'

Persian Gulf 1988 – Robocruiser: 'The Captain says it's definitely an Iranian fighter. But there again, he's definitely got his binoculars the wrong way round.'

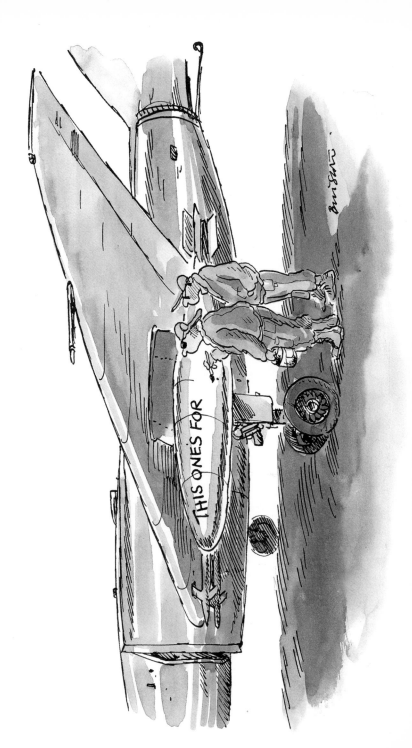

Kosovo 1999: 'I should leave it blank. Who knows where it's gonna fall?'

Kosovo 1999 – The Chinese Embassy: 'It was an Embassy? So the fortune cookie lied...'

enemy fire. Kahn and his colleague, Sergeant Sheppard, found the break and managed to mend it. Sheppard was at once in touch with his brigade headquarters. 'For God's sake stop shooting,' said Sheppard, 'you're firing on our own men.' 'Who is speaking? What authority have your for stopping the guns?' was the reply. 'Linesman here,' said Sheppard, 'if you will hang on a moment we will have the line mended quickly and then you can speak to an officer.' Kahn and Sheppard had risked their lives, running out under the British barrage to find the broken lines, but they had saved far worse casualties. Although five men were already dead and seven wounded. Kahn commented that the guns had just adjusted their range and would soon have been putting shells right into the Australian dugouts, causing appalling slaughter.

5

The Second World War in Europe

The factors that returned mobility to the battlefield in 1918, namely tanks and aircraft, were also those that offered the greatest threats of amicide in the Second World War. With far more fluid combat situations and with operations stretching across a much vaster area the problems of locating and maintaining contact with friendly forces became very great. With fast-moving armoured formations pushing the battlefront back at speed there was always the threat of friendly casualties from indirect artillery fire and tactical ground-support aircraft. In spite of improved communications, errors were frequent. And the difficulties of terrain added substantially to the problems of identification. The campaigns in Europe, notably in Italy in 1943 and in Normandy in 1944, frequently involved house-to-house fighting, sometimes amidst rubble that could conceal both friendly and enemy troops. In the North African desert, with its absence of landmarks and identifying features, and where sandstorms and dust concealed vehicle identification, mistakes were frequent. Perhaps worst of all was the jungle fighting in Burma and New Guinea, where it was often impossible to follow the moments of friendly units and where tactical air support had at best to be something of a hit-or-miss affair.

The performance of inexperienced American soldiers in North Africa in 1943 has been well documented, as have incidents of friendly fire among the green troops. Under-trained and too soft, the GIs seemed fuelled only by a kind of naïve faith that things would work out in the end. One American officer, apparently aware of the fragility of his company's morale, wrote:

> We never really thought we were hot in camp. We always thought that out in the theater they would do it better – the sentry would never daydream, the communications would always work and our units would always be where and when they were supposed to be – we could see a hundred flaws in everything we did, a hundred ways in which an alert enemy could beat us by capitalizing on our errors. Sometimes we made big talk about what our unit could do in action but we always knew it was just that.[23]

Writing of the ill-fated airborne operation in Sicily on 10–11 July 1943, Charles Shrader has shown that even when the paratroopers landed they were not safe from the friendly fire of American ground troops. Landing well to the south-east of Gela, Chaplain Kuehl and a small group of the 504th Parachute Infantry were immediately brought under fire by friendly forces. Even though they knew the pass word and yelled it at their attackers this did not stop the fire. It was only after the chaplain had crawled to the rear of his assailants to reason with them that they stopped firing. On the same night – 11 July – the American 171st and 158th Field Artillery Battalions were in action against Colonel Rueben Tucker's paratroopers. As one of the gunners pointed out quite reasonably, 'since no news of the American paratroopers had reached this headquarters, they were assumed to be hostile and the Battalion was deployed for all round defense.' The outcome of this engagement was that one of the paratroopers was killed. Clearly, as we shall see elsewhere (see pp. 184–197), co-ordination between the three armed services during Operation Husky (the codename for the invasion of Sicily) reached an all-time low. On the other hand, the ground troops appear to have shown a complete absence of initiative. While the gunners shot the easily identified C-47 transports out of the sky without a thought, they also kept up a steady fire against men who called out to them in their own language and supplied the right password. In view of the overwhelming evidence that a mistake had been made, American troops continued to fire at and kill their own men without anyone showing the initiative to call a halt or radio through the information to their headquarters that they had doubts about the identity of the troops they were engaging. Certainly night added to the fears of individuals and the strategic situation, namely that they had just landed on an enemy-held island, must have contributed to their unease, yet these soldiers should have been more than unthinking automatons. The men on the US destroyer *Beatty* who kept firing at a ditched C-47 which was clearly identifiable, and the tank crews who machine-gunned the paratroopers as they descended, had succumbed to the primitive urge to kill in which conscious thought played no part. In such situations friendly fire is an inevitable consequence.

During the fighting around Salerno, Italy, in September 1943, green American troops reacted badly to rumours. Norman Lewis, attached to US Fifth Army Headquarters, wrote of what he saw:

> Outright panic now started and spread among the American troops left behind. In the belief that our positions had been infiltrated by German infantry they began to shoot each other . . . Official history will in due time set to work to dress up this part of the action . . . with what dignity it can. What we saw was ineptitude and cowardice spreading down from the command and this resulted in chaos.[24]

The Second World War saw a transition in the use of artillery, from the massive, static bombardments seen on countless occasions on the Western Front in 1915–18, notably on the

Somme in June 1916 and at Passchendaele in the summer of 1917, to a more mobile and much more flexible use of guns after 1940. This did not mean that the massive barrage did not play a part in battles of this period, as for example by the British under General Montgomery at El Alamein in 1942, but that the blitzkrieg tactics introduced by the Germans against Poland and France stressed mobility as well as firepower, and because battlefronts could change so quickly, particularly on the eastern front, that immobile units of artillery would have been overrun and left miles behind the action. Combined with this increased mobility came the almost universal employment of indirect fire, requiring a precision in target-identification that was difficult to achieve at the time. This resulted in many friendly-fire incidents that have had to be accepted as a small but inevitable part of modern warfare. Charles Shrader has expressed surprise at the relatively small number of cases of artillery amicide reported from the North African theatre of operations in 1942 and 1943. Here, green American troops were responsible for numerous examples of aerial and ground amicide, and it may be the case that there are fewer available sources from which to trace artillery amicide instances. Or, indeed, it may reflect the fact that blue-on-blues were so regular that they provoked less notice. For whatever reason, artillery incidents of amicide during the Second World War produced none of the truly horrific examples cited by both the French General Percin and by British write during the First World War.

The role of the artillery during the Allied advance through Italy from 1943 to 1945 was very significant. The campaign involved fighting in both mountainous terrain and in heavily built-up urban areas. In each, German forces offered tenacious opposition, generally needing to be dug out of powerful defensive positions. Mobility was far less a factor than in North Africa or Normandy, and the attrition struggle was often far more like those typical of the First World War. The result was that Allied artillery played the vital part in 'softening up' the enemy prior to an assault, and in consequence friendly casualties were often heavy, notably where front-line troops became intermingled with those of the enemy in street fighting.

During American assaults on the Gothic Line at Monte Altuzzo in September 1944, a series of blue-on-blue incidents occurred. On three successive days, 14–17 September, elements of US 85th Division suffered casualties from American artillery on four separate occasions. Fighting on the steep and rocky slopes of Monte Altuzzo, men of the 1st Battalion, 338th Infantry, were hit by mortar fire and by artillery shells, pinning them down and wrecking their assault. The Germans were threatening to break the American hold on the mountain by vigorous counter-attacks and the shots fired by their own gunners forced the Company B commander, Captain Maurice Peabody, to pull his men back to Paretaio. Even while engaged in withdrawing, the 338th were not safe from their own guns. Before they reached Paretaio they were hit by American shells, which had been called in to support a neighbouring company of the 2nd Battalion against a major German attack.

Meanwhile, Company C of the 1st Battalion were holding the south-west slopes of the mountain, and on 15 September they were also hit by incoming American fire. One shell struck a group of soldiers, killing six of them including an officer and wounding several others. The commanding officer of 1 Platoon, Lieutenant William Corey, rightly guessing that the shells were American, tried to get the firing stopped but found that his telephone lines had been cut in the explosion. When he did eventually get this message through to the supporting artillery – 329th Field Artillery Battalion – they vehemently denied that the shells had come from them. In fact, the truth was never discovered. But as Charles Shrader has shown, this incident – minor indeed compared to the aerial holocausts of Operations Cobra and Totalize (see pp. 200–213) – was very significant in the effect that it had on the morale of the infantrymen. As Shrader writes:

> Although only one shell actually struck the platoon, the resulting confusion and the belief that it was from friendly artillery had a demoralizing effect on the survivors. The

dazed and angry men had quickly scattered down the hillside and Lieutenant Corey had an extremely difficult time reorganizing his position to face the expected German counterattacks. The shaky men were scarcely capable of maintaining a stubborn defense.[25]

A few misdirected shells had an effect out of all proportion to the casualties they inflicted or the damage they had caused. They had seriously weakened the morale of troops who were already at full stretch holding back a difficult enemy. For the American soldiers in this instance to feel that they were as vulnerable from behind as they were from the front was a blow to a fundamental aspect of warfare: security to the rear. As we saw in the case of General Braddock's British troops on the Monongahela River in 1755, it was the belief that they were being encircled that caused morale to collapse and panic to set in. On Monte Altuzzo, the effect of the few friendly casualties was that the infantry felt unwilling to call in or even accept mortar and artillery support, and without this support infantry assaults became almost impossible. Later attacks by A and C Companies of the 338th were carried out without support from their mortars for fear of having front-line troops hit by their own shells. In consequence, the German defenders were free from artillery bombardment and no doubt inflicted heavier casualties on the advancing Americans than would have been the case had they had to keep their heads down. And yet all the evidence suggests that soldiers would much prefer to risk enemy fire than incur a real – if much smaller – danger of being hit by their own shells. What was lost on Monte Altuzzo was not just artillery support, it was trust. And if soldiers within a unit – battalion, regiment or division – cannot trust each other, and lost confidence in their supporting artillery, then not only does morale suffer but the fighting efficiency as well.

After D-Day, 6 June 1944, the historical record of the progress of the US 30th Infantry Division through the Normandy battlefields has provided Charles Shrader with much evidence of the problems of friendly fire in the European theatre of the war. Examples of amicide were so common during the fighting of 1944–5 that it is only possible to deal with a few of the cases that affected this single division which, in a sense, can stand as an exemplar of what was happening generally in the American sector of operations.

On 7 July, Lieutenant-General Charles Corlett, commanding XIX Corps, of which the 30th Division formed a part, hoped to effect a breakout by using part of the US 3rd Armored Division – the CCB – to cross the Vire river and attack southward in conjunction with the 30th Division. This decision was to set in train a series of confused events that led to incidents of amicide. When the tanks and armoured vehicles of the CCB reached the Vire River at Airel on the night of 7–8 July, they found the whole area crowded with 30th Division infantry. In the milling confusion it was difficult for them to get their heavy equipment across the river by the single bridge. In a startling modern re-run of the Austrian disaster at Karensebes in 1788, the frustration felt by the American troops caused them to begin firing in the air and then, shockingly, firing at each other in their frustration. Even machine guns were brought into action against their fellow Americans. The 30th Division's commander, Major-General Leland Hobbs, shocked by the previous night's madness, complained to the corps commander, Corlett, that his men had suffered 16 casualties, all shot by members of the CCB. There were no casualties reported by the CCB, though the intensity of the firing made it unlikely that they escaped unscathed.

Even when day came on 8 July the situation did not improve. It was very hard to separate the thousands of infantrymen from the heavy equipment because there was no obvious place for them to reassemble once they had become crammed into the streets of the small Norman town. To add to the confusion, the whole area was under counter-attack by German forces of the 2nd SS Panzer Division. General Hobbs tried to keep an even temper, which was difficult in view of the fact that forward units of the 30th Division were in contact with German forces and could not be supported by the divisional artillery, which was trapped in the logjam in Airel. The only answer was to put the two units under the same command and that is what Corlett decided to do, place the CCB under 30th Division command, not entirely to the satisfaction of General Hobbs, who had had a bellyful of the troublesome tankers.

By 9 July, Hobbs may have felt that he was free at last of the problems of Airel, of friendly fire and of the CCB when he was able to order the armour to attack south-west and capture a vital strategic position known as Hill 291. But Hobbs was wrong. The unholy marriage of the CCB and 30th Division was just over the honeymoon period. The commander of the CCB, Brigadier-General Bohn, was having trouble moving his heavy vehicles through the Normandy bocage, the difficult hedgerow terrain that held up Anglo-American forces in the first weeks after the Normandy landings. To make matters worse heavy rain had made the ground thick with mud. Even had he wished to press on and get out of the way of the 30th Division he was finding that the very elements were against him. Eventually everybody lost patience with what they saw as his delaying tactics. His new commander, Leland Hobbs, gave Bohn an ultimatum: either get going and take Hill 291 by 1700 hours or get sacked. This spurred Bohn into action. He ordered one of his tank companies to cross the St Jean de Daye-Pont Hébert road and head straight for Hill 291 and not to stop for anything. At once eight Sherman tanks set off toward Haut-Vents, firing as they went and spraying machine-gun bullets into the surrounding hedgerows. For the moment they were out of the picture but they would be back in time to steal the show in the last reel.

General Hobbs had other things on his mind besides the progress of Bohn's tanks. 30th Division was about to become the meat in a sandwich, attacked by the 2nd SS Panzer Division from the west and the Panzer Lehr Division from the east. During a day of heavy fighting Hobb's attached armoured unit, the 743rd Tank Battalion, was virtually wiped out in a German ambush. Hobbs's 823rd Tank Destroyer Battalion, armed with 36 3-inch and 76mm anti-tank guns, had also been under

intense pressure from German thrusts. On the afternoon of 9
July, 1 Platoon, Company C of the 823rd, led by Lieutenant
Ellis McInnis, was in a defensive position south of the St Jean
de Daye crossroads. Retreating infantrymen reported as they
passed him that German tanks were not far behind and
shellbursts overhead indicated that his unit would soon be in
action against the enemy. Right on cue – at 1800 hours –
McInnis spotted an unidentified tank about a thousand yards
form his position. The lieutenant radioed headquarters to
check if there were any friendly armoured units in that area
and was given the unhelpful reply, 'What you are looking for
is in front of you.' This could almost qualify as one of the great
misleading statements in military history. What was McInnis
looking for? His inquiry was about friendly tanks. Was he
looking for them? Or was he looking for enemy tanks? And
how could headquarters be certain about what McInnis was
looking for? In the event, the tank provided an apparent
answer and saved the young lieutenant from racking his brains
about the meaning of headquarters' enigmatic reply. The tank
set off to the north, spraying the 1 Platoon positions with
machine-gun fire. Soon seven other tanks were seen, which also
fired their machine guns at McInnis's men and opened up with
their 75mm turret guns. At the distance of a kilometre and in
the drizzly, misty conditions, McInnis was unable to make a
positive identification of the tank types but their fire was real
enough to leave him in no doubt that he was in contact with
the enemy. As a result, he ordered his platoon to open fire. In
fact, his men were itching to hit back at the tanks, one of them
already having been slightly wounded by their fire, and with
the first shot they disabled the lead tank, leaving it pouring
smoke and flames. Two or three more shots were fired but no
more certain hits were achieved. But the tanks now headed
straight for McInnis's unit, firing all the time. When they were
no more than 400 yards away one of the anti-tank gunners
identified the tanks as Shermans and called everyone to stop
firing. But the tanks kept firing and they kept coming. Although
Sergeant Nunn courageously stood up and waved at the tanks

he could do nothing more to stop them as they closed in and his men dived for cover. The tanks simply crashed through 1 Platoon's position and continued northwards. McInnis's men suffered only light casualties but a nearby unit led by Lieutenant Raney was not so lucky. As the tanks rumbled past, one of his men was killed by a direct hit from a 75mm shell and two others were wounded. Two Platoon of Company C, led by Lieutenant Connors, also fell foul of the tanks. At a range of just 15 yards, one of the Shermans pumped bullets and shells into an unarmoured half-track, severely wounding the driver. At such range it is inconceivable that the tank crews could have failed to realize that they were destroying American vehicles and killing American troops. It was easy for the soldiers of the 823rd to identify individual tanks, one of which was No. 25 from the 3rd Armored Division and another carried the name BE-BACK on its hull. What is incredible is that nobody in the tanks could make a similar identification of the vehicles and equipment so liberally marked with national and unit insignia. So ferocious was the tank attack that at one stage Raney, McInnis and several others tried to shelter behind a stone building. But as if compelled to exterminate everything in its path, one tank blew the building down with high-explosive shells. At a range of just twenty feet, another of the tanks turned its main armament on Lieutenant McInnis, but after a heartstopping moment it did not fire and moved away. As the seven remaining Shermans moved off northwards they opened fire on another American unit – the 30th Reconnaissance Troop under Lieutenant Curry – and blew a hole in one of their M-8 half-tracks.

This incredible incident had lasted under half an hour and yet it seems to encapsulate all that is inexplicable in amicide. However much one allows for poor visibility, battle fatigue, the fog of war or any other comfortable euphemism, one is left struggling for an explanation for what happened here. The casualties and material losses had fortunately been relatively light but the 823rd were, in the words of their commander, Major Lohse, 'mad as hell'. He described the aftermath of the engagement, by saying that the unit 'took two prisoners which were its first, suffered its first fatal casualties, was shot up by its own Infantry and Armored Force but under all circumstances came through their first critical engagement in fairly good shape and without too serious losses.' The following day Major Lohse carried out an investigation of the curious 'battle' with the Shermans. In the first place he needed to find out why McInnis's platoon had opened fire on the Shermans. His conclusion was that McInnis had been given information by retreating infantry and by headquarters that enemy tanks were classing on his position. The poor visibility on 9 July made identification difficult or indeed impossible at a range of a kilometre and the 823rd had received no reports of friendly tanks in the area. Once the tanks opened fire, Lohse felt, McInnis was entitled to assume that the mystery armour was unfriendly, and as soon as the Shermans began heading north, when the main movement of all Anglo-American thrusts was at that time in a southerly direction, the 823rd were right to assume that they were German. On the other hand, when the tanks were within 400 yards, the 823rd gunners were able to identify them as American and effect an immediate ceasefire. When this did not stop the tanks, several individuals tried to identify their units as American but to no avail. Nothing seemed to stop the tanks and Lohse was at a loss to understand the thinking of the tank crews, who had every opportunity, notably when within a few yards of the 823rd positions, to see that their opponents were American.

The tanks, or course, were those sent by Brigadier-General Bohn to take Hill 291 with all possible urgency. It would be kind if hardly complimentary to the tank commander to suggest, as Charles Shrader does, that he 'became confused'. He had apparently taken a wrong turning at a crossroads and instead of heading towards Haut-Vents he blundered straight into the 823rd TD Battalion position. It can hardly have helped when the lead tank, presumably containing the commander, was knocked out by McInnis. Without proper guidance the other tank crews seem to have lost their heads. Once the remaining Shermans had passed through 823rd's lines they reversed their direction and headed back towards Hill 291 at Haut-Vents, which they reached as darkness fell. Incredibly, no sooner had the tanks actually arrived at their correct position than they were attacked and strafed by American aircraft. Apparently, these strikes had been called in earlier when the hill was occupied by enemy troops, but having been delayed by bad weather they were eventually launched after the Germans had gone and been replaced by friendly units. This illustrated the problems, in terms of amicide, of an increasingly fluid battlefield.

The problems faced by the 823rd were only the top of a very large iceberg. In the early period of the fighting in Normandy, before the breakout, Allied troops were so crowded together that there was bound to be confusion and, in consequence, friendly casualties. On 10 July, the 30th Division again came under fire from American tanks and five days later a more serious blue-on-blue occurred north of St Lô. As the US 29th Division began its assault on the French city, it found itself under fire from units of the neighbouring 35th Division.

During the battle of Schmidt in November 1944 there were many incidents of inaccurate American artillery fire, resulting in friendly casualties. American troops of the 112th Infantry were in retreat from their position in Vossenack, intending to re-establish their lines farther back. Before they left the infantry had summoned artillery fire but, to their consternation, when it came the first four volleys of shells landed right on the new defensive line that was being set up. One shell demolished a barn in which soldiers from 1 Platoon of E Company were sheltering, killing one man and seriously injuring three others. The commander of E Company, Lieutenant Melvin Barrilleaux, rushed to the command post to try to stop the guns but before he had gone more than a few yards another shell killed his sergeant and wounded him. Barrilleaux and the wounded men were evacuated to a casualty clearing station and by the time the friendly fire was halted the entire American position had been fatally weakened so that the retreat continued.

The difficult terrain and the harsh weather conditions made artillery support a very questionable commodity at this stage of the European war. Shrader cites several other examples from this period, including one on 14 December, when men of the US 9th Infantry Division near Wahlerschied, were hit by their own artillery. Later in the same week, men from the 343rd and 344th Infantry Regiments endured a heavy fire from American artillery that so shattered their morale that they nearly panicked and abandoned their posts. Eventually, the American guns were only stopped by an officer running ahead to an observation post and signalling their predicament.

In fairness to the American troops engaged in a confusing and bitter struggle in appalling conditions, Charles Shrader evens things up by citing examples of German friendly fire. On 4 October 1944, near Uebach, troops from the German 49th Infantry Division were hit by their own guns, while on 28 December, not far from Sadist in Belgium, the 25th Panzer Grenadier Regiment called up artillery support only to find that mortar bombs began dropping into their own lines. The problems of a night battle and the difficulty of communicating precise references were clearly at fault here.

An unusual blue-on-blue involving rumoured forces occurred at Oberembt on the night of 26–27 February 1945. The American 30th Infantry Division was engaged with units of two German divisions, the 9th and the 11th Panzer along the Roer River. As the flat terrain provided poor cover for tanks, most of the armoured operations were taking place at night, improving the possibility of concealment but also increasing the likelihood of misidentification. The 117th Infantry regiment had already taken the town of Oberembt and the plan was to push on that night to seize two villages and the town of Putz. As night fell on 26 February, the 3rd Battalion of the 117th was detailed to take the village of Kleintroisdorf, while the 1st Battalion simultaneously captured Kirchtroisdorf. Once these targets had been captured, the 2nd Battalion would move through its sister units and go to take Putz. To overcome the danger from minefield, the infantry was to be supported by

American tanks from the 743rd Tank Battalion and British flail tanks of the Lothians and Border Horse, which had been specially designed to precede the infantry exposing and exploding mines with their flailing chains.

The operation started well and by midnight the two villages had been captured and the 2nd Battalion had begun its advance to take Putz. But the success of the mission was compromised by an unfortunate incident involving the British and American tanks. The four British flail tanks had been ordered to support the 1st Battalion's attack on Kirchtroisdorf; unfortunately, they turned left instead of right and followed the 3rd Battalion towards Kleintroisdorf. After travelling a few hundred yards, the platoon leader, realizing his mistake, turned his tanks round and headed back in the right direction. As they did so they were spotted by American tanks and wrongly identified as German. The American tanks opened fire and destroyed all four of the flail tanks before they could identify themselves. As usual, human error was at the root of a blue-on-blue. A simple navigation error, coupled with poor visibility and a failure to distinguish friend from foe, produced a tragic and wasteful incident.

The friendliest of friendly fire occurs when one side in wartime helps its enemy to inflict casualties on itself. This might sound so unlikely that it is beyond the bounds of historical truth and yet the response of the American people to the threat of enemy action during the early months of war in 1942 can hardly be explained in any other way. When one of the German U-boat commanders involved in Operation *Paukenschlag* or 'Drumbeat' was asked by his crew if he had a map of their area of operations he responded by pulling out a tourist guidebook of New York. This said it all. Maps were unnecessary; the lights of New York City would guide the Germans to their targets and American complacency would do the rest.

Operation Drumbeat, during which dozens of German U-boats patrolled the coastal waters of the eastern seaboard of the United States and sank hundreds of merchant ships illuminated by the brightly lit coastal communities, proved to be the most expensive and disastrous American defeat in the whole war, costing 5,000 lives and threatening the US domestic economy with collapse. The United States came closer to defeat than most Americans realized during the first few months of 1942. It would not have been a defeat involving conquest of American territory but its effects on the oil industry and the rest of the American economy – domestic and military – would have been unprecedented. The crisis also strained relations with the British navy, which felt that it had risked everything to escort the merchant ships across 3,000 miles of Atlantic ocean only for them to be sunk in the last fifty miles when they came under American jurisdiction.

The United States had drifted into war in a fit of absent-mindedness from which the Japanese had awoken them at Pearl Harbor. In January 1942, they had just three cutters or converted yachts operational, to defend an eastern coastline 1,500 miles long. As recently as 1940, plans for 52 new destroyers had been abandoned for reasons of economy. In explaining why were there no coastal defence craft, particularly when war against Germany had been imminent for many months and the Germans were renowned as the most potent submarine power, one must look for the answer in America's 'love affair' with the big gun. Only impressive big-gunned battleships could persuade Congressmen to support naval expenditure, particularly as each battle-wagon that came down the slipway carried the name of one of America's proud states, filling taxpayers with local as well as national pride. Roosevelt was quite aware of this problem when he told Churchill, 'My Navy has been definitely slack in preparing for this submarine war off our coast. As I hardly need not tell you, most naval officers have declined in the past to think in terms of any vessels of less than two thousand tons. You learned the lesson two years ago. We still have to learn it.'

The biggest problem in the defence of America's coastlines in the first few months of the war was to get the American people to take the war seriously. The newspapers they read might speak of battles in Africa, Asia or Europe, but the American people had never previously been persuaded to take any notice of such far-off places. Their troops had gone 'over there' in the First World War and might do so again now, but none of 'over there' ever came 'over here' and therefore most Americans preferred war by proxy. Foreign troops had not been seen on American soil by any living American. The outcome was that Americans expected life to go on normally for them, however unpleasant it might be for the Europeans. The way in which this attitude was displayed was in the American attitude towards 'blackouts' or even 'dimouts'. The lights of the coastal cities illuminated all shore installations and defensive positions, as well as silhouetting targets at sea, like merchant ships. In the case of the main combatant powers coastal blackouts had been rigorously applied but, in the first three months after Pearl Harbor, the Americans made no concessions towards dimming their lights at all, and coastal command did not even suggest it. It was 'business as usual' in the land of free enterprise and no war was going to turn out the lights. America's admirals, at least those who had been to sea, must have been aware of the way in which cities like New York turned night into day, so that merchantmen who tried to hug the coast to avoid discovery by U-boats were lit up by neon lights.

The Germans could hardly believe their luck, fighting a foe who did not seem to mind how many blows he suffered as long as he could pretend that it was business as usual in the shops. Admiral Dönitz would normally expect there to be some reason in this madness and waited to feel the keen edge of retribution at any moment. Instead, all he detected was the kind of token reaction that showed that the Americans were still thinking as individuals and were rejecting the advice that the British gave them. As in the First World War, convoys were the obvious answer. How long would it take the Americans to realize this?

As so often during the Second World War, Hitler's interference with the military planning of his service chiefs came to the help of his enemies. In this case it was the fear of a

British invasion of Norway. Hitler ordered Dönitz to relocate 20 U-boats off the coast of Norway. This was a misuse of resources and it helped the Anglo-American escorts to turn the tide in the battle of the Atlantic, but it owed nothing to coherent American policy. It has often been said that victory in war goes to the side making the fewest mistakes. Even if it is doubtful if the Allies actually made 'fewer' mistakes, their mistakes were certainly less decisive than those made by the Germans and the Japanese.

By mid-March shipping losses off the US coast were so heavy that US naval commander, Admiral King, was beginning to panic, unaware that victory was about to be handed to him on a silver salver bearing Hitler's initials. As far as he could see, matters were absolutely desperate. Moreover, the British were losing their traditional phlegmatic approach to disaster and were beginning to blame their American allies for being incompetent. The British First Sea Lord, Sir Dudley Pound, complained that he safely escorted ships all the way across the Atlantic and as soon as they entered American coastal waters they fell an easy prey to U-boats. Admiral King retaliated by telling Roosevelt that the problem of the U-boats was not an American one but a British one. It was Britain's responsibility to bomb the U-boats and repair yards even though he knew that there was no bomb either in Britain or in the United States that could penetrate the seven-metres thick bunkers which protected the submarines.

If the British were angry at the inadequacy of American methods against the U-boat, the American oil industry was positively furious. In the first two months of 1942, 27 oil tankers had been destroyed off the American east coast and if this continued insurance companies would not cover any merchant ships and oil supplies to American industry would fail. Incredible as it may seem, the American war effort would simply grind to a halt. So heavy were losses among merchant seamen that new men could not be found to fill the ranks. As a result, representatives of the oil industry made demands of the US Navy. These hard-headed businessmen got to the nub of a problem that the naval men had avoided for months: there must be a total blackout on the coast so that merchant ships were not illuminated and rendered easy targets for the U-boats. King responded by requesting dimouts on amusement parks and beaches, not blackouts as was obviously preferable. This was another of King's blunders. The need for blackouts was only later proved after dozens more ships went to the bottom, lit from behind by mindless funseekers ignorant of the price of their neon lighting. Survivors from one vessel torpedoed off Atlantic City later reported that the lights that night were like Coney Island and the whole area was lit up like daylight all along the beach.

If the propaganda campaign next launched by the US Navy had been perpetrated by Josef Goebbels in Germany or Josef Stalin in Russia, Americans would have nodded sagely and reflected on the virtues of democracy and a free press. Instead the campaign was all-American and was used to conceal the failures of the same navy department and of its leader, Admiral Ernest King. Basically, the Navy department began issuing lies. They claimed 28 U-boats had been sunk off the east coast whereas the correct figure was nil. Those citizens who lived in coastal areas must have found these figures surprising for the U-boats were apparently like the heads of the hydra. If 28 had been sunk why did there seem to be more than ever, popping up and disturbing the children paddling in the sea? Also, why was there never any debris from sunken U-boats whereas the beaches were covered in the flotsam from wrecked merchantmen? But the Navy PR officers were not so easily defeated as their anti-submarine operation. They came up with a brilliant idea, one so devious that Goebbels might have surrendered the Sudetenland to own it. They appealed to the public to help to keep their success against the U-boats secret from the enemy. Therefore anyone witnessing the destruction of a U-boat, or photographing it, or finding wreckage on the beaches must keep it to themselves or risk the enemy finding out. Thus the absence of any reports of U-boats being sunk in the press was explained by the fact that the American people was doing its patriotic duty of keeping quiet about it. The fact that, no doubt, dozens of U-boats were being blasted to 'Davy Jones's Locker' warmed the hearts of those who may not have seen it themselves but felt that many others had.

Today this might be called a 'virtual victory' for the American Navy. In 1942 it was a sign of desperation. It was not until somebody whispered the word that had won the U-boat war in 1917 and would do so again by 1943 – 'convoy' – that matters took an upward turn. If the Americans were prepared to find enough small craft to escort convoys near their coasts, the U-boats would find that the 'Happy Time' was over and now they had to pay. Even now Admiral King squirmed at the thought of adding pleasure craft and yachts to his navy at a time when his flat-tops and battle-wagons were fighting it out manfully with the Japanese in the Pacific. Using the argument that had been rejected in Britain in April 1917, King claimed that convoys would merely crowd ships together so that they could more easily be sunk by fewer U-boats. If he had been doing his homework he would have known that the statistics proved him wrong. Meanwhile, something had to be done urgently. In the first six months of 1942 over 400 merchant ships had been sunk off the east coast of America. Though the service chiefs may not have understood the significance of such economic warfare the Army Chief of Staff, General Marshall, slowly realized how serious the situation was. He tried to tell Admiral King of his fear that in another month or two their means of transport would be crippled and they would be unable to bring sufficient men and planes to bear against the enemy to influence the war.

The subsequent blacking out of the coastline and the adoption of convoys saved the Americans from themselves. Operation Drumbeat was one of the strangest examples of friendly fire but one as potentially deadly in its implications as any in this book.

6

The Second World War in the Pacific

The ground war in the Pacific – either the island-hopping operations of the Americans or the jungle fighting of the British in Burma and the Australians and Americans in New Guinea – contained at least as many examples of friendly fire as the more traditional fighting in the European theatre. Added to the normal ingredients for disaster, such as inexperienced troops, poor visibility, misidentification, poor co-ordination, difficult terrain and a hostile environment, must be added the cultural shock brought about by a conflict between Allied and Japanese codes of behaviour. Many green American troops regarded the Japanese as quite unlike themselves: either sub-human through their capacity to survive in the jungle on a handful of rice, or super-human in the early years of their triumphs in South-East Asia. The outcome was that it was not until later in the war that either American or, or for that matter, British troops came to a realistic estimate of their Japanese opponents. This contributed to the feeling of unease felt by American troops in their early engagements with the Japanese and resulted in many blue-on-blue incidents. General Eichelberger described one particular characteristic of American troops: 'Excitedly firing at noises during the night was a common fault and seriously restricted the use of patrols and other important movements after dark.' Indiscriminate firing – later to be a problem in Vietnam – was thus a habit that had to be addressed in an attempt to reduce friendly casualties. On 25 February 1944 a report by Colonel Horace Cushman contained the following:

Killing or wounding our own troops

During recent operations a number of officers and enlisted men have been killed or wounded at night by our own troops who fired with the belief, or for the fear, that the Japs were infiltrating into their areas. The majority of cases reported occurred among troops bivouacked well to the rear of the front line infantry battalions. Some of the men and officers were sleeping in their jungle hammocks when shot. The majority of this 'trigger happy' firing, although not restricted to troops which had not been previously in action, was among newly arrived units.

Officers with battle experience in this theater are of the opinion that this condition is contributed to by the overemphasis placed on the ability of the Jap to infiltrate into our rear areas and by the often heard statement 'stay in your slit trenches after dark, assume that everything that moves is a Jap.'[26]

Fear of the unknown or, for many green American soldiers in 1942 or 1943, the unknowable, in the shape of the Japanese, was at the root of these early friendly-fire incidents. What was rarely understood, of course, was that the Japanese were basically an urban people and most of their troops had been no more accustomed to living and fighting in a jungle than the Americans. In such a case the Americans were victims of their own cultural stereotypes. It was not until the Americans and the British came to terms with their own prejudices about Asian people in general that they were able to encounter them on equal terms. It is noticeable how this problem had still not been overcome by the 1960s in America's long involvement in Vietnam. Even by then American troops had not learned that the enemy should neither be underrated nor overrated. A soldier should fight the enemy that faces him not the one he imagines, otherwise he becomes a victim of his own fears. This 'painting of pictures' has hindered the performance of European and American troops in their conflicts with Japanese and Asiatic troops in the twentieth century.

One of the most extraordinary instances of friendly fire – and one closely linked to the problems of 'painting a picture' – occurred on 15 August 1943, when large numbers of American and Canadian troops were landed in the Aleutians, on the island of Kiska. So severe were weather conditions in the area, with frequent storms, persistent fog and heavy snow, that for weeks at a time it had been impossible even to locate the island. Through a serious intelligence failure, the American commanders expected to face a fanatical resistance by Japanese troops, even though there were, in fact, none whatsoever on the island. The Allied troops selected for this operation had never seen combat before and had obviously been building up an expectation of the struggle of a lifetime against enemies larger than life, tenacious, resilient and fanatical. On 15 August, a huge armada of ships, including two battleships and five cruisers, converged on Kiska. The island had been subjected to more than a fortnight of bombing – when the aircraft had been able to locate the island – and by nightfall 35,000 troops had been landed. By the end of a day of sustained fighting, 28 American servicemen were dead and a further 50 seriously wounded. All of the casualties, it transpired, had fallen victim to their own comrades during gunfights taking place in a thick mist. Upon landing the American troops fanned out in the heavy fog, expecting to face enemy resistance at every turn. The American columns frequently exchanged fire and when night fell the inexperienced soldiers lost even the confidence that daylight had given them. A prey to their own fears, and those of their officers, they fired at every walking shadow. As one survivor, Lieutenant Murphy, later wrote, 'the troops were shooting at anything that moved.' One American soldier, convinced he was attacking a Japanese unit, had to be deliberately shot down by his comrades as he insisted on charging and flinging grenades as he ran, even though they shouted at him to stop in English. The Kiska fiasco was written off by the commanders as good experience. Casualties were unfortunate but it had been a good exercise with live ammunition. As Admiral Kincaid, the invasion commander, later wrote, 'We had no way of anticipating our men would shoot each other in the fog.' As we have seen before, this is not a fair comment. Locate green troops in an area of expected enemy activity, add fog to the equation and one gets a situation ripe for blue-on-blue. Admiral Kincaid should have known better than to blame it all on the men.

At first, American soldiers found themselves completely disorientated in the fighting for the Pacific islands. As one corporal wrote, 'Get used to weird noises at night. This jungle is not still at night. The land crabs and lizards make a hell of a noise, rustling on leaves. And there is a bird here that sounds like a man banging two blocks of wood together. There is another bird that makes a noise like a dog barking.' The result was that many GIs found it difficult to sleep and were constantly alert for the slightest sound. They fired indiscriminately and caused many friendly casualties. One war correspondent wrote about Japanese scare tactics:

> The constant roar of artillery and mortars made it impossible to sleep at night. In addition, the Japs used night harassing tactics. Most of the night fighting was done with knives and machetes. Muzzle blast from rifle fire at night gave away positions and locations of troops. During the night men rested in foxholes three or four feet deep. Usually there were four men in a foxhole, sometimes less. Japs sneaked in pairs towards the foxholes. One would often jump into the middle of our men and try to stab them. The others stood by to see the outcome. Sometimes the Japs would jump in the foxhole and then jump out quickly hoping our troops would become excited and stab each other.[27]

On New Georgia, there was an outbreak of friendly fire among green troops. Terrified by Japanese psychological tactics, American soldiers sprayed bullets about and even threw grenades, killing a number of their comrades. On Hollandia, units of the US 24th Division lost all control and fell victim to their fears. According to General Eichelberger, the men who had been ordered to guard his headquarters:

> . . . carried on a terrific war. Tracer bullets from all directions made fireworks in the camp. Automatic rifles were fired and grenades were thrown. Troops on the inside and on the outside thought they were being attacked by the Japanese . . . the battle of Brinkman's Plantation was . . . a battle among Americans. A master-sergeant was killed, a number of troops were wounded. It was a disgraceful exhibition.[28]

General Omar Bradley, when questioned about the main shortcomings of inexperienced troops, listed 'reliance on rumor and exaggerated reports' as one of the most debilitating factors. This weakness was clearly in evidence during a large number of the Pacific friendly-fire incidents. It was only necessary for the word to spread that there were Japanese troops on the loose for green troops to begin spraying bullets about. It was not so much the Japanese soldiers themselves who inspired the fear, it was the 'idea' of them, the strangeness and the fierceness of their behaviour, the fanaticism and cruelty with which they fought, their willingness to give up their lives and fight to the end. In open combat the American soldiers were at least the equals of the Japanese but, in the jungle environment of so many of the Pacific battlegrounds, the American soldier felt isolated and alienated. As he fired his bullets indiscriminately into the tropical vegetation, it was not just the Japanese soldier that he was trying to keep at bay but the primal fear he felt in himself of darkness and the unknown. American military training failed to help their men to adjust to jungle fighting, both in the Pacific, in New Guinea, and later in

Vietnam. A British sergeant, reflecting later on American training methods, made the following valid observations:

> It appeared that the American infantrymen were not trained in 'battle noises'. They seemed to drop to the ground and fire wherever shots were heard close by . . . It was purely a matter of lack of experience. They were shouting at each other and firing at nothing.[29]

A common feature of friendly-fire incidents in the Pacific war was poor co-ordination between different units, notably between army units and the Marines. During the invasion of the Gilbert Islands, in November 1943, the planners of US 27th Division devised a system for occupying the island of Makin that almost guaranteed friendly casualties. The island was divided virtually in half by a deep and wide trench, known as the West Tank Barrier. In order to overcome this obstacle the plan was for 1st and 2nd Battalions of the 165th Infantry Regiment to co-ordinate an attack from both east and west simultaneously. The two battalions would stay in radio contact throughout and signal to each other with coloured smoke flares, to avoid friendly casualties. It must have seemed a foolproof system to the planners aboard some US naval unit in the Pacific. But to the battalion commanders on Makin – Lieutenant-Colonel Gerard Kelley of the 1st and Lieutenant-Colonel John McDonough of the 2nd – it soon became a nightmare. In the first place, each failed to establish radio contact with the other. Next, the 1st Battalion soon found themselves pinned down by what they assumed was friendly fire from their sister battalion. In spite of every effort to get the 2nd Battalion to stop firing, Kelley was ordered to get his men moving forward to meet up with McDonough. While the Americans were making things harder for themselves, Japanese snipers were adding to the confusion by picking off stragglers. So panicky did the American soldiers become that they kept firing throughout the night of 20–21 November, inflicting more friendly casualties and wasting huge quantities of ammunition, without ever having much idea where the Japanese defenders were. Dawn on 21 November only brought more absurd incidents. Landing craft approaching Yellow Beach machine-gunned two empty hulks, which had already been rendered uninhabitable by air attacks. But, convinced that they harboured Japanese troops, first the LCIs strafed them, then further air strikes were called in to attack them and finally tanks were brought on to the beach to bombard them with their main armament. Apart from being a waste of ammunition this mad attack on 'phantom enemies' resulted in many friendly casualties, as bullets and shells went over or through the hulks and wounded American troops in the jungle behind. The problem was that the troops were mainly inexperienced National Guardsmen, in action for the first time, who allowed themselves to be pinned down by even small pockets of Japanese defenders. At night they were demoralized by Japanese scare tactics, including simple techniques like uttering threats in English, throwing firecrackers and keeping up a regular sniper fire. The American troops of the 27th Division were thoroughly rattled and kept firing indiscriminately at unseen targets, exposing themselves to counter-fire. As one soldier wrote:

Smoking out the snipers that were in the trees was the worst part of it. We couldn't spot them even with glasses and it made our advance very slow. When we moved forward it was as a skirmish line, with each man being covered as he rushed from cover to cover. That meant that every man spent a large part of his time on the ground. If one of our men began to fire rapidly into a tree or ground location, we knew that we had spotted a sniper, and those who could see took up the fire. When we saw no enemy we fired occasional shots into trees that looked likely.[30]

Some of the Americans lost their nerve complete and one ran along the beach shouting, 'there's a 150 Japs in the trees.' This only added to the hysteria as the men of the 27th peppered the trees and each other with wild fire. It took nearly four days to complete the occupation of the island of Makin, during which time Japanese submarines exacted a heavy toll on American support ships which should have been able to move away from the island in the first 24 hours.

The co-ordination of artillery fire was sadly amiss during the Buna campaign in Papua. Relations with Australian troops in the operation were strained when a mortar bomb from an American battery fell on a command post occupied by Captain Jack Blamey, nephew of General Sir Thomas Blamey, C-in-C of the Australian Army and Supreme Commander, allied Land Forces, South-West pacific. Captain Blamey was killed along with another soldier and six other ranks were wounded.

A further dimension to friendly fire in the Pacific War was added by the role played by naval gunfire in supporting American ground troops. The situation for the naval gunners was fraught with difficulties, not least because they were always firing blind and frequently had to find their targets after bombing runs by aircraft. The consequent smoke and dust clouds made targeting almost impossible. On 22 February 1944, American ships were due to support a landing at Parry Island. The planes had already plastered the Japanese defences and much of the island was masked by smoke. As the landing craft approached the shore they disappeared entirely into the murk and unfortunately were hit by shells fired from the American destroyer *Hailey*, resulting in 13 deaths and 47 men wounded. On the same day, further 5-inch shells from American destroyers hit friendly troops and destroyed a number of tanks. In view of the fact that the naval gunfire had helped in the suppression of Japanese resistance on the island the friendly casualties were accepted as the price that has to be paid for such indirect fire in difficult conditions.

In April 1944, during the occupation of Bougainville, Company K of the all-black 25th Regimental Combat Team, on its first patrol, encountered a Japanese machine-gun position. Coming under enemy fire for the first time, the men of Company K panicked and began firing wildly, and then more carefully, at each other. In spite of every effort by the company commander to stop the firing, by the time the company fled in disorder it had suffered ten men killed and 20 wounded, many of whom had fallen to the bullets of their comrades. The American operation on Saipan in June 1944 was controversial less for the numerous incidents of friendly fire than for the relief from his command of Major-General Ralph Smith, GOC 27th Division, by Lieutenant-General Holland Smith, commander of V Amphibious Corps. The dispute revolved around the slow and uncertain performance of Ralph Smith's men, which had already been seen during the occupation of Makin. On Saipan, the 27th were frequent victims of their own artillery. But what made matters worse was that the 27th's artillery also distributed its shells on neighbouring marine units, causing heavy casualties. In Charles Shrader's opinion, 'Although Ralph Smith's relief was ostensibly based on the slow and uncoordinated advance of his division on June 23, there can be little doubt that Holland Smith's decision was influenced by the unwarranted shelling of his marines by the 27th Division's artillery.' In a sense, therefore, Ralph Smith was himself a victim of friendly fire.

The Americans were not the only troops on Saipan guilty of friendly fire. Japanese soldiers, unwilling to accept defeat and surrender, chose suicide for themselves and killed any of their own people less eager than they to follow the military code of honour. Japanese civilians, mostly women and children, had been fleeing from the advancing Americans until, on the cliffs at the northern tip of the island, there was nowhere else to go. It is believed that as many as two-third of the 12,000 civilians on the island committed suicide by drowning or leaping from the 800-foot cliffs. Japanese snipers shot down any of their people who tried to surrender.

The occupation of Guam in July and August 1944 was fraught with difficulties of co-ordination between army and marine units, as on Makin and Saipan. The dense jungle and fanatical Japanese resistance was responsible for holding up to the advance of the 77th Infantry Division to capture Mount

Barrigada. Part of the trouble was the roadblocks set up by the Japanese. As a result, a platoon from the 307th Regiment, supported by a tank, was ordered to pass down Finegayan Road to clear them. Having successfully removed two blocks the tank opened fire on a suspected third roadblock, only to find that it was manned by men from the 3rd Marine Division. The marines had been warned that the army patrol was coming but clearly the patrol had not been told to expect the marines. The army men had expected friendly forces to identify themselves with red smoke but nobody had told the marines. The army patrol would not stop firing until the marine company commander risked his life by waving his helmet and running down the road towards them. Seven marines had been wounded in the snafu (the common term for a military blunder).

A few days later the marines got their revenge. A patrol from 2nd Battalion of the 306th Infantry was moving along the Salisbury Road when it came under rifle fire. The suspicion was that the fire was coming from the 3rd Marines and this suspicion became a certainty when the rear company of the 2nd Battalion got into a fire-fight with marines at a road junction. When a complaint was lodged at 3rd Marine Division Headquarters, the army was told categorically that there were no marines in the area of the incident. No sooner had this reply been received by the army than the command post of the 306th Infantry Regiment came under fire from marine howitzers, while another army patrol was machine-gunned along Salisbury Road by men suspected of being marines.

It seemed that the Japanese were not needed: the Americans were content to fight themselves. Co-ordination between army and marine units had reached a new low-point and it seems impossible to attach an 'accidental' label to all of these incidents. On 8 August, units from the 77th Infantry Division, the 1/306th and 3/307th Regiments, engaged in a costly fire-fight. Each had come under mortar fire from the general direction of the other and, apparently using this as justification and making no attempt to identify the enemy – who could have been Japanese, after all – they returned mortar fire. Each radioed that they were engaged with a Japanese counter-attack and then began spraying bullets in the general direction from which the mortar bombs had come. As the firing increased, both battalions became increasingly certain that this could not just be friendly fire but must now involve the Japanese. Tanks supporting the 306th Infantry joined in and shelled the 307th's position. As if this was not enough, each battalion then called for artillery support and a barrage was fired by the 902nd Field Artillery Battalion. Eventually the situation was brought under control but not before both battalions had suffered significant casualties. It was another example of the effects of mass hysteria. Officers who should have known better shot first and looked for excuses afterwards.

7

Ground Warfare Since 1945

Friendly-fire incidents in the Korean War of 1950–53 resulted from the poor training and often low morale of an American army which was raised hastily and had to learn its profession on the battlefield rather than the parade ground. A few selected from the depressingly large number illustrate the difficulties a pampered, peacetime force encountered in coming to terms with the harsh realities of a war situation. On 7 July 1950, the 3rd Battalion of the 34th Infantry, in action against North Korean regulars near Ch'onan, was targeted by its own artillery and hit by mortar fire. Only when Major John Dunn went to the rear himself was the fire brought to a halt. Later, as the American troops were forced to retreat, men of the 21st Regiment were bombed and strafed by American planes.

Later in the year, with the intervention of the Communist Chinese on the North Korean side, matters became even more desperate. The American retreat from the Chongchon River revealed an army in disintegration. Green troops sprayed bullets in all directions and a machine-gunner, in a state of shock, turned his weapon on his own colleagues. The fact that the American troops were fighting under the flag of the United Nations only served to make things more difficult. With 14 nations committing combat troops, misidentification between allies made amicide a strong possibility. To make matters worse, there were Koreans on both sides and this latter point resulted in a disastrous blue-on-blue on 26 November 1950. The South Korean II Corps, fighting on the right flank of the American 2nd Division, was broken by Chinese attacks and forced to retreat southwards. During the early afternoon, the commander of the US 38th Infantry Regiment, Colonel Peploe, witnessed a mass of disorganized Korean solders fleeing through his lines. It was the 3rd South Korean Regiment, in full retreat. But the American soldiers had not been told to expect Koreans heading south and opened fire on them, believing them to be assault troops of the North Koreans. After some difficulty Peploe managed to halt the American friendly fire. But at American divisional headquarters the decision had already been taken to bolster the front weakened by the South Korean collapse with troops from the Turkish Brigade, newly arrived at the front and quite unaware of the identity of the fleeing Korean troops. No senior American commander briefed the Turks as to their task; they were simply thrown in at the deep end to sink or swim. Undeterred, the Turks – 5,000 strong – immediately set about the first Koreans they met. Unfortunately, they turned out to be the fleeing South Korean 3rd Infantry Regiment. Near the village of Wawon the Turks came under fire and responded fiercely. Soon the American 2nd Division Headquarters was deluged with reports from the Turks that they had just routed the enemy, inflicting many casualties and taking numerous prisoners: unfortunately, they were the South Koreans. While the Turkish Brigade was licking its wounds and relishing its victory, it was suddenly hit by overwhelming numbers of Chinese. For two days it hung on but when it eventually fell back it was found to have been so badly depleted that the Americans felt obliged to apologize officially to the Turkish government. A further setback occurred the next day when the South Korean troops attached to Colonel Peploe's 38th Infantry command tried to launch a counter-attack against the Chinese and were brought under a crushing fire from nearby American tanks.

One of the most tragic cases of amicide on record occurred during the Korean War. Whilst fighting along the Imjin River on 23 April 1951, the British 29th Brigade, containing the 1st Battalion of the Royal Northumberland Fusiliers, the 1st Battalion of the Royal Ulster Rifles and the 1st Battalion of the Gloucestershire Regiment, was ordered to withdraw from its positions to avoid being overrun by heavy Chinese concentrations. Most of the brigade got away but the Glosters were surrounded by a full division of Chinese regulars. They soon ran short of ammunition, medicines and food and although American planes tried to drop supplies, most of them fell into Chinese-occupied areas. Wave after wave of US fighter-bombers swept in, drenching the rocky hills with napalm, but in spite of artillery and air attacks the Chinese tightened their grip on the beleaguered British troops. Throughout 23 April, the Glosters beat off attack after attack by waves of Chinese, but at dawn on the 24th, A Company was overrrun, while B Company was reduced to just one officer and fifteen other ranks. Of the original 622 officers and men, the Glosters had been reduced to a small but tough group of men holding a perimeter of just a few hundred yards. Lieutenant-Colonel J P Carne, commanding the battalion, called for helicopter support to evacuate his wounded but the enemy fire was too fierce to risk bringing the choppers in. On the afternoon of 24 April, several attempts were made to relieve the British but they were driven back by overwhelming Chinese numbers. As night fell on the 24th, the Chinese renewed their attacks but all through the hours of darkness the Glosters drove the enemy back, until the hillsides surrounding their position were covered with thousands of enemy dead. At dawn on 25 April, Carne's battalion was down to less than 300 men and ammunition was so low that the British only fired when the Chinese were within fifteen yards of their lines. With the rest of the 29th Brigade in full retreat the Glosters were now entirely on their own, in a sea of Chinese troops. There was nothing left for the survivors but to try to break out as best they could. Colonel Carne again called in air support and once again the US dive bombers answered the call, blasting out the Chinese from within thirty or forty yards of the British position. Yet however many Chinese fell there was still no way out for the Glosters and Carne called his company commanders together to offer them the choice of surrendering or trying to fight their way clear. Most chose the second option, though there was no chance of taking the numerous wounded men with them and Carne himself volunteered to stay with the injured. With Carne, the battalion doctor and the chaplain, stayed the Regimental Sergeant-Major, Hobbs, a man who had spent his whole adult life with the regiment.

Once the decision was made, the remnants of B, C and D companies set off southwards to try to break through Chinese lines. Captain Michael Harvey led the 100 men of his group north instead, then westwards, circling round the Chinese positions, before heading south to where he hoped to find friendly positions. At first Harvey's group was lucky, wiping out small Chinese sections but encountering no large enemy units. But their luck did not hold. Moving down a valley they found the hills on both sides swarming with Chinese. Harvey later estimated that 40 artillery pieces opened up on his grim band and several of the Glosters were killed or wounded. Yet Harvey had made it clear from the outset that there could be no stopping for casualties; every man knew that. The survivors of his party found refuge from the Chinese fire in a foot-deep ditch which ran along much of the valley. Still men fell while the rest struggled on, their hands and feet bleeding from the jagged rocks over which they were forced to crawl. Just as the survivors felt their suffering would never end, they saw a sight that must have lifted their hearts: about 500 yards away was a line of American Sherman tanks, stretched across the valley, which were firing at the advancing Chinese troops. Harvey and his men struggled to their feet and ran and crawled towards the tanks. The young American lieutenant in charge of the tanks had received no instructions to keep a lookout for friendly troops in the area and certainly would not have expected to see them coming towards him from the direction of the Chinese. As Harvey and his men got closer to the tanks, the lieutenant ordered his Shermans to open fire on them with machine guns and main armament. In seconds at least six Glosters were cut down. It was a tragic case of misidentification. An American plane, identifying the men as British, swooped down low over the tanks, waggling its wings and trying to distract the Shermans from their prey, but the lieutenant continued firing.

Captain Harvey, lying flat on the ground to allow the tank fire to pass over his head, found a stick within reach, stuck his cap on it and crawled forward, waving it at the tanks, but to no avail. Trapped between a pursuing enemy behind and friendly fire ahead, many of the exhausted Glosters were caught and bayoneted by the Chinese. Desperate to end this atrocious blue-on-blue, the circling US plane flew low over the tanks and dropped a hastily scrawled note. The truth at last dawned on the unhappy US tankers, who realized they had been machine-gunning friendly forces who had just fought their way out from the midst of overwhelming Chinese forces. The tanks stopped firing and the wretched survivors were able to crawl into American lines. Together the tanks and what was left of the Glosters retreated down the valley to safety. Harvey would never admit to the Americas how many of his men had fallen under their fire. Harvey's 38 men were the only survivors not to be captured from the entire 1st Battalion of the Gloucestershire Regiment, known to the world ever afterwards as the 'Glorious Glosters' for their heroic resistance. Rather fewer people know the dismal fate of Harvey's survivors, victims of a tragic blue-on-blue; perhaps it is better that way.

A second and much more famous blue-on-blue, immortalized in print by S L A Marshall and on celluloid by a famous war film, *Pork Chop Hill*, occurred during the Korean War. In the last few weeks of the fighting, in April 1953, American and Chinese forces were contesting possession of a hill, named Pork Chop Hill. Two companies – K and L – of the 31st Infantry Regiment, part of the American 7th Division, were ordered to attack and take the hill but from opposite sides. Poor co-ordination between the units contributed to a classic blue-on-blue. No sooner had Company K reached the top of the hill than they came under fire from the machine guns of Company

L. Believing the hill to be held by the Chinese, nothing could convince 1 Platoon of Company L to stop firing until they literally ran out of ammunition.

Incidents of amicide among ground troops were so frequent during the long American involvement in Vietnam (1965–73) that it would be tedious to attempt to do more than indicate some of the main problems experienced there. At least five per cent of all casualties during the war were due to accidents and friendly fire. Ten thousand Americans died from non-combat causes, including amicide, and deaths from the latter cause were always listed as KIA – killed in action. According to Charles Shrader, incidents of amicide in Vietnam 'were precipitated by nervousness and lack of fire discipline or by inadequate coordination.'

The American military philosophy in Vietnam, as in Korea, was to employ technology as substitute for using highly trained infantry. This fallacious policy, sometimes referred to as spending bullets rather than lives, resulted in the application of aircraft, helicopter gunships and artillery to a situation that could better have been handled by the men on the ground. This application of hardware often hampered the work of the infantry, as well as inflicting unnecessary casualties on them from blue-on-blues. However, the use of firepower rather than manpower was popular with the troops and with public opinion in the USA. Although it reduced casualties from enemy fire, in many ways it revealed an underlying lack of commitment on the part both of the generals and the politicians, who feared the political effects of a high body count more than they feared the Communists.

The majority of the American troops involved were not regular soldiers and lacked a high degree of dedication or self-motivation. Most, as civilian draftees, were naturally much concerned with self-preservation and their commitment to the military profession or the cause of saving Vietnam from the Communists was questionable in many cases. The unpopularity of the war both among soldiers in Vietnam and amongst the public in the United States only served to lower morale. Racial stereotyping, of the kind that had affected American and British soldiers in their attitude towards the Japanese in the Second World War, was even more marked in American attitudes towards the Vietnamese people as a whole, and this obviously contributed to a wide range of friendly-fire incidents, some of an undisciplined nature like fragging. Two brief examples from Shrader can serve to represent the kind of errors that were regular occurrences in the confused jungle fighting. In October 1966, during a patrol near Bong Son, a soldier of the 12th Cavalry stepped off the jungle path his unit was following to relive himself. When he returned his was mistaken for an enemy and shot dead by his own best friend. A second incident, five years later, involved a soldier who, becoming disoriented, wandered out of his unit's defensive perimeter. Finding himself lost, he returned to his lines from a different direction and was shot dead by one of his colleagues. Casualties from this cause – carelessness and panic by inexperienced troops operating in a threatening environment – make no headlines. Nor is it always possible to tell how patrol casualties were caused, whether killed by the enemy or accidentally by their friends. One can only surmise that these accidental killings must have made up a far from insignificant percentage of the total American casualties in Vietnam.

An incident involving Australian troops offers a rarer and yet more substantial example of ground amicide from Vietnam. It emphasizes the problems of co-ordination between small platoon-size units and how in the difficult environment of a jungle battleground mistakes of identification are almost inevitable. On 19 September 1971, Lieutenant Gary McKay was part of a company-size operation in thick, leafy jungle to the south-east of an area known as the Courtenay Rubber Plantation in Phouc Tuy Province in the very south of Vietnam. While out on patrol McKay received a warning from company headquarters that he could expect to encounter enemy troops within a thousand yards of his position and so he issued verbal warnings to each member of his platoon before moving on. His platoon had gone no more than another 150 yards when firing broke out at the front of the column. McKay called out 'Contact front' to his signaller to inform the rest of the company but was surprised when the signaller replied that their neighbouring unit – 10 Platoon – had already reported that they were in contact with the enemy as well. In McKay's words, 'My mouth went dry and my heart skipped a beat as it struck me what was happening. I sprinted forward screaming out for everyone else to cease firing . . .' It was a blue-on-blue. McKay's platoon had blundered into another Australian unit: itchy trigger fingers had done the rest, with inevitable results. McKay's scout had shot one of the other platoon members in the head, inflicting a shocking, certainly mortal wound. McKay remembers, as he passed by the other platoon, one of the soldiers 'mouthed an obscenity at me and I turned on him and let loose with all the venom I could muster. I knew how he must have felt having lost a mate because of a mistake on my part, but I really didn't need that kind of hassle just there and then.'

McKay next set out to investigate how the accident had occurred. The forward scout had apparently fired at an unidentified movement which McKay explains was exactly what his platoon had been trained to avoid. But no amount of practising could prepare troops for the real thing and once exposed to a situation in which troops were told they were within a thousand yards of the enemy, men were inclined to shoot first and feel guilty afterwards. And, of course, the guilt felt by men who had shot comrades was something impossible to quantify or permanently to remove. McKay admitted that he felt much of the responsibility himself for having chosen the wrong track. Although he had not pulled the trigger he could not rid himself of the feeling that he was responsible for the actions of the men in his platoon. Both McKay and the forward scout benefited from continuing on the search-and-destroy mission, although no contact was made with the enemy. It was vital that neither man be allowed too much time to think about the blue-on-blue or else morale in the platoon would have been irrevocably reduced. McKay was pleased that there was no contact with the enemy as he was doubtful how his platoon would have responded. It was possible that they would have been so aware of the need for caution that they would have fallen into the error of being too cautious, thus reducing combat efficiency. In the event, the patrol passed off peacefully, except for the blue-on-blue.

McKay had already expressed his unease at being dependent for artillery support on neighbouring American units, some of which he believed to be less than combat efficient as a result of the drugs that so many of the soldiers seemed to regard as essential to their survival in Vietnam. McKay feared that if they were to fire in support of his unit, there was every chance of a blue-on-blue. As he wrote:

> The platoon were visiting the US 155s as they hadn't seen these huge guns before and so I took the opportunity to speak to the lieutenant in charge . . . He was a decent sort of a bloke but who had a real load on his plate.
>
> . . . I asked him quite bluntly what all the noise was the night before. He looked at me and said, 'Oh yeah, last night was our beer ration night and everyone was letting off a little steam.' I commented that they must have had a truckload of beer from all the noise they were making; he said 'Shit, no man, they smoke dope.' I couldn't believe my ears. Here was a direct support battery of 155mm guns firing in support of us and the battery was full of pot heads! I questioned him further and asked how he controlled this sort of thing and he said that they had a weekly 'shake-down' when they search the soldiers' tents, but when the soldiers ran past his bunker on the way to muster, they would throw the dope into his bed space to avoid detection. He was quite sincere when he said that he considered he was pretty lucky since 'none of my guys are on to hard stuff.'
>
> I was stunned and had to thank God that we didn't have a drug problem in our army like the Americans had. It still worried me a lot that these soldiers were likely to fire in

support of us whilst we were patrolling in this area . . . I made a mental note that if and when we called for fire support in future I would try not to use that American battery.[31]

The thick foliage in the Vietnamese jungle accounted for a number of blue-on-blue incidents. In his recent autobiography, General Norman Schwarzkopf describes the cause of the incident that gave rise to C D B Bryan's book, *Friendly Fire*:

On the night of February 18, 1970, C Company had dug in on a jungle hilltop. They'd made a routine request for our artillery to zero in on the trails near their position in case the Vietcong attacked during the night. One of the test rounds detonated directly above them, spraying the men with shrapnel and killing Michael Mullen and another soldier. A subsequent investigation concluded that a lieutenant at the artillery fire direction centre, in calculating trajectories, had forgotten to take into account the vegetation on the hilltop. The round had been meant to sail over C Company; instead it had hit a tree and exploded.[32]

Gary McKay describes a similar incident, involving shells fired by the Australian artillery:

The forward observer started adjusting artillery fire as close as we could get it and the plan was that we would keep the artillery falling just in front of the assault to keep any enemy in depth to our assault line from interfering with our attack. This proved more difficult than anyone had imagined: as the trees were so tall they were catching the odd shell, and we took a few minor casualties from our own artillery fire. The wounds were not too bad – mainly shrapnel wounds to the backs of the legs.[33]

The risk of shells being deflected by tree branches is further demonstrated in two more incidents recorded by Charles

Shrader. In the first, US Special Forces operating on the Cambodian border in April 1968, lost four men killed and 15 wounded when an 8-inch shell exploded in the treetops, directly over their position. On 10 May 1968, four men of the 327th Infantry Regiment were killed when a shell with a delayed-action fuse hit a tree and was deflected into their position.

The computations made by artillerymen are sometimes prone to error and this contributed to inaccurate or short firing with consequent friendly casualties in Vietnam, as elsewhere. In addition, the miscalculation of powder charges by gun crews can be fatal. Shrader cites several examples of this problem. In 1968, an inexperienced member of a gun crew selected different lots of powder for individual shells during a fire mission. The result was that the shells showed great inconsistency, falling short or well over the target and also landing among friendly troops. In 1970, at a fire-support base near Hue, a howitzer battery made the same mistake, resulting in a shell hitting a company from the 101st Airborne Division, killing a man and wounding others. But the worst case, according to Shrader, was an incident in late 1967 in which a gun-crew error in handling charges result in Charge 7 being used rather than the correct Charge 4. When the guns were fired shells landed in an American base camp, causing 38 casualties. The unit that had been hit promptly responded with counter-battery fire and hit the perpetrators of the error, killing 12 men and wounding 40 more. It was an object lesson in the dangers of indirect fire. Human error had created a chain reaction that lasted 25 minutes and cost 90 casualties.

The confusion of the fighting in Vietnam was at the root of many blue-on-blue incidents, as Eric M Bergerud recalled so memorably in his book, *Red Thunder, Tropic Lighning*, describing the experiences of the men serving in the 25th Combat Division. In the first, an unconsidered action by a tank crew had serious results:

A fight ensued, with shots right and left. Although I didn't realize it until the next day, while the shooting was going on, there was an American tank nearby. He heard the action and decided that he wanted to get into it. He fired two fléchette [shell containing hundreds of small steel darts, scattered on detonation] rounds. Unfortunately, one of the rounds went right into my platoon, and eleven men were wounded, a couple very seriously.[34]

Misidentification of friend and foe is not only a problem for artillery, miles behind the front, or aircraft operating above the clouds. It is at its most deadly when it applies to small units or even individuals. In this instance soldier Dan Vandenberg describes the sort of incident that must have occurred on countless occasions not just in Vietnam or the jungle fighting of the Second World War, but in house-to-house operations in the European theatre or night patrols in the First World War. What is apparent is the ever-present fear felt by the individual soldier and the ease with which mistakes can be made. Just a split second to decide whether to fire or not and on that moment's thought your life may depend. It is hardly surprising that so many soldiers have pulled the trigger, and lived only to regret the error.

Marsh and I were walking parallel to each other as we entered the woods. You're all pretty jittery because you know Charles [the Vietcong] is in there someplace, and instead of staying 10 to 15 yards apart, we started coming closer together without knowing it because you can't really see through the thick terrain. All of a sudden, we came to a break in the woods, and out of the corner of my eye, I saw something. I turned and started to pull the trigger, and I was looking right at Marsh, and he was pulling his trigger. If a fly would have sneezed, that's all it would have taken for each of us to have ripped off a magazine at each other. That's when I saw the ultimate look of fear. When I looked at his eyes, all I saw was white. I imagine my face looked the same.[35]

And with the error came the guilt – the knowledge that you had been responsible for killing one of your comrades. As we saw in the case of the Australian officer, Lieutenant McKay, the guilt can so affect the morale of not just an individual but of a whole unit, that they become incapable of combat.

> Track 13 [tracked armoured personnel carrier] was in flames: They had taken a pretty heavy hit from an RPG [rocket-propelled grenade] . . . One of the guys from 3rd Squad came walking on down towards us, walking away from the burning APC . . . I leaned out of my turret and asked if anybody up there was hurt. He just looked up and said, 'Dave's dead.' Dave was probably my best friend I had over there, the .50 gunner on Track 13. He was killed instantly, a direct hit. I was stunned and my mind locked up on me, and I didn't want to believe it . . . So we stayed in position for maybe five minutes until some of the other tracks backed up and turned round and we figured a way to get the hell out of there . . . They carried this guy right by my APC on a stretcher. To make it worse, we were told a little later, that he had been killed by a .50 calibre round from one of our own machine guns. Either I killed him or the APC behind me did. They were the only two. 50s that were in the action. I like to think it wasn't me because of the direction I was firing in relation to the firefight, but I'll never know.[36]

In the confusion of battle accidents occur. They are tragic but who can take responsibility for chaos? Here an American NCO is hit by an artillery round from a friendly gun:

> The VC [Vietcong] broke through the lines. They were shooting behind you: they were shooting in front of you. When the artillery guys lowered their guns, they were firing these bee-hive rounds point blank at the charging Vietnamese. They were opening the breech, sighting down the bore, slamming in a bee-hive round and just firing. Our sergeant ran in front of an artillery piece, and the bee-hive round cut him to pieces.[37]

And, as in all other wars, non-combat accidents accounted for a high proportion of casualties in Vietnam. Lieutenant-Colonel Carl Neilson wrote of one such incident:

At the end that day, we had a terrible accident where a box of claymore mines went off in an armoured personnel carrier and killed 5 soldiers. We had fought all night and all day, had swept the battlefield, had suffered 5 or so men killed and about 10 men wounded, and had inflicted 400 casualties, and then, right at the very end, 5 guys were killed through the carelessness of somebody who had left a set of detonators in with the claymore mines. I guess that is kind of the story of Vietnam combat.[38]

During the Falklands War of 1982 there were a number of blue-on-blue incidents, the details of which have only recently been made public. Even the high professionalism of the British troops on the islands did not prevent at least two tragic and costly mistakes. In fact, in the case of the death of 'Kiwi' Hunt, an SBS (Royal Marines Special Boat Squadron) NCO, it was rather an excess of professionalism rather than its lack that cost him his life. Hugh McManners relates the incident in his recent book *The Scars of War*. Not long after the British landing on East Falkland, at San Carlos, G Squadron of the SAS (Special Air Service Regiment) ambushed an SBS patrol of four men led by Sergeant 'Kiwi' Hunt. The elite SBS troops had 'blundered' into the equally elite SAS operation area and the SAS men were following every movement of Hunt's patrol through night-vision equipment. The senior officer commanding G Squadron had placed himself alongside his machine-gunner and the two men were trying to decide whether the approaching figures were friendly troops or not. The machine-gunner, convinced that no friendlies should be operating in their operational area, wanted to fire first and ask questions afterwards but the officer held him in check, still anxious over the identity of the men approaching. When Hunt's men were just thirty feet away they were challenged by the SAS officer.

Hunt apparently stood stock still and held his weapon away from his body at arm's length, as did the two men directly behind him. But the man at the back, possibly not hearing the challenge, tried to get away in the darkness. This threat to the ambush overrode the officer's hold on his machine-gunner and the man immediately opened fire, killing Hunt instantly. It was a tragic mistake but for men operating at the peak of their profession it was not allowed to become a matter of deep regret. The SAS reaction was that Hunt had made a mistake and had paid for it with his life. In the hard world of these special forces Hunt had allowed himself to be ambushed and had suffered the inevitable consequences. The rivalry between the SAS (Army) and SBS (Royal Marines) undoubtedly played its part in absorbing the tragedy of this useless loss of life and neither unit wanted to be seen to be 'giving quarter' or even asking for it. As McManners observes, 'Violence is the SAS trade-mark.'

A second and potentially more serious blue-on-blue occurred when A and C Companies of the 3rd Battalion of the Parachute Regiment fought a gun battle in the hills north of San Carlos Water, on East Falkland. Late on 21 May 1982, two British Gazelle helicopters were shot down in the area by Argentine soldiers and the two companies of the Paras were hunting these enemy troops when they encountered each other. According to Hugh McManners, A Company saw about 30 members of C Company coming round a headland and assumed that they had located the Argentine forces; unfortunately, C Company reached the same conclusion when they sighted their fellow paras. Each company commander contacted battalion head-quarters, asking for a fire mission on the other. At this point, of course, the problem ought to have been recognized by the artillerymen, who should have noticed that the friendly grid references were exactly the same as the supposed Argentine ones. But as usual in blue-on-blues, human error intervened and made a tragedy out of a crisis. The grid references relayed to headquarters by A Company's commander placed his men apparently a thousand yards away from where they actually were. Alarm bells therefore did not ring at battalion head-quarters and the gunners duly followed instructions to open fire, assuming that there were two, rather than one, enemy sightings. The fire-fight began. One of the participants, Sergeant McCullum of A Company, reported what happened next:

> So there we were, with a strong section struck on a forward slope with three machine guns, and a whole platoon of C Company lined up with at least five machine guns, ready to shoot at them. So you carry on, you go for it! And in the fog of war it was a classic blue-on-blue.[39]

For both sides it was their first taste of battle. Hyped up and raring to go, as these two companies of tough young men undoubtedly were, there was no second thoughts and everyone began firing. It was what they had been trained to do and few of them would have had any time to worry about whether the men they were firing at were really the enemy. In addition to rifle and machine-gun fire, the battalion mortars – which both young officers had called up – now began bombarding the battlefield. If the A Company commander had had any doubts he would have found it difficult to resolve them as within seconds his radio was shot to pieces. Soon the superior firepower of C Company was driving the patrol from A Company, with nine men already seriously wounded, to find cover. But the rest of A Company, following the best military principles and marching to the sound of the guns, soon came up to the rescue. From the area of Findlays Rocks, two Blues and Royals Scimitar light tanks appeared and, in response to emergency flares from their beleaguered comrades, fired 12 rounds at C Company. No sooner did it seem that A Company's patrol had been saved than the battalion's supporting artillery, which C Company had called up, dropped over 40 shells on and around the desperate survivors.

It was a scene of chaos. On top of the slope McCullum and his comrades were sitting ducks for the artillery, while lower down the slope they would be machine-gunned by the rest of C

Company. By now two more men had suffered severe head injuries but, when a Sea King helicopter came in to evacuate them, it crashed in trying to land too quickly. A second helicopter was called in, this time carrying 3 Para's CO, Lieutenant-Colonel Hew Pike, who had deduced that the battle that was raging was in fact a blue-on-blue. Orders swiftly circulated to stop all firing. There were no Argentine troops in the area, only friendly forces.

Incredibly, in view of the ferocity of the fire-fight, there were no fatalities, though 11 men were seriously wounded. The pride of these professional soldiers had been deeply hurt. Sergeant French of A Company was angry because the disorder of that night challenged his profound belief in discipline and co-ordinated activities:

> I get more angry now thinking back on the blue-on-blue than I did at the time, when I thought of it as part of the fog of war. It need never have happened if certain individuals (not in the patrol or in the defending company) had been doing his job – however, who am I to criticize?
>
> Co-ordination of defensive positions is vital. You learn that it is far more important in war than it has ever been on exercise. The effect of the tragedy was to make everyone very much more careful.[40]

Human errors have contributed to ground amicide throughout history. In the words of Charles Shrader, 'Sometimes incidents resulted from human failures as simple as the inadvertent pushing of a button at the wrong time, the transposition of numbers, or a mistake in arithmetic. On other occasions, the human failure was more complex in its origins, and commonly the fear and confusion so prevalent on the battlefield played a major role.'

Part II

Air Warfare

8

Air Warfare up to 1939

The introduction of aircraft as an aspect of warfare is an entirely twentieth-century phenomenon. Nevertheless, though recent in origin, it has not taken planes long to revolutionize warfare to such an extent that command of the air has become a prerequisite of victory in modern battles. However, in terms of its threat to friendly as well as enemy troops, the aeroplane has introduced a new and terrible dimension to the concept of amicide. Unlike ground weapons, it seems that technological developments in air warfare have moved far beyond the capacities of human operators to control them. Charles Shrader lists no less than 99 separate cases, taken almost entirely from the records of the United States, of aircraft engaging friendly forces. Naturally Shrader's figure reflects only the tip of an iceberg. If one were to study the records of the RAF, the Luftwaffe or the Soviet Army Air Force in the Second World War, with the same intensity that Shrader brought to his work on American sources, one would expect to be confronted by an equally large figure. In simple terms, aircraft profoundly influence modern warfare and can inflict terrible damage on friend or foe from a height and with a speed that is almost beyond the capacity of the ground soldier to resist. The tragedies of blue-on-blue incidents in the Gulf War, notably that involving the Royal Fusiliers in their Warrior IFVs, illustrate quite starkly how swiftly death can come from the skies. In terms of amicide, air warfare is the 'growth' area.

Shrader has likened the effects of air amicide to those of artillery errors in previous wars. Yet, with the capacity of modern air-to-ground missiles to penetrate even the toughest armoured vehicles, air amicide is far more severe and much more destructive. The effects of the accidental saturation bombing of the US 30th Division during Operation Cobra in Normandy in 1944 reveal almost total disorientation and collapse of morale among the survivors. Nor do the ground troops resent artillery 'shorts' as much as they do short bombing aircraft. The way that American troops in Normandy renamed their airmen the 'American Luftwaffe' and shot at them on sight is a very clear indication of the views of the infantry.

Since 1945 technology has made far greater strides in the field of air warfare than in land or sea warfare, with planes having greater speed, range and far more terrible weapons of destruction. Each of these improvements carries with it dangers for friendly forces. Clearly the control of aircraft operating ever further from their bases, flying faster so that decisions need to be made in split second, and carrying even more lethal weapons, some of which may be nuclear, makes the likelihood of errors in targeting very real. In conflicts involving fast-moving ground action, the problems of ground support revolve around the difficulty of accurately identifying targets. Failures of this kind on the part of pilots have contributed a heavy toll of friendly casualties. Desert fighting – with its notable problems of dust and sand – contributed to heavy friendly losses in the Gulf War, and even the marking of coalition vehicles with painted signs and fluorescent coloured panels did not provide a solution that only advanced electronic tagging will every really achieve. As Shrader writes, 'It is too much to hope that a pilot, diving at 600 m.p.h. through smoke while taking evasive action and attempting to deliver area-type ordnance accurately, could instantaneously and correctly identify camouflaged friendly ground troops making maximum use of available cover and concealment.' On the other hand, one should note the advice to pilots on bombing raids made in the Second World War, which was echoed by Chuck Horner in the Gulf, 'If in doubt, don't . . .' Do not drop the bombs or fire the missiles. This is something easily said at briefings, with blood pressure normal and without the adrenalin coursing through the veins as is bound to happen to a pilot facing a potential enemy and in a 'you-or-him' situation. Then, with your life on the line, how easy is it to remember instructions not to fire if there is any doubt?

Although there were many friendly-fire air incidents during the First World War, few of them achieved notoriety. The slow speed of the attacking aircraft and their very limited bomb loads reduced their capacity to cause serious casualties when set against the ossuary of artillery victims. Nevertheless, two curious examples were recorded at the time, the first by Captain (later Major-General Sir) Edward Spears in 1914. During the early weeks of the war, the French sought to exploit the advantage they enjoyed over the Germans in the area of air warfare. Short of a really effective aerial bomb they employed a curious device like a large metal container filled with tiny steel fléchettes, which could be tripped on to ground troops below. The weapon was abandoned when, in error, one French pilot dropped the fléchettes on to a unit of French Zouaves. The effects were surprising – indeed, they almost qualified as a form of chemical or bacterial warfare. While in their container the fléchettes were immersed in oil. However, when they were tipped out they still retained the oil on their sharp edges and so infected the wounds they caused on the wretched Zouaves, contributing to blood poisoning. Curiously, at the very time that the French abandoned these fléchettes, and the British adopted heavy darts, the Germans took up the French idea and used fléchettes until they had perfected a suitable hand-dropped bomb.

The second notable friendly-fire incident involving aircraft also concerned the French. On the morning of 12 May 1916, the French airship AT-O took off from Le Havre and proceeded along the coast, looking for German U-boats. There was a mist over the sea and visibility was not very good so that from a height of 1,600 feet the airship commander, Lieutenant Saint Rémy, found himself in a quandary when he faintly discerned a ship below him, travelling on the surface. In fact, it was the British submarine D-3, commanded by a Canadian officer, Lieutenant Maitland-Dougall who, like Saint Rémy, was on anti-submarine patrol.

From the airship Saint Rémy at last made out the shape of a submarine below him, but he detected no signs of identification. At that moment, rockets were suddenly fired from near the stern of the submarine and passed close to the French airship, convincing her crew that she was under fire. It could mean only one thing: the submarine was German and had opened fire on them. Neither Saint Rémy nor any of his crew seemed to have given any thought to the possibility that the rockets were for identification rather than an attempt to ignite the airship. Instead, the French opened fire on the submarine with their machine-gun and the crewmen who had been firing the rockets scuttled back for safety to the conning tower. Soon the French saw the submarine begin to dive. As it did so, Saint Rémy dropped a total of six small 70-pound bombs, two of which hit the submarine on the tower and forced it back to the surface. As they watched from above, the submarine foundered and began to sink beneath the waves, while a few small figures struggled in the sea. Saint Rémy was delighted that he had sunk a U-boat and took his airship down to just a hundred feet so he could confirm his kill. But once he neared the waves and called out to the men swimming in the sea he discovered that they were British. Unable to rescue them, he flew off to fetch help but by the time a ship reached the scene the men had drowned.

It was a sad and quite unnecessary disaster, caused almost entirely by the problem of misidentification. The signals used by the British ship to identify itself had been quite unknown to the French commander and although D-3's crew had painted a recognition symbol on a forward hatch, which corresponded with those agreed between the French and British authorities for 1–15 March 1916, the French failed to understand the significance of it. Maitland-Dougall had been confident to stay on the surface precisely because he had already identified the airship as French. Why the submarine would stay on the surface and allow itself to be bombed if she really was German does not seem to have occurred to Saint Rémy at any stage. And why the French regarded the signal rockets as offensive weapons we can only surmise. Obviously flying in an airship was a hazardous occupation and fire was an ever-present fear. Thus the rockets may have posed a greater threat to the French airship than the British crew can have understood. However, once the airship opened fire with her machine gun the submarine had no alternative but to dive to escape the strafing, which appears to have confirmed Saint Rémy in his suspicions that the vessel was a U-boat. If the outcome had been less tragic the whole incident could be dismissed as a farce, a kind of comedy of errors. But in wartime few things are merely funny, and Saint Rémy's errors caused the loss of a British submarine and her entire crew.

The novelty of seeing aircraft employed in reconnaissance operations never quite wore off for many of the poorly-educated peasant-soldiers of the Tsarist armies. There are several reports of Russian aircraft being shot down by Russian infantrymen, who wrongly identified them as German. Their reasoning for shooting the planes down is interesting. When questioned by an officer, one group of soldiers claimed they had shot at the aircraft because they believed that it must be German rather than Russian, because no Russian was clever enough to design such a thing.

During the great German offensive of March 1918, when the British Fifth Army was shattered by Ludendorff's decisive stroke, the Royal Flying Corps played an important part in helping to support the ground troops. Unfortunately, as French troops were brought in to bolster the British lines, the British airmen frequently mistook the powder-blue uniforms of the French for the *feldgrau* of the Germans, attacking their allies with bombs and machine guns. Where they were spotting for the artillery, British pilots sometimes reported that German troops were operating behind British lines and also erroneously called down artillery fire on French troop concentrations.

9

The Second World War

The vast majority of examples of air amicide occurred during the six years of the Second World War. On fronts throughout the world, aircraft played a vital role in all aspects of the fighting, both on land and at sea, and they contributed as well to the swelling numbers of friendly casualties. Both in strategic bombing and in tactical ground support, pilots, navigators and bomb-aimers made mistakes that cost thousands of lives. Yet even in the early days of the war, before the scale and intensity of operations placed unbearable pressures on aircrew, relatively simple errors reflected a carelessness among the young men who took to the air.

On 6 September 1939, Britain's secret weapon – her newly installed radar – gave a false reading and appeared to indicate that a massive German air attack was under way. Everyone was prey to panic and the fear of the all-powerful bomber. As a result fighters were scrambled and a tragic dog-fight ensued in which two RAF Hurricanes were shot down by Spitfires from another squadron, with the loss of one of the pilots. As if this was not bad enough, ground anti-aircraft batteries joined in the battle and shot down one of the Spitfires. Clearly at this early stage, with nerve ends showing, there were always likely to be mistakes. And again, as in almost every example of friendly fire in this book, the fundamental problem was a human one. In January 1941, during the British campaign to

drive the Italians from Eritrea, the RAF strafed General
Savory's 11th Indian Brigade, though fortunately casualties
were light. But later the same year, in November, during the
Crusader battles in North Africa, the 1st Essex Regiment
suffered 40 casualties when their ground-support aircraft
dropped bombs amongst them, instead of ahead of them on the
escarpment they were attacking.

Between 1939 and 1941 this problem of 'early nerves' and
poor identification systems was by no means a specifically
British failing. The German Luftwaffe was responsible for a
series of blue-on-blue incidents during the campaign against
France in May 1940. Germany's blitzkrieg campaigns in
Poland and the Low Countries had been dominated by the
Luftwaffe, which provided close ground support for German
tanks and armoured vehicles. However, this close co-operation
between ground and air forces was always a finely judged line
and things could and did go wrong, as General von Mellenthin
experienced in Poland. He remembered how on one occasion a
low-flying aircraft passed over his headquarters, whereupon
his flak gunners – without attempting to identify the intruder –
opened fire with all their guns. An air liaison officer rushed
about trying to stop the gunners, telling them it was a German
plane – a Stork reconnaissance aircraft – but the gunners were
so excited that they took no notice. By an incredible stroke of
luck the old plane was not hit and landed unharmed. As the
gunners – now chastened by seeing the plane's identification
marks – gathered round to see if the pilot was all right, out
stepped the Luftwaffe general who was responsible for close air
support. As von Mellenthin observed, 'he failed to appreciate
the joke.'

The Ju87 Stuka dive bomber was one of the most feared
weapons of the German blitzkrieg in Poland and France. One
German commander was to find out what it was like to
experience a Stuka attack from the point of view of the victim.
On 14 May 1940, a group of Stukas mistakenly attacked the
2nd Panzer Brigade at Querrieu, near Amiens. Their mistake
was quickly brought home to them by the brigade's

commander, General Heinz Guderian, who ordered his flak gunners to open fire on the German planes. Only days before Stukas had seriously damaged a column of German tanks near Cheméry, narrowly missing Field Marshal von Rundstedt, commander of Army Group A, and Guderian was taking no chances. As he said, 'It was perhaps an unfriendly action on our part, but our flak opened fire and brought down one of the careless machines.' The two crewmen escaped by parachute and landed in the midst of the German infantry who, not surprisingly, told the airmen what they thought of them. Guderian called off his enraged men and having himself torn the flyers off a strip, 'fortified the two young men with a glass of champagne.' Guderian could afford to be magnanimous. The Stukas had done no harm on this occasion and their work elsewhere was winning the war for Germany.

While the British and German airmen made their early blue-on-blues and learned from their mistakes, the Americans came fresh to the battlefields of North Africa in 1942 and tended to replicate the mistakes that the other combatants had made earlier in the war. One was in the field of aircraft accidents. An astonishing fact was that in a single year – 1943 – 2,264 American pilots and 3,339 aircrew were killed in a total of 16,128 accidents, while training in the United States. So often were B-26s destroyed that a popular saying at the time at one Florida airbase went, 'One a day at Tampa Bay'. In case it is assumed that the Americans were alone in suffering this dreadful, accidental attrition, it should be pointed out that according to German records, 45 per cent of all German planes lost between 1941 and 1944 were victims of non-combat destruction. So common was accidental loss as a reason for aircraft destruction and aircrew casualties that it threatened Germany's prospects in the war.

Charles Shrader lists a large number of amicide incidents involving American aircrew in North Africa, from November 1942. Near Madjez-el-Bab in Tunisia in the last week of November 1942, a company of the American 701st Tank Destroyer Battalion, attached to the British 11th Brigade, was attacked by American P-38 Lightnings and lost virtually all its vehicles to air attack. After two weeks of intense effort, the company engineers had managed to repair some of the tank destroyers and get them back into action, only for another wave of P-38s to attack them, strafing the vehicles and killing three men and seriously wounding two others. It is hardly surprising to find that in the unit's campaign diary the author had some hard words for this 'inexcusable' example of mistaken identity. Eight weeks later units of the same 701st were bombed by American B-25s near Station de Sened, in Algeria. During the battle of the Kasserine Pass a flight of American B-17s lost their bearings and instead of bombing German troop concentrations in the Pass they destroyed an Arab village more than a hundred miles from the battle area.

There were also examples of the ground troops striking back, wrongly identifying aircraft types and shooting friendly planes down. During the crisis in Tunisia of February 1943, following the American defeats at Sidi Bou Zid and the Kasserine Pass, it is hardly surprising that the anti-aircraft gunners were feeling edgy. On 21 February 1943, in rain and fog, aircraft from XII Air Support Command were helping ground troops of 1st Armored Division hold back an Axis advance towards Thala and Tebessa. Poor training in aircraft identification played a major part in the AA gunners wrecking five US planes and then, the following day, shooting down a further five P-38s, in spite of a detailed warning to the gunners that low-flying friendly aircraft would be supporting ground troops. The gunners were also reminded that the enemy usually used yellow or white paint on the noses of their planes against the black or brown of the American ones. To aid identification the P-38s even tried rocking their wings as they flew over friendly positions, but all to no avail. Shrader is scathing about these incidents, which he puts down less to identification problems than to poor training. In view of the near hysteria which was sweeping through American troops in Tunisia at this time, after their first exposure to veteran German units, it is as well to judge the gunners with appropriate indulgence. In an attempt to prevent further losses, American ground troops were forbidden to fire at aircraft until they had themselves come under attack. The view that these inexperienced American gunners were trigger-happy received further support once Allied troops had left Africa and moved across the Mediterranean to Italy. Yet it is as well to point out that the enemy were hardly faultless in this regard. The Italian Governor of Libya in 1940, the famous flyer Marshal Italo Balbo, was shot down and killed by his own anti-aircraft gunners on returning to his headquarters at Tobruk after inspecting the Egyptian front. Flying a clearly identifiable Savoia-Marchetti S79 bomber, Balbo fell victim to the nerves of his edgy gunners who had just received news – false as it turned out – of a mass RAF attack on Tobruk. How Balbo's single Italian bomber could have been mistaken for a 'massed' anything is difficult to understand. Nevertheless, the gunners fired and achieved a friendly 'kill'.

After the Japanese attack on Pearl Harbor one can understand why the American anti-aircraft gunners developed a bout of 'itchy-fingers', but one cannot excuse it. It was yet further evidence of the kind of panic among American gunners that was apparent around Gela in Sicily in 1943.

On the evening of 7 December 1941, six fighters from the aircraft carrier *Enterprise*, which had fortunately not been in the harbour during the Japanese attack, flew past Diamond Head and asked permission to land. In view of the nervous condition of the anti-aircraft gunners throughout the island of Oahu, clear instructions were circulated to every unit that six friendly aircraft were coming in to land. There could have been nobody in charge of a gun in Oahu who was not made absolutely aware that the incoming planes were Americans. Yet it was not enough. As a naval officer said later, 'Kids were sitting on those guns who had been shot at all morning, and they were jittery and trigger-happy.' As the planes flew over the battleships in 'Battleship Row' the flagship *Pennsylvania* opened fire with every gun it had got. Where the flagship led, everyone else followed. The problem was that the panic was infectious. Even those gunners who knew the six planes were American joined in firing because everybody else was firing. One fighter tried to crash land at Wheeler Field but it was so full of bullets that it cartwheeled in and burst into flames. Another of the aircraft was brought down over a residential area and exploded causing heavy civilian casualties. One plane crashed on Ford Island and was machine-gunned even after it had landed. Fortunately, the firing was as inaccurate as it was wild and the pilot sprinted away from the wreck, dodging bullets as he ran. Two other pilots parachuted down from their stricken planes, but when Ensign Eric Allen tried to follow suit he was machine-gunned as he hung in the air and later died in hospital. As if this was not bad enough, the gunners kept firing and inflicted casualties on nearby ships. The loss of the six planes ended the Day of Infamy for the American people.

The bombing of the French port of Le Portel by the RAF on the night of 8/9 September 1943 was one of the heaviest inflicted on any town in the history of aerial bombing. A recent study by Michael Cumming (*The Starkey Sacrifice*) has revealed that this single small French town, in the Pas de Calais, south of Boulogne, sustained a raid of such intensity that it was saturated by more high explosive than was used in the 'thousand-bomber' raid on Cologne in May 1942, and that its death toll on that single night exceeded that inflicted by the Luftwaffe in their infamous raid on Coventry in November 1940, a raid that Winston Churchill always insisted was the most devastating ever inflicted on Britain during the Second World War. Le Portel, according to Cumming, was hit in that single night by 678 tons of high explosive, more than was used on the whole of Berlin in two raids during 1943. The RAF chose to use this enormous hammer to crack the tiny nut of Le Portel without ever publicly revealing its reasoning. In fact, this tremendous raid, carried out by over 200 RAF bombers, is scarcely mentioned in any of the histories of the bombing service, nor in the numerous histories of the British war effort during 1943. The reason for this reticence is that all the damage and casualties inflicted on Le Portel must be considered within the definitions of military blunders and friendly fire. Five hundred French civilians were killed on one night by British and Allied airmen and their town virtually wiped off the map as a result of human error. To make matters worse – if that is possible – the raid was part of a charade in which the Germans refused to play their part and which left Winston Churchill and senior RAF leaders with both red faces and a butcher's bill which they were only too keen to hush up.

Operation Starkey, of which the raid on Le Portel was a part, was aimed at misleading the Germans in Normandy into believing that the Allies were planning an invasion of Europe in 1943. It was hoped that the Luftwaffe would commit vital parts of its fighter defences to an air battle over the supposed invasion scene which would enable superior Allied air power to score a decisive local victory. In addition, should the circumstances become propitious, the operation was to exploit any opportunity to make a real invasion if there were signs that the German defences were weaker than expected. This was the worst kind of planning, for which 'wishful thinking' is too kind a description. The areas chosen for the dummy landing were the beaches between Audresselles and Ambleteuse, six miles north of Boulogne, and those between the River Brone and Hardelot, seven miles south of Boulogne. However, it proved to be the invasion that never was and failed to arouse any interest in the enemy. Unfortunately, the Germans had powerful coastal artillery in the area which would endanger any real operations in the Channel opposite Boulogne and it was these that 200 bombers of the RAF were ordered to target. Tragically, the little town of Le Portel was situated between two of the key gun sites and it was this that cost so many French lives in the bombing attacks.

In the event, the accuracy of the RAF bombing of the coastal guns on the night of 8/9 September 1942 was no worse than usual. The average inaccuracy of RAF bombers at the time was accepted as half a mile which meant that the targets, which were a mile apart, would merge into a single target on the maps used. The problem was that the War Office maps included the town of Le Portel within the same square as that used for the target guns. Thus the saturation bombing of the guns would inevitably mean that many bombs would hit their target square and yet massacre French civilians in a built-up area. This is what happened as Cumming's book so graphically describes: one of the least-known yet still one of the deadliest examples of aerial friendly fire in history.

The Anglo-American invasion of Sicily in July 1943 witnessed some of the most shocking examples of friendly fire ever recorded in military history. Mass hysteria seemed to be the problem on several occasions. It was decided by Allied planners that the airborne attack on the island should involve four distinct and separate airborne strikes, all to be conducted by night, even though many of the American paratroopers involved had no night jump experience. The first assault – Operation Ladbroke – would be carried out by the British 1st Air Landing Brigade, led by Brigadier Hicks, which would land in Sicily from 147 Waco and Horse gliders, towed almost entirely by American C-47s. Once landed, their task was to secure the strategic Ponte Grande Bridge and hold it until British ground troops could move out of their beachhead. The second stage of the assault involved the airborne troops of Colonel James Gavin's 505th Parachute Infantry Regiment, who would be carried over Sicily by 266 C-47s and dropped on four zones north of Gela. Their job was to prevent any German counter-attacks developing against General Patton's US Seventh Army on its beachhead. The next night more C-47s would bring in Colonel Reuben Tucker's 504th Parachute Infantry to reinforce Gavin's men at Gela. Tucker would be accompanied on the flight by the assistant divisional commander, 'Bull' Keenens, while Major-General Matthew Ridgway, commander of US 82nd Airborne Division, considered too old to parachute in to take overall command of the operation, arrived by sea. The final part of the operation had been allocated to the most experienced part of the Allied airborne troops, the British 1st Parachute Brigade, led by Brigadier Lathbury, whose job was to capture the vital Primosole Bridge.

Ridgway had become uneasy about the danger of friendly fire even before the operation began. He knew that his airborne troops would be crossing the path of the Allied invasion ships and was anxious to ensure that the ships would not open fire on the C-47s by mistake as they flew over. Quite reasonably he addressed his views to Admiral Cunningham, the British C-in-C of naval operations, but found that the latter was not prepared to guarantee the safety of his force. Having fought through three years of intense naval warfare in the Mediterranean, and having suffered grievous losses from German aircraft, Cunningham was not prepared to risk allowing friendly aircraft a free flight close to his ships. Ridgway was shocked at this attitude, commenting 'We were informed that the Navy would give no assurance that fire would not be delivered upon aircraft approaching within range of the vessels at night.' This should have been enough to persuade the planners to rethink the flight paths but instead they refused to change those already decided. Ridgway was even more worried to learn that his division's second strike, by Rueben Tucker's 504th Regiment, would fly not only over the invasion ships but along 35 miles of the invasion beaches, sitting target for Allied guns below. All he could do was press the Navy to give him the guarantee he wanted, warned that, 'unless satisfactory assurances are obtained the Navy, I would recommend against the dispatch of any troop movements.' Ridgway's courageous stand seem to have some effect at last when General Patton at Seventh informed him that the Navy would withhold fire provided the airborne troops flew along certain prearranged and came no closer than a distance of seven miles ships. Ridgway was relieved to hear this, yet he would been so pleased if he had realized the sheer impossibility controlling the activities of hundreds of anti-aircraft spread across miles of front. It would only take itchy trigger finger to set the whole lot off. In fact, either because of secrecy or sheer administrative incompetence, neither the naval gunners nor those manning guns on the merchant ships in the invasion fleet had been informed that there was going to be an airborne invasion and so nobody was expecting to see friendly planes overhead. Even Admiral Hewitt, commanding the naval forces taking Patton's Seventh Army to Sicily, only found out about the airborne attack on the day it was due to take place. In such an administrative muddle it is hardly surprising that the gunners were the last to learn.

On the evening of 9 July 1943 the British 1st Air Landing Brigade took off from six airfields around Kairouan in Tunisia. They were travelling in 137 Waco and 10 Horsa gliders, piloted by men from the 1st Battalion of the Glider Pilot Regiment. The gliders were being towed by C-47s of Colonel Ray Dunn's American 51st Troop Carrier Wing. Dunn's men were, in the main, pilots from civil aviation and few had seen action or flown through flak. This proved to be a serious problem and contributed significantly to the catastrophe that was about to ensue.

As the C-47s and the gliders approached Sicily a number of factors threw the entire air convoy into chaos. In the first place, the high winds made glider flying difficult, while the heavy flak coming up from Italian gunners forced the American pilots to take evasive action. To make matters worse, the gunners on the Allied invasion convoys joined in along with the enemy gunners and soon the sky was filled with planes and gliders going in every direction. In the words of Carlo D'Este, 'The factors of inexperience, wind and enemy flak were a fatal combination and enough to ensure that Operation Ladbroke would be a first class disaster.'

As they approached the shores of Sicily, the C-47 pilots made a decision which condemned hundreds of British airborne troops to a watery grave. According to Charles Whiting in *Slaughter over Sicily*, the decision was taken to increase altitude to 1,800 feet, apparently to allow the gliders two free miles of flight once they were released from their tows. It also allowed the C-47s to release their gliders earlier than had been planned so that they did not need to fly through so much flak. Whatever the reasoning, the result was tragic. As Charles Whiting wrote:

> Some pilots decided that they had had enough. They did not even try to unload their tows. Instead they turned about and headed for North Africa again. Others released their gliders miles away from the landing zone and fled for safety . . . But the main fault, which led to the disaster to come, was that the gliders were released not two miles out to sea, but at twice or even three times that distance.[41]

Gliders now began to dive into the sea, miles from the shore line. The glider carrying General Hopkinson, commander of the British 1st Airborne Division and planner of Operation Ladbroke, was one of those to fall into sea. Hopkinson managed to get clear of the wreck and hang on to piece of wreckage until he was picked up by the British destroyer, HMS *Keren*. Ironically, Admiral Lord Ashbourne, flying his flag in the *Keren*, knew Hopkinson. As he wrote, 'I saw a body floating in the sea almost alongside and evidently alive. I told the captain of the *Keren* to pick him up. A few minutes later a dripping soldier arrived on the bridge. He turned out to be Major-General G P Hopkinson, commanding 1st Airborne Division. The last time I had seen him was in 1922 when I had rowed in the same boat with him at Cambridge. We wrung out his clothes, gave him a plate of eggs and bacon and then sent him off to catch up with the rest of his soldiers.' Hopkinson was not going to find it an easy task to 'catch up with the rest of his soldiers.' The 1st Air Landing Brigade had been destroyed and scattered to the four winds. And Hopkinson knew who he thought was to blame – Colonel Dunn's tow pilots. Of the 147 gliders that had left Tunisia that evening, 69 had crashed into the sea, drowning 326 of the British troops. Of the other gliders, just two had been shot down – by friend or foe – several had been towed back to Tunisia and 59 had landed somewhere in Sicily, though they were spread out across an area of 25 square miles. Resentment against the American tow-pilots was so severe that when they got back to Tunisia, British troops there had to be confined to camp to avoid a lynching. In fact, two gliders even landed on different islands, one in Sardinia and another in Malta.

The tragedies of war often have a comic side for those with a black sense of humour. The fate of one glider was truly farcical. Expecting to land on a rocky coastal area in Sicily, the men found themselves instead on a broad, sandy beach. Far from encountering Italian troops – or even German ones – the soldiers were amazed to find that their whole invasion force had apparently been beaten to Sicily by a British mobile bath unit that passed them on the road. Then the truth dawned on them. They were not in Sicily at all; they had landed back in North Africa! Another glider crashed into the sea not far from a large, shadowy ship. The glider troops swam over the ship, climbed up the anchor chain and on to the deserted deck. Suddenly, a sailor emerged on deck carrying a slop bucket. As he saw the soldiers he called for help and soon the twelve wet men were being attacked by British sailors. Only with some difficulty were they able to explain that they were not enemy saboteurs but gliders troops, somewhat off target. Perhaps the most ridiculous of all the landings was by the glider that reached Malta. Its occupants immediately organized them-selves for action and got ready to move off towards their rendezvous point. Suddenly a jeep drew up with two occupants who wanted to know what these 'invaders' thought they were doing there. The young lieutenant leading the commandos replied that he was heading for his assigned LZ (landing zone) at Syracuse. A voice replied from the jeep, 'We are sorry to inform you that you are not in Sicily, but on the main airstrip at Malta, and what's more, you are blocking one of the runways and the fighters cannot take off. So please take the jeep and pull not only the trailer [that is, the jeep and trailer that had been carried in the glider] but also this bloody glider 200 yards in that direction.' Even so, there was no disguising the fact that hundreds of British lives had been needlessly thrown away by the incompetence or cowardice of their tow-pilots. The disaster had not been accidental: mass hysteria on the part of inexperienced pilots had resulted in the ditching of gliders into the sea at night, miles from the shore and far from any chance of rescue. It had been a disgraceful and discreditable example of amicide.

While the massacre of the British glider troops was taking place, the second stage of the airborne attack was under way. Colonel James Gavin and the 505th Regimental Combat Team was already flying towards Sicily, following a patch between the ships carrying Patton's US Seventh Army and Montgomery's British Eighth Army. Gavin was well aware that if one of the naval gunners lost his nerve and opened fire on the hundreds of C-47s a general massacre would ensue. But if Gavin's luck held while he passed over the ships it began to run out when the air armada reached Sicily. As had happened with the British gliders, some of the American-C-47 pilots panicked in the face of the heavy flak. The American paratroopers were scattered over 1,000 square miles, many dropped at too low an altitude so that their chutes failed to open and they were killed outright or broke bones. Some pilots ordered the troops out over the sea, while others simply turned around and flew straight back to Africa. The American paratroopers who fell into the British sector found in the early hours of 10 July that the British troops, not expecting to see Americans there, opened fire on them. Nobody had given the Americans the British passwords and accidental casualties were common.

General Ridgway, from his floating headquarters, could only wince as news of the Gavin fiasco was added to the sorry tale of the gliders. None of the American troops had landed where they were supposed to, many being up to 60 miles from their LZs. Some had not even landed in Sicily at all, but were in Sardinia, Malta or even – in a few tragic cases – in the mountains of Southern Italy, where their bodies lay undiscovered for many years.

If a more dismal fate was possible than that which had

overtaken the British 1st Air Landing Brigade or Gavin's 505th Regiment, then it was about to happen to Colonel Reuben Tucker's 504th Regiment. While American and British infantry were coming ashore on the beaches of Sicily, General Patton was worried by the fact that few of Gavin's paratroopers were in position to hold up enemy counter-attacks. He therefore ordered Ridgway to bring in the second part of 82nd Airborne's contribution to Operation Husky (the code name for the invasion of Sicily) – the 504th. Ridgway radioed to 'Bull' Keenens in Africa to prepare the 504th for a drop that night. But the danger of friendly fire – so fearful a prospect to Matthew Ridgway – had increased during the day. The invasion fleet had been in constant action against German and Italian planes and the flak gunners on the beaches and on the ships had endured a harrowing day of almost relentless battle. German planes were continuing to stage hit-and-run attacks, while Stuka dive bombers, sirens wailing, continually fell from the skies, spilling bombs on to the crowded decks of the transports. It was a day of high tension and of bitterness. The British hospital ship *Talamba* was sunk by German bombs and as night fell the whole of the landing area was illuminated by the flames that had engulfed the American ammunition ship *Robert Rowan* as it was bombed. And into this scene of chaos soon would fly the slow C-47 transports carrying their precious cargo of American paratroopers. Their divisional commander, with a prescience of disaster, continued to press for guarantees of no naval fire. Earlier in the day Ridgway had been told that the navy could make no such promises, whereupon he had warned Patton at Seventh Army headquarters that unless he got his guarantee he would 'officially protest this follow-up drop.' This appeared to do some good; Seventh Army headquarters gave Ridgway at least the impression that he had got his guarantee. In fact he had not, because nobody could guarantee any such thing. Tucker's flight path would take him over 35 miles of invasion beaches, packed with Allied troops and defended by hundreds of anti-aircraft guns, not to mention the hundreds more on the ships just off shore. With every gunner tired, nervous, blazing with anger at the loss of the hospital ship, how could anyone guarantee that these men would not fire at the first planes they saw, planes which, for all they knew, were carrying bombs with their names on them? When Ridgway checked around the AA battery commanders he found, to his horror, that more than one knew nothing at all about the order not to fire. An artillery liaison officer then reassured him that all would be taken care of at a briefing that afternoon. What more could Ridgway have done? He had to trust someone.

On 11 July, Colonel Tucker in Tunisia had no reason to think that the drop would pose any special problems. With better weather than the previous night, and much lighter winds, and with Gavin's men already – presumably – in position, his role was simply as a back-up. The flight to Sicily was straightforward and aboard the lead C-47s the paratroopers were preparing themselves for the drop. Behind them the bulk of the regiment was being brought in at 700 feet over the massed ships, landing craft and land troops of US Seventh Army. Suddenly the sound of a single machine-gun was heard, firing up at one of the passing transports. It was like a signal for an ambush. The first bursts were followed by a few more desultory rounds from other guns and then there broke out a roar as hundreds of guns began firing into the sky. The C-47s desperately fired recognition flares but they were answered with a deluge of bullets, shells and rockets. When the gunners were later questioned, most simply explained that they thought the low-flying transports were German bombers and that they had taken so much punishment during the day that they were looking to get some of their own back. Some of the more inexperienced men admitted that they could not recognize a C-47 from a German bomber and others claimed they thought the planes were dropping German paratroopers on to the beaches. In fact, it was one of history's clearest examples of mass hysteria. So tight was the tension felt by all the combatant soldiers on the Gela beaches that night that a single incident could make a hundred – a thousand – men act as one, without rational thought. With the C-47s flying at just 700 feet it was almost impossible for the gunners to miss. Aboard the transports paratroopers were killed in their seats, shot by machine-gun bullets or ripped by shrapnel. Below, watching the slaughter, Ridgway and Patton stood staring in horror, Ridgway in tears for the massacre of his fine division, Patton simply repeating 'Oh, my God! Oh, my God!' But there was no divine intervention that evening. Tucker's men were beyond salvation. Planes were crashing into the sea or on to the beaches. For days afterwards the bodies of paratroopers were washed up at Gela.

During the initial drop, 33 out of the original 144 C-47s were shot down in minutes, while another 60 were so badly hit that they would never fly again. A total of 318 paratroopers were killed or wounded, over one in five of the men involved in the operation, and all were victims of friendly fire. Captain Adam Komosa later described his experiences:

> It was the most uncomfortable feeling known that our own troops were throwing everything they had at us. Planes dropped out of formation and crashed into the sea. Others, like clumsy whales, wheeled and attempted to get beyond the flak which rose in fountains of fire, lighting the stricken faces of men as they stared through the windows.[42]

Colonel Tucker was one of the fortunate ones who landed on the correct dropping zone. As he touched down he found, to his horror, that not far away a group of turret gunners in Sherman tanks were firing wildly into the sky at the passing planes. Tucker's meeting with these men can better be imagined than described. When the plane that transported the colonel got back to Tunisia, it was found to have been holed over a thousand times by bullets and shrapnel, all of which were fired by American guns. But now the perpetrators of this shocking amicide let their madness take them over the line that separates war from atrocity. It seems that the naval gunners, exhilarated by this massacre of what they believed to be German planes, now began a 'turkey shoot', killing the parachutists as they helplessly floated down, many of them jumping only to escape from their burning C-47s. The night sky was illuminated by the burning planes and parachutes, and by the tracer fire arching upwards. One witness of that night, Herbert Blair, spoke poignantly of what he saw:

Hit after hit we scored until ship [C-47] after ship bursts into flame or falls spiralling into the sea. But something is wrong. From the wounded ships parachutes come fluttering down, some in flames, others to billow out in a slow descent. Then some trigger-happy gunner aboard another ship decides to pick off the supposedly helpless Jerries. Soon every gunner is firing at the troopers who dangle beneath the umbrellas of their chutes . . .

'Cease firing! Cease firing! Stand by to pick up survivors! Stand by to pick up survivors!'

Only then does the dreadful realization descend like a sledgehammer upon us. We have wantonly, though inadvertently, slaughtered our own gallant buddies. I feel sick in body and mind.[43]

An American destroyer, the *Beatty*, fired on a plane that had ditched in the sea and continued firing for quite some while before it was recognized as American and boats were launched to rescue the survivors. With the grimmest of all grim humour, one of the C-47 pilots remarked later: 'Evidently the only safe place for us over Sicily tonight is over enemy territory.'

By the next morning the full extent of the catastrophe was clear. Of a total of 5,307 paratroopers who had flown in the previous day, less than 2,000 were still fit for combat and over 1,200 of them had died from acts of amicide. General Eisenhower was shocked by the outcome of the whole airborne operation. Essentially, the elite troops of the American 82nd Airborne Division and the British 1st Airborne Division had been frittered away as the result of what came to be known as the 'Sicily Disaster'. Eisenhower wrote to Patton: 'If the cited report is true, the incident could only have been occasioned by inexcusable carelessness and negligence on the part of someone. You will institute within our command an immediate and exhaustive investigation into the allegation with a view to find responsibility. Report of pertinent facts is desired and if the persons found responsible are serving in your command, I want a statement of the disciplinary action taken by you. *This will be expedited.*' How could Eisenhower possibly account for the loss of so many Allied lives when the enemy had not even been involved? There had been a scandal and he wanted a scapegoat. But where could one begin? Certainly not with the green gunners who panicked after a day's aerial battering by Stukas.

Even as the search for scapegoats began the last phase of the ill-fated airborne assault was under way: this time the elite British 1st Parachute Brigade, commanded by Brigadier Lathbury, was on its way to Sicily. In terms of casualties Lathbury's men did no better than their predecessors, for chaos was still the order of the day. The commander of the 1st Battalion, Parachute Regiment, Colonel Pearson, had to force his American pilot to fly on through the flak by threatening to shoot him and by holding a revolver in his back, after the man had tried to turn back. But when the time came to jump, many of his men were killed by enemy fire as soon as they jumped from the transport. The 3rd Battalion, under Colonel Yeldham, was just as unlucky, losing many men to enemy fire and, as he recorded in his diary, to 'the fire of our flak ships'. Of 16 gliders that accompanied Lathbury's flight, four were shot down by friendly fire and most of the others succumbed to enemy guns. Of Lathbury's paratroops, most went the same way that Gavin's 'All Americans' had gone, scattered to the winds, some ending up on the Italian mainland but far too many others not reaching land at all and perishing in the dark waters of the Mediterranean. One group even landed on Mount Etna, though as many as 30 per cent were taken straight back to Tunisia. In order to fight the full strength of two German regiments supported by Tiger tanks, Lathbury found himself at the dropping zone with just 295 men out of his total force of 1,856.

If Eisenhower was looking for someone to blame he should have started with whoever planned the transport for the airborne troops. The poorly trained American pilots who flew the C-47s, many of whom were airline or freight pilots in civilian life and had no experience of such tough and dangerous work, were guilty of at best funk and at worst a scandalous disregard for the safety of their passengers. Both in the British and American sectors, the pilots were responsible for the deaths of hundreds of paratroops, most simply ditched into the sea at night. But so disgraceful were the facts when they reached him that Eisenhower decided the whole fiasco must be hushed up. There were too many reputations at stake. As a result it was interesting to note the skill with which the buck was passed when the investigations began. The officer commanding the troop-carrying operation placed the blame fairly and squarely on the shoulders of the army and navy anti-aircraft gunners, who frankly panicked at the sight of so many low-flying planes. This view was supported – unsurprisingly – by air commanders involved, like General Carl Spaatz, head of the USAAF in the Mediterranean. The shooting-down of Tucker's planes, according to Spaatz, was the result of a breakdown in co-ordination between all three services. To spread the guilt even further and thinner, Spaatz blamed command decisions at headquarters in Malta, Tunisia and even Egypt. No attempt was made to find out who had fired first on the night of Tucker's martyrdom.

The real cause of the problem was the fact that the airborne troops were there at all. And at this point, Eisenhower's deputy, Air Chief Marshall Arthur Tedder, entered the fray. Tedder's well-known antipathy towards Eighth Army Commander General Montgomery was clearly at the root of his criticism of the whole operation. It had been too dangerous, according to Tedder, for the airborne troops to be carried across an area of open battle. Tucker's men had to fly over 35 miles of beachhead, where the troops had only just suffered air attack by the enemy. It was far too risky to expect men in such a state of tension not to respond to such a potential danger, as Tucker's C-47s must have seemed to offer. It was risking amicide and nobody should have been surprised when the paratroops suffered disaster. In a way Tedder was right. After all, General Matthew Ridgway had been worried about friendly fire from the beginning and had pressurized his fellow commanders to guarantee that the gunners would not fire at his men. This they proved unwilling to do for a reason that Tedder was at pains to explain. The British Air Chief Marshal wrote, 'Even if it is physically possible for all the troops and ships to be duly warned, which is doubtful, any fire opened up either by mistake or against enemy aircraft would almost certainly be supported by all troops within range. AA firing at night is infectious and control almost impossible.'

Admiral Cunningham, Britain finest fighting sailor of the Second World War, was less than helpful. As far as he was concerned it would have been far better to keep friendly planes away from his ships. He had made it quite clear from the start that he would not guarantee that his guns would not fire at British and American planes for the simple reason that he could not risk the safety of a ship on a rapid identification of a distant aircraft at night. He applied the rule that his gunners would fire at any aircraft that flew too near. If the planners had selected better routes and if the pilots had navigated better the disaster need not have happened. With the navy blaming the army planners, it was incumbent on the latter to reply and they duly did through Lieutenant-General Frederick Browning, commanding I Airborne Corps, who returned the blame to the pilots: 'The navigation by the troop carrier aircrew was bad . . . It is essential both from the operational and moral point of view that energetic steps are taken to improve greatly on the aircrew's performance up to date.' But Eisenhower was not having any of this. He agreed with the view that the operation was just too dangerous and he prohibited any further airborne operations by the 82nd

Division. But Montgomery felt that there was still a future for British airborne operations, provided that the transport system and pilot performance were improved. The prickly and chauvinistic British general was notably blunt about the American pilots. 'The big lesson is that we must not be dependent on American transport aircraft, with pilots that are inexperienced in operational flying. Our airborne troops are too good and too scarce to be wasted.'

But the final word was left with Ridgway. It was elegantly expressed but it was a lie. 'The lessons now learned could have been driven home in no other way, and these lessons provide a sound basis for the belief that recurrence can be avoided. The losses are part of the inevitable price of war in human life.'

It was also during the conquest of Sicily that American aircraft first earned the uncomplimentary epithet from the GIs of the 'American Luftwaffe'. In Sicily, the North American A-36 Invader, admittedly a first-rate dive bomber, had a depressing record of hitting friendly troops by mistake. During the progress of the 2nd Armoured Division's pursuit of the 15th Panzer Grenadier Division, American planes made repeated attacks on their own troops, killing and wounding 75 men. Even when the ground forces displayed luminescent identification this did not seem to stop an A-36 once it had started its dive. General Omar Bradley narrowly missed falling victim to an A-36, which dive bombed and strafed him while he was visiting General Allen's HQ. Bradley observed that he was getting used to it; it was his third strafing that day by American planes. The A-36s were also responsible for the loss of Monte Cipolla to the Germans. A group of American GIs were desperately holding a position on the mountain until seven A-36s bombed them, killing or wounding 19 men, destroying their last four howitzers and driving them headlong down the slopes. In the same area, near the town of Troina, A-36s also dive-bombed British XXX Corps Headquarters, mistaking it for a German-held position. The attack was actually witnessed by General Omar Bradley himself:

For three days [General] Allen's attack on Troina was thrown back by savage resistance . . . Troina itself was to be bombed until it surrendered or was smashed into dust.

On the late afternoon of 4 August I waited at a bend in the road, high up in Cerami, to witness there air attack, the heaviest to date in our Sicilian campaign. Across the bowl-like depression, now half obscured in dust, the fire from eighteen battalions of artillery hammered the enemy's AA positions.

Thirty-six fighters circled high overhead, each loaded with 500-pound bombs. The artillery slackened and the bombers peeled off in a near-vertical dive. Soon the crown of Troina was wreathed in dust. By the time a second flight of thirty-six planes had bombed that stricken city, Troina lay half obscured under a column of grey dust that partially hid the cone of Mount Etna. Once more the infantry started forward, but once more the enemy held and lashed back in counter-attack.

The following day we renewed the offensive. This time Major-General Edwin J. House, Patton's tactical air commander, accompanied me to Cerami to view the air bombing. H hour passed with no sign of air. As we were about to leave in dismay, a drone sounded far off to the south. There, high in the sky, three A-36s were high-trailing for home.

'Holy smokes,' I turned to House, 'now just where in hell do you suppose they've dropped their bombs?'

'I'll be damned if I know,' he said.

'Maybe we'd better get back to your headquarters and see what went wrong.'

On our arrival the phone was ringing. It was [Lieutenant-General Sir] Oliver Leese from British XXX Corps.

'What have we done that you chaps would want to bomb us?' he asked.

'Where did they hit?' I groaned.

'Squarely on top of my headquarters,' he said, 'they've really plastered the town.'[44]

Eventually, when A-36s shot up an American tank column in spite of yellow recognition signals, the GIs lost patience and shot one of them out of the sky. The pilot parachuted down and was furious when he found out that he had been shot down by friendly troops. 'Why you silly sonofabitch,' said the tank commander, 'didn't you see our yellow recognition signal?' 'Oh,' said the pilot, 'is that what it was?'

Even after the Allied troops had crossed the Straits of Messina into mainland Italy, American airmen continued to exact an alarming toll on friendly troops. Heavy bomber strikes caused widespread havoc, inflicting heavy friendly casualties at Venafro, during the bombing of Monte Cassino. Vanafro was 15 miles from the target area and the American planes managed to destroy the British Eighth Army commander's caravan (the long-suffering General Leese, who had succeeded Montgomery as GOC Eighth Army, was fortunately not in it) and a Moroccan military hospital, causing 150 casualties among the civilians, as well as among gunners from the 4th Indian Division. During the advance on Rome, American Mustang fighter-bombers strafed columns of American troops by mistake, inflicting hundreds of casualties. American General Mark Clark was furious about the Venafro fiasco, during which 57 Allied soldiers and friendly civilians were killed, putting it down to 'poor training and inadequate briefing of personnel'. But a New Zealand officer was more perceptive: 'Heavy bombers from 14,000 feet are not accurate enough for this class of close support. Medium and light bombers are excellent.' If only Omar Bradley could have come to the same conclusion the Cobra tragedy might have been avoided.

10

Operation Cobra and Afterwards

Far from promising a prompt end to the war against Germany, the D-Day landings in Normandy in June 1944 seemed to offer a prospect not very different from the dreadful, static warfare of 1914–18. British and American planners, possibly blinded by their enormous material advantage over the Germans, notably in air power, had blundered in underestimating the problems posed by the difficult Normandy terrain, particularly the bocage, the thick hedgerow country that slowed down even the Allied tanks. At the end of the war General Bedell-Smith admitted:

> All commanding officers were theoretically aware of the hegerow terrain, but none had seen it. You cannot imagine it when you have not seen it. I had seen air photos of it but I could not imagine what it was like. Field Marshal Brooke, who had fought there, was very pessimistic about our chances.[45]

This bocage was skilfully used by the German defenders to slow up the Allied advance and the unusually stormy weather in early June 1944 hampered Allied air units from supporting their troops. In fact, the whole huge enterprise, which had begun on 6 June, was being held up by the slow progress out of the bridgeheads. Huge numbers of troops, with all their heavy equipment as well as their air support, were waiting in England and in the United States to ship to France but there was literally no space ashore to take them all.

There was a clear need for a breakout from the Normandy bridgeheads and among ground commanders the belief was that heavy bombers acting as ground-support aircraft could carpet bomb sections of the German front lines in order to force passages through for the Allied troops. Such use of heavy bombers would require very close liaison between ground and air commanders, yet the pressures of the war situation were such that this close relationship was never possible. The main point at issue was over the role of the heavy bomber, which had never been designed for ground support. In the eyes of the air commanders heavy bombers were a vital part of the strategic bombing campaign against Germany and in this role alone they would contribute to Allied victory. The transfer of such bombers to ground support was extremely ill advised if not actually counter-productive. Certainly their capacity to carpet bomb was not in question, but their capacity to bomb precisely at a time when friendly troops were within range was a very different matter. As Supreme Allied Commander, General Eisenhower was under pressure to use everything available to get his ground troops moving again and if heavy bombers could assist then he was prepared to use them. But there was a fundamental disagreement between the Allied air commanders. The Deputy Supreme Commander, Air Chief Marshal Tedder, backed by United States Strategic Air Force Commander Lieutenant-General Spaatz, was at odds with SHAEF air commander Air Chief Marshal Sir Trafford Leigh-Mallory. Tedder and Spaatz had no intention of handing over their heavy bombers to Eisenhower and Leigh-Mallory for their ground-support operations. They both doubted Leigh-Mallory's strategic grasp of the war and Spaatz in particular was no fan of the British airman's judgement. Nevertheless, Leigh-Mallory retained Eisenhower's confidence and he continued with his plans for carpet bombing to precede an Allied breakout from the Normandy bridgeheads, threatening to resign if Tedder or Spaatz tried to stop the operation. The situation favoured Leigh-Mallory in that ground operations had virtually come to a halt. Something was needed to regain the impetus of the Anglo–American invasion.

The plan for carpet bombing was targeted on General Omar Bradley's US First Army front at St Lô and was to be known as Operation Cobra, but first he needed to win the close and precise co-operation of the air chiefs in England. What Bradley wanted was something that had never been tried before in war: the sort of saturation of the enemy front in 60 minutes that had taken thousands of British guns days and weeks to achieve on the Somme in 1916 and at Passchendaele the following year. The bombers would concentrate on an area five miles wide and one mile deep, using light bombs to achieve minimum cratering and maximum anti-personnel effect. It was hoped that the impact on the German defenders would be so tremendous that they would be incapable of offering much resistance as VII Corps drove through them. Unfortunately, professional jealousy among the Allied leaders was rife. The airmen regarded Bradley as a dilettante in air matters and felt that his plan was simply unrealistic. Heavy strategic bombers simply did not have the tactical capacity he was demanding. Bombing so close to friendly forces was just asking for trouble. They wanted a safety zone of at least 3,000 yards, and even this was scarcely enough to guarantee that there would be no mishaps like friendly casualties. But a 3,000-yard safety zone was flatly ridiculous in Bradley's eyes. What was the use of pounding the enemy until he was dazed and then positioning your assault troops so far back that by the time they had crossed the safety zone the Germans had recovered and were ready to repel the assault? To Bradley a distance of 800 yards was the maximum he would ask his men to fall back. To the airmen this was tantamount to suicide. And so the dispute dragged on; airmen and footsloggers might as well have been speaking a different language. One group knew the realities of air warfare, the limitations in bombing technique of heavy bombers designed to blast areas rather than precise targets and the near certainty of friendly casualties if the safety margins were cut too fine. The other group was versed in the problems of land warfare, in which to hand over 3,000 yards of hard-won ground to the enemy was unacceptable. Eventually a compromise solution was reached which satisfied neither side. Bradley would order his men to fall back 1,500 yards and the airmen would try to operate within the constraints of an infantryman's scenario. It was a formula for catastrophe.

Omar Bradley had given a lot of thought to how the heavy bombers should approach the area to be bombed. Aware of the dangers of friendly casualties, he wanted them to come in parallel to the road from St Lô to Periers, so that they did not overfly his own ground troops. To Bradley – on the ground – the road was the most important and the most obvious feature of the area. However, from 15,000 feet or so, the airman did not consider the road to be as prominent a feature as Bradley felt it to be. To make maters worse, experienced airmen saw obvious flaws in Bradley's plan to fly in parallel to the road. With a time limit of just 60 minutes it was stretching the bounds of possibility to expect 1,500 heavy bombers to fly in over an area just one mile wide. The air chiefs insisted that only a north-south approach, using the Normandy coastline for reference and the St Lô–Periers road as a sighter for the bombardiers, was feasible for an operation on such a large scale. And so the matter stood, with Bradley insisting on a parallel approach to the road, with the bombers overflying German lines, and the air chiefs insisting on a north-south approach, with the bombers overflying American troops. The problem was that, at the meeting in Stanmore, in England, Bradley and air chiefs like Leigh-Mallory failed to appreciate the substantial differences that existed between them. Bradley left assuming that the airmen agreed with him and after the fiasco that followed on 24 and 25 July, he accused them of deliberately misleading him. This was unfair, for he was asking them to do something that they considered impossible.

Preparations for Operation Cobra now speeded up and the attack was earmarked for 21 July. Troops of US VII corps were instructed to 'vigorously push the attack across the highway to insure annihilation of any remaining enemy.' The emphasis on 'any remaining enemy' was significant and shows the confidence the ground commanders had in the efficacy of the proposed bombing. It was supposed that the Germans would be so shattered by the bombing that few would survive and those that did would offer only feeble resistance to a determined American push. However, ground commanders were less happy to receive orders to withdraw nearly a mile to offer a safety zone. This mile had been fought over and won with the lives of their soldiers.

Had Bradley heard the instructions that were being given to air force bombardiers he would have been gravely concerned. They were instructed not to bomb short 'because the penetration route is directly over friendly troops'. This would have alerted him to the fact that his insistence on a parallel approach by the bombers to avoid friendly casualties had been rejected in favour of a north-south approach, at right angles to the St Lô–Periers road. The misunderstanding between Bradley and the air chiefs was going to exact a high price in American lives.

Operation Cobra involved a vast commitment in airpower by two tactical air commands, IX TAC and XIX TAC. At the start, fighter-bombers would attack a strip along the St Lô to Periers road, to be followed by an attack from 1,586 heavy bombers, coming in over the English Channel at a height of some 15,000 feet. These US Eighth Air force 'heavies' were to attack in three waves, each over the target for 15 minutes, with a five-minute interval between waves. The target area would be hit by 50,000 general-purpose and fragmentation bombs, most of relatively small size – 100-pounders. Formations of 12–14 bombers would follow the example of a lead aircraft and drop their bombs to conform with the lead bombardier. As if that was not enough, once the heavies had delivered their payloads, German rear areas were to be attacked by medium bombers from the US Ninth Air Force. It would be a prodigious display of Allied air mastery and, according to the standards of the time, it should have been adequate to achieve the saturation of German defences that Bradley was seeking. But with operations on such a scale some things were bound to go wrong. The first problem was the weather. On 23 July heavy cloud made flying impossible and an irate Bradley commented, 'Dammit, I'm going to have to court martial the chaplain if we have much more weather like this.' But the following day Leigh-Mallory overruled another Eighth Air Force request for a postponement and gave the order to begin.

In the last few days before Cobra began it was obvious that there was still general confusion among the air chiefs about the approach to the target area to be followed by the Eighth Air Force heavy bombers. Leigh-Mallory and his deputy, Hoyt Vandenberg, continued to question the planners involved in bringing in the heavies. They were unhappy to learn that the Eighth Air Force men considered Bradley's plan for a parallel approach impracticable; there just was not enough time to bring in more than 1,500 bombers along that path. Vandenburg was told by Major-General Fred Anderson that, 'he was worried about the repercussions that might arise and that he wanted it clarified that the time factor which was sent by AEAF [American Eighth Air Force] was the controlling one for their direction of attack.' Vandenburg told Leigh-Mallory that Bradley's plan was a non-starter and that the general might prefer to extend the time beyond one hour to allow the parallel approach that he preferred. But the British air chief replied that he had already discussed this with Bradley and he was unwilling to extend the bombing time. According to Leigh-Mallory, Bradley 'had decided to accept the additional risk of perpendicular to the road bombing.' This statement was later vehemently denied by Bradley. But in view of the catastrophe that followed the saturation bombing nobody was in a hurry to accept responsibility and it is doubtful if we will ever know where the truth lay.

Heavy cloud on 24 July postponed the operation by the

fighter-bombers but by the time Leigh-Mallory decided to call the whole show off it was already too late to prevent many of the Eighth Air Force's heavy bombers from taking off. The 2nd Bomber Division, however, aborted their own attack as heavy cloud cover over the target area made identification impossible. A minor incident when a single bombardier accidentally unloaded his bombs on an allied air field was not too serious a problem for such a large operation. The 3rd Bomber Division also failed to locate the target, though perhaps 40 planes did drop their bombs in the vicinity. The real problems began when the 1st Bomber Division arrived over France and found that conditions were improving. Although some of these aircraft received the recall signals, most did not and 317 heavy bombers dropped a total of 10,124 high-explosive bombs and 1,822 fragmentation bombs. In the confusion some of these bombs fell short. Individual problems – one lead bombardier had a faulty bomb-release mechanism – were magnified many times over. This unfortunate airman, by dropping short, was followed by a further 12 or 14 planes which took their lead form him. On the ground, men from the US 30th Division were already diving for cover in ditches. In seconds, 25 soldiers were killed and a further 131 wounded. The Cobra fiasco had begun.

General Omar Bradley was shocked when the news reached him. It was exactly what he had feared and what he had tried so hard to avoid. How had it been possible? When he realized that the bombers had flown in on a perpendicular line rather than the parallel one on which he insisted, he was furious. The airmen had lied to him. He asked Leigh-Mallory for an explanation. Leigh-Mallory promised to get one – from Eighth Air Force. But, according to Vandenburg, the matter had already been discussed some days before. Was Leigh-Mallory really ignorant of Eighth Air Force's intentions to fly in perpendicular rather than parallel? Again it seemed that someone was lying.

On the ground, news of the postponement gave VII Corps' commander, General Lawton Collins, no real alternative but to reoccupy the safety zone that he had abandoned only hours before. There were a lot of disgruntled GIs after the zone had been recaptured at the expense of some casualties. At least the Germans were left with the impression that the day's fiasco meant that a major American attack had been repulsed.

Meanwhile, Leigh-Mallory had decided to try again the next day – 25 July – when the meteorologists promised better weather. But first he had to persuade Bradley to accept another perpendicular approach by the heavy bombers. As he pointed out, it was now far too late to change Eighth Air Force's mind about the time needed for a parallel run, and so – uneasily – Bradley accepted. The operation was now timetabled for 0900 on 25 July.

On the morning of 25 July the weather had improved but there was still cloud cover at 14,000 feet, making it necessary for the heavy bombers to fly at a lower altitude than planned and requiring the bombardiers to recalculate their bombing data. In itself this should not have posed many problems but in an operation on such a vast scale small errors were likely to have great effects.

The first problem was that a wind coming from the south blew a huge column of smoke from the target zone – which had just been hit by Ninth Air Force's fighter-bombers – northwards, directly into the path of Eighth Air Force's armada of 1,495 heavy bombers, B-17s and B-24s. Even without the problem of cloud cover it was extremely difficult for navigators and bombardiers to pick out landmarks, for the whole area was covered by immense clouds of smoke, dust and red marker flares. Nevertheless, the American bombers succeeded in dropping over 4,000 tons of bombs into and around the target area. Errors were inevitable and they were on a scale that matched the entire operation. According to the official report by Walter E Todd, human error contributed to extensive friendly casualties. Two lead bombardiers released their bombs without first achieving satisfactory identification and were then followed by their entire units, while a command pilot caused short bombing when he assumed his wing was supposed to bomb as a single unit. The results, on the ground, were catastrophic. The 30th Infantry Division, which had suffered casualties the previous day, was again in the forefront of the blue-on-blue. A total of 61 men were killed, 374 wounded, 64 others were listed as missing and 164 men suffered total nervous collapses as a result of shell shock or 'combat fatigue'. Other parts of VII Corps also suffered losses and included in the final list of 111 fatalities was General Leslie McNair, the most senior American officer lost during the entire war. McNair had been in a forward position – despite warnings that he should stay at the rear – observing the effects of the saturation bombing. He died when his bunker suffered a direct hit. Bradley was horrified when he received the news. 'Oh Christ,' he said, 'not another short drop.' War correspondent Ernie Pyle was with the troops on the ground and recorded the shattering effects of the bombing:

> As we watched there crept into our consciousness a realization that windrows of exploding bombs were easing back towards us, flight by flight, instead of gradually forward, as the plan called for. Then we were horrified by the suspicion that these machines, high in the sky, and completely detached from us, were aiming their bombs at the smokeline on the ground, and a gentle breeze was drifting the smokeline back over us! An indescribable kind of panic comes over you at such times. We stood tensed in muscle and frozen in intellect, watching each flight approach and pass over us, feeling trapped and completely helpless.[46]

Lieutenant-Colonel George Tuttle of the 30th Division described his experiences: 'The ground was shaken and rocked as if by a great earthquake. The concussion, even underground, felt as if someone was beating you with a club.' Young Lieutenant Sidney Eichen of the 120th infantry, like many of the American soldiers that day, felt proud as he saw the seemingly endless lines of American planes flying towards him.

Their power seemed limitless. Suddenly, he had the awful realizaton that, just as they had yesterday, these bombers were going to drop short over American lines. As he wrote afterwards, 'My outfit was decimated, our anti-tank guns blown apart. I saw one of our truck drivers, Jesse Ivy, lying split down the middle. Captain Bell was buried in a crater with only his head visible. He suffocated before we could reach him.' The bitterness of the GIs towards the airmen who killed them knew no bounds and many of them fired their rifles impotently into the skies at the planes that had earlier filled them with such pride.

Nevertheless, in spite of the appalling casualties to friendly forces the bombing went on and was immediately followed up by American infantry assaults on German fronts. Disappointingly, the first waves of American troops found the Germans, apparently unruffled by their ordeal, waiting for them and resistance was firm. It transpired that German losses were only marginally heavier than those of the Americans – 700 to 601 – which was a good advertisement for the effectiveness of German tunnelling. Unlike the Americans, few of whom had dug foxholes, the Germans had been thoroughly prepared for anything less than the Day of Judgement. On the other hand, American troops can be excused for not expecting to need such protection against their own aircraft.

German resistance on the afternoon of 25 July was unexpectedly strong. A German commander, General Fritz Bayerlein, explained that although German forward positions had been destroyed, reserves had been held back beyond the target area and were quickly rushed to the front once the bombing had stopped. As a result, American progress was slow and when First Army failed to achieve the expected breakout, the search began for scapegoats. The army blamed General Doolittle's Eighth Air Force for 'lacing enthusiasm for ground support'. But the air chiefs responded by blaming Bradley. He had been warned that if he reduced the safety zone below the 3,000 yards that had originally been demanded as the minimum safe distance for heavy bombing, then friendly casualties were almost inevitable. As General Spaatz said, 'We were attempting to place too heavy a concentration in too small an area.'

But all was not as it appeared. German defences were a façade. Bayerlein described the experiences of the German troops on 25 July:

> It was hell . . . The planes kept coming overhead like a conveyor belt, and the bomb carpets came down, now ahead, now on the right, now on the left . . . The fields were burning and smouldering. The bomb carpets unrolled in great rectangles . . . My front lines looked like a landscape on the moon, and at least seventy per cent of my personnel were out of action – dead, wounded, crazed or numbed. All my front line tanks were knocked out. Late in the afternoon, the American ground troops began filtering in. I had organized my last reserves to meet them – not over fifteen tanks, most of them from repair shops. The roads were practically impassable. Then next morning the bombing began all over again. We could do nothing but retreat.[47]

If the Americans pushed hard the whole edifice would collapse and they would get their breakthrough. General Collins had already decided to fling in his armour on the morning of 26 July and this would prove decisive. Cobra would be a success after all but it would be one achieved at the price of one of the worst aerial blue-on-blues in history.

Who was to blame for the dreadful Cobra fiasco? Omar Bradley was convinced that he knew the answer. It was the air chiefs of the Eighth Air Force, who had refused his reasonable plan for a parallel approach over German lines and instead opted for the perpendicular approach that took the planes over friendly troop concentrations. 'It was duplicity,' Bradley wrote bitterly in his autobiographic *A General's Story*, 'a shocking breach of good faith.' But this was untrue and Bradley must have known that even as he wrote those angry words. He had been told repeatedly that 60 minutes was far too short a time for 1,500 heavy bombers to carry out the operation if they approached parallel to the St Lô-to-Periers road. Nor was it certain, even if they did approach in that way, that no bombs would fall on friendly troops. A safety margin of 3,000 yards was the minimum the airmen thought advisable, and Bradley was being unrealistic by reducing it to 800 or even the 1,500 yards that was the final unwilling compromise. Bradley simply did not understand and was apparently unwilling to try to understand the problems of the strategic bomber asked to become a tactical bomber for a 'one-off' mission. He was expecting the flyers to bail out his First Army at a low point in its fortunes.

If blame was to be apportioned Bradley had to be prepared to shoulder his share. Aware of the dangers from blue-on-blue bombing he still made no attempt to take safety measures to minimize the danger when the time came for the saturation bombing. Why were the American troops out in the open, cheering on the 'heavies' rather than in foxholes and trenches like the Germans? The simple answer, of course, is that he was relying on being able to attack the Germans straight away, while they were still groggy from the bombing. To have dispersed VII Corps and sent them under ground would have used up vital minutes when the time for the infantry assault came. This was a senior command decision. Friendly casualties might need to be risked in order to reduce casualties from enemy fire. It was an equation to be balanced by the officer commanding but it reflected little credit on Bradley that when he got his sums wrong he tried to blame someone else for his own failings.

In terms of blame, Bradley did not stand alone. Air Chief Marshal Leigh-Mallory failed in his task to co-ordinate ground and air units during Operation Cobra. His own experience had mainly been with single-seat fighters and he really knew little and understood less of the problems of the heavy bomber. In his role as liaison between the British and the Americans, Leigh-Mallory was something of a disaster and even a British officer at SHAEF wrote him off as having a reputation for incompetence and 'a pompous, arrogant attitude'. His decision to let the 'heavies' set off on 24 July, even overruling in the process the opinions of the weather expert, before recalling them, too late in some cases, contributed to the tragic friendly casualties on that day. In addition, it also meant that the American troops who had abandoned the safety zone on 24 July had to fight to regain the territory when the news came that the operation was postponed. A further, extraordinary decision that formed part of the Cobra bombing was the use of Ninth Air Force's fighter-bombers as a preliminary to the work of the heavy bombers from Eighth Air Force. The obvious problem – and one that should have been manifest at the time – was the obscuring effect of all the smoke from the fighter-bombers' ordnance. With a wind from the south, all this smoke would be blown across the approach paths of the 'heavies', with the result that target identification would be difficult, the St Lô-to-Periers road invisible and careless bombing much increased. It was a disastrous formula, particularly for airmen flying over territory occupied entirely by friendly forces. In such a case, blue-on-blue was not so much a possibility as a certainty.

In August 1944 the Canadians and Poles launched an armoured offensive against German troops at Caen. As in the case of Operation Cobra this operation – code named 'Totalize' – was to be prefaced by an aerial bombardment of German positions. On 7–8 August, 1,000 bombers from RAF Bomber Command were due to saturate the forward German positions but such was the build up of smoke and dust that at least a third of the planes did not drop their bombs for fear of hitting friendly troops. The next day the US Eighth Air Force took over ground support and unfortunately inflicted 300 casualties on the Canadians and Poles. This error was followed up by the RAF and RCAF on 14 August, during their support for the assault on Falaise, code named 'Operation Tractable'. At first all went well until 77 Lancaster and Halifax bombers of the second wave flew over the Canadian and Polish lines, dropping their bombs on friendly troops, causing 65 deaths and wounding over 400 men. By an incredible oversight, nobody had informed Bomber Command that ground troops were identifying their positions by yellow smoke: the fact was that yellow smoke was Bomber Command's target-identification colour. The more desperately the ground troops burned their yellow flares the more the bombers rained death on them. Worse casualties were only avoided when an Auster reconnaissance aircraft took off and flew in front of the bombers, waggling its wings and trying to draw them away from the Canadian lines.

Aerial amicide continued to exact a heavy price during the late summer of 1944. So heavy had been the friendly casulaties during the massive heavy-bomber raids in Operations Cobra, Totalize and Tractable that the use of heavy bombers was discontinued and ground support was left to the more flexible medium bombers and fighter-bombers. However, although this decision reduced the severity of the incidents, it did not necessarily reduce their number. The very scale of operations and the increasing fluidity of the battlefield that followed the Allied breakouts from Normandy contributed to a rash of minor friendly-fire incidents. Human errors among pilots and navigators led to numerous strafings and bombings of Allied troops so that few units even bothered to record them all. Among the ground troops it was merely a sign that they had a new enemy in the sky – the American Luftwaffe. As usual, US 30th Division was in the thick of it. On 29 July, near Troisgots, American fighter-bombers bombed and strafed several units from the division. A few days later, during the heavy fighting around Mortain, the division was frequently attacked by American P-47s and British Typhoons. On 7 August, the 120th Infantry recorded ten separate incidents of friendly fire by Allied fighter-bombers, while two US tanks from the 3rd Armored Division were destroyed by friendly aircraft. Near Laval, American fighters shot up Third Army and XIX Tactical Air Command headquarters. Tired of taking this aerial punishment, anti-aircraft gunners around Laval promptly shot down one of the attacking planes.

The fact that Anglo–American troops were having to fight their way through France, Belgium and Holland to liberate them from the Germans involved the obvious difficulty of trying to destroy a tenacious enemy without harming the friendly population of the countries concerned. And when one adds the extra difficulty of using close air support and tactical bombing to support the ground troops, the chances of friendly casualties were much increased. On 2 October 1944, American planes made 'a gross error of navigation' and attacked the Belgian town of Genck, 35 miles from the intended target inside Germany. The result was that 34 Belgian civilians died and 45 others were injured.

Just before Christmas in 1944, the Belgian town of Malmédy suffered further attacks by American planes. The apparently ubiquitous 30th Infantry Division was in combat with 1st SS Panzer Division near La Gleize. Ordered to support the ground troops six B-26s missed their designated target, which was Zulpich, the railhead for the German Seventh Army, and instead dropped their bombs on Malmédy, killing at least 37 soldiers of the 30th Division, many Belgian civilians and burning much of the town in the process. This incident was blamed on palpable human error. The terrain around Malmédy was quite different from that near Zulpich, 33 miles away, and misidentification in good visibility had seemed impossible.

On Christmas Day itself, four B-26s revisited Malmédy and dropped a further 64 250-pound bombs into the ruins. Aware that they had missed their target – St Vith – the pilots were apparently satisfied that they had hit an alternative target in Born. Again visibility was excellent and once again the blue-on-blue was put down to human error.

So frequent were these 'human errors' that many American ground troops opened fire on their own planes as soon as they saw them. A staff officer of 1st Division reasonably opined on 7 July 1944, 'I wish you would tell the Air Corps we don't want them over here. Have them get out in front and let them take pictures, but no strafing or bombing.'

The German offensive in the Ardennes in the winter of 1944, popularly known as the Battle of the Bulge, saw some of the most confused fighting of modern times. In the appalling conditions – low cloud, mists and snow blizzards – friendly fire was common, much of it provided by American aircraft. On 24 December 1944, however, flying conditions were excellent with good visibility, yet this did not prevent a series of friendly-fire incidents. A squadron of P-38s attacked the village of Buisonville, recently occupied by units of the US 2nd Armored Division, and killed an American officer and wounded another. At Bastogne, P-47s strafed and bombed troops of the US 101st Airborne Division.

In the fighting between the Salm and Ourthe rivers, units from the American 3rd Armored Divisions were heavily hit by friendly fighter-bombers. On Christmas Day, 1944, near Grandménil, American tanks were attacked by a flight of eleven P-38s from the 430th Fighter Squadron which mistook them for Germans. In the carnage that followed the Americans lost 39 men killed and over 100 wounded. In the event, the responsibility from this blunder lay not so much with the pilots as with the neighbouring American 7th Armored Division which had called in the air strike. In spite of the fact that the tanks of 3rd Armored were carrying orange identification panels, the American pilots were not deterred and continued to attack them. Clearly co-ordination between divisions and their allocated air supports was highly suspect. Human error, whether bureaucratic or military, was at the root of the problem and yet one wonders why individual pilots could not have responded with the individual initiative that has increasingly become a demand of modern warfare.

Hitler had been unprepared to accept that the war was lost at the end of 1944 and launched a tremendous counter-attack against the Americans in the Ardennes which has become known as the Battle of the Bulge. Alongside the ground assault he also drew together all the remaining strength of the Luftwaffe and launched them in surprise attacks on British and American airfields around Brussels. As many as 439 Allied aircraft were apparently destroyed on the ground, including B-17s, Lancasters, Spitfires and Typhoons. It was a stunning achievement which cost the Germans just 93 aircraft shot down by Allied fighters or flak. Unfortunately, the butcher's bill became much larger as the triumphant German squadrons returned to their bases. The German anti-aircraft defences had been kept in ignorance of the operation and when the low-flying German aircraft flew over them they massacred them with a violent explosion of flak, which shot down an incredible 184 friendly planes, including 59 unit commanders and senior staff. It was a death blow to the old Luftwaffe which was never able to launch so powerful an operation again. It was also probably the most expensive blue-on-blue mishap every recorded, certainly in terms of material if not in lives lost.

11

America's Undeclared War
With Switzerland

On 5 September 1927, George and Ira Gershwin's new musical *Strike Up the Band* opened in Philadelphia. Based on a script by George S Kaufman, the show was a satirical comedy which included the most unlikely situation that even the most ardent of American patriots could contemplate – a war with Switzerland, and in defence of Fletcher's American Cheese at that. In 1927 it was all good, harmless fun, of course, and in the show the Swiss seemed to take that war as an opportunity for a display of Swiss hospitality when Kaufman's fantasy became reality and American bombs rained death and destruction on the undefended Swiss town of Schaffhausen. The undeclared Swiss–American war of 1944–5 had begun. Soon Swiss fighter planes were shooting down American bombers, killing American aircrew, while Swiss towns suffered a number of damaging raids in which many civilians died. And in spite of the best efforts of politicians and diplomats on both sides of the Atlantic the killing went on, unintentionally on the part of the Americans but in grim earnest by the Swiss, who were determined to defend their territory and their rights as a neutral state. This fantasy war was one of the strangest manifestations of friendly fire and one imbued with the most serious consequences.

Allied bombing of southern Germany after 1943 was fraught
with great difficulty. Bad weather over the mountainous terrain
on the Swiss–German border, combined with faulty navigation
and pilot error, produced a series of friendly-fire incidents in
which American and – to a much lesser extent – British aircraft
invaded Swiss air space and dropped their bombs by mistake
on Swiss targets. In such cases it was hardly adequate to inform
the Swiss authorities that some accidental damage or friendly
casualties were to be expected in modern warfare. To the
neutral Swiss such 'attacks' were acts of war and would
provoke immediate retaliation. The Americans were politely
informed that single aircraft violating Swiss air space would be
escorted to a landing field and forced to land there, while
formations of two or more bombers would be attacked
without warning. Soon after the Schaffhausen raid Swiss
aircraft, acting on this policy, shot down an American bomber
and impounded another, after forcing it to land at Dübendorf.
The Swiss hoped that they had made their point. Yet friendly-
fire incidents increased rather than diminished after this
display of force. To the embarrassment of the American
authorities their air commanders could find no foolproof
system to stop their crews flying over Switzerland. When
ambassador Leland Harrison apologized to the Swiss for the
Schaffhausen raid and offered to pay compensation, he was
presented with evidence of what the Swiss foreign minister
described as the 'deliberate attack' by 50 American planes on
Schaffhausen causing casualties of over 100 dead and wounded.

At first the Americans were unwilling to accept all the blame,
point out that there had been earlier incursions of Swiss air
space by British planes. But when General Spaatz, commander
of the US Strategic Air Force in Europe, collated all the evidence
it was obvious where the fault lay. On 1 April 1944, two
American bomber groups had indeed flown over Schaffhausen
by mistake, though their crews were insistent that their bombs
had missed the town. Spaatz duly apologized to the Swiss
though he frankly felt he had more important things to worry
about, like the D-Day landings in Normandy, only a few weeks

away. He knew that bad weather and heavy cloud cover was a common feature over Switzerland and southern Germany at that time of year and felt that it was all much ado about nothing. But when Spaatz's views were leaked to the press there was an outcry in Switzerland, intensified by meteorological evidence which showed that weather conditions over Schaffhausen on 1 April had been excellent, with near perfect visibility. In Germany the Nazi propaganda machine accused the Americans of 'war crimes'. The Americans were faced with a public relations disaster. Only generous compensation combined with measures to ensure that there was no repeat of such friendly bombing would satisfy the Swiss.

An investigation of the Schaffhausen raid revealed that adverse conditions over France, with heavy cloud and strong winds, had broken up the bomber formations, scattering the planes over a wide area. Their original target had been the German town of Ludwigshafen am Rhein but, when gaps in the cloud enabled the Americans to identify a city on the east bank of the Rhine, they did not realize that they had been blown across the Swiss border and were, in fact, 50 miles from their target, flying over Schaffhausen. At this stage there was still a chance that the tragedy could have been avoided. Standard American procedure precluded bombing a target within 50 miles of Germany's borders unless a positive identification could be made. Two important targets – the benzol storage plant and the butadiene factory (butadiene is used in the manufacturing of synthetic rubber) – should have shown the pilots whether they were over Ludwigshafen or not. In fact, no American pilot achieved a positive identification of either target, so no bombs should have been dropped. On the other hand, human nature being what it is, it was asking a lot of a pilot to fly back across Occupied France with a full bomb load, particularly after having risked so much already. As a result, through human error, the target was not identified and American bombs were dropped on a city in neutral Switzerland causing over 100 civilian casualties. As a one-off the Schaffhausen raid would have been bad enough, but even as

American officials tried to smooth the ruffled Swiss feathers, news of more incidents became public. The Swiss air force fought fire with fire and, on 13 April, its fighters shot down a damaged American bomber, killing the six crewmen. Now it was the turn of the Americans to protest.

In the space of three days in July 1944 a total of 23 American bombers were forced to land by Swiss fighters. The situation was getting out of hand. Yet, however much the politicians might fume at the diplomatic embarrassment, in the skies over southern Germany American pilots were facing the choice of flying their bombers, sometimes damaged by flak or short of fuel, across France and the English Channel to their bases in England, or to take the easier and safer option of seeking internment in neutral Switzerland. Many chose the latter option, even jettisoning their bombs on Swiss territory rather than attempt a crash landing loaded with high explosives. On 19 July, the castle of Weyden, home of the president of the International Red Cross, was struck a direct hit by a damaged US bomber abandoned by her crew.

Although these repeated incidents of friendly fire were viewed in an extremely serious light by US politicians and diplomats, not everyone in the armed forces shared their concern. Senior members of SHAEF – both British and American – were convinced that the Swiss General Staff was full of German sympathizes. Moreover, the fact that Switzerland – quite legally as a neutral state – had continued to trade with Nazi Germany, convinced some commanders that the Swiss deserved everything that was coming to them. Yet this was no answer to the most important question that needed to be asked: why were so many American planes flying off course and bombing the wrong targets? One optimistic – and specious – theory was that German pilots were flying captured and repaired American planes over Switzerland in an attempt to score a sensational propaganda victory. But this was grasping at straws. There were quite enough verifiable incidents of American friendly fire to render any German co-operation quite unnecessary. On 29 October 1944, American bombers attacked the railway junction at Noirmont, even though Swiss flags were painted on a number of the village roofs and were quite unmissable in the good visibility that day.

On 25 December, bombers from the US 1st Tactical Air Force bombed the town of Thayngen in Switzerland, on the mistaken assumption that they were attacking the Singen railway bridge in Germany. The American pilots blamed cloud cover but again it was obvious that a serious error in identification had been made, in which case the bombs should not have been dropped. In the early days of 1945 the Swiss were in the front line again, as US bombers attacked Chiasso and the hydro-electric plant at Brusio in the Puschlav valley. On 22 February, President Roosevelt sent a special representative, Laughlan Currie, to Switzerland to apologize for the serious and continuing violations of Swiss air space. Currie went to Schaffhausen to lay a wreath on the graves of the civilians killed by American bombs on 1 April 1944, but his timing could hardly have been worse. As he was honouring the dead in Schaffhausen, American bombers made their most widespread attacks on Swiss territory. Thirteen separate incidents occurred and at Stein am Rhein – just twelve miles from where Currie was making his gesture – seven civilians were killed and some sixteen injured. This time it was impossible to blame adverse weather conditions for it was bright and sunny. Currie's mission was fatally undermined. All he could do was offer compensation.

At SHAEF General Eisenhower was smarting from the criticism he was receiving from all quarters. He knew that the percentage of friendly-fire incidents was minute compared to the thousands of successful missions carried out by British and American planes over Nazi-occupied France and Germany. Yet it was the mistakes that were getting all the headlines. When, in early March, six US B-24s dropped 12 tons of explosives on Zürich, while others hit Basle with more than 16 tons, the reputation of the US Army Air Force seemed on the line. In Washington, General George Marshall, Chief of Staff of the US Army, ordered Eisenhower to send Spaatz to Switzerland to see if he could do a better job of explaining why his bombers could not fly straight or bomb the right targets. At a crucial stage in the war it was an incredible decision to uproot Spaatz from his London office and send him to the small French town of Annemasse, dressed in civilian clothes and a Tyrolean hat, to meet the Swiss top brass. It could have been a scene from *Strike Up the Band*. But the Swiss did not appreciate the honour that was being paid them. Perhaps Spaatz should have come barefoot and dressed in a sheet. They presented him with a full list of grievances and it was a pretty long list at that. Their demand for compensation was readily accepted by the American delegation and Spaatz expressed his readiness to prohibit bombing within 150 miles of the Swiss border unless precise identification was possible. Within 50 miles of Swiss territory no bombing of any sort would take place. Had these restrictions been applied a year earlier they could have had a significantly weakening effect on the Allied bombing campaign against Germany. At last it seemed that the problems caused by friendly fire were coming to an end. The compensation finally paid to Switzerland for bomb damage amounted to some $18 million, settled in October 1949. Yet no one ever really solved the problem of why so many American pilots mistook their targets over so long a period. The bombing of Zürich in March 1945 was particularly puzzling. Situated as it was on a substantial body of water – Lake Zürich – the city was clearly identifiable and was most unlikely to have been confused with any nearby German target. Moreover, to attack Zürich the American bombers needed to have travelled deep into Swiss territory and no sort of navigational error or adverse weather conditions seemed to provide an adequate excuse for bombing the city by mistake. In fact, the Zürich fiasco gave rise to one of the very few occasions where those responsible for friendly-fire incidents were both named and subjected to court martial. On 1 June 1945, the pilot and navigator of the lead aircraft in the squadron that bombed Zürich were tried by court martial at Horsham St Faith in England. As it happened the presiding officer on that occasion was none other than Hollywood star

James Stewart, then a USAAF colonel. Both men were acquitted on a charge that they 'wrongfully and negligently caused bombs to be dropped in friendly territory'. In their favour it was shown that their plane had been subject to equipment malfunction as well as poor visibility. Nevertheless, the final decision to drop the bombs was taken by the pilot and the responsibility for the civilian casualties was his. As in most friendly-fire incidents in was human error that played the most significant part in America's unfortunate 'war' against Switzerland.

12

Air Warfare in East Asia

Although air amicide was much less of a feature in the Pacific than in the European theatre of operations, it must not be regarded as insignificant. Distinguishing friendly forces from enemy troops was notably difficult in the jungle terrain of New Guinea, where there were numerous accidental bombings of friendly forces. According to Charles Shrader, the American troops involved in the recapture of Guam in July 1944 were constantly subject to friendly-fire incidents. On 21 July, the first day of the assault, members of the 22nd Marine Regiment on Agat were attacked by American aircraft. Three days later, units of the marines trying to break out of their bridgehead called in air support from the navy's planes. When it came it proved to more damaging to them than to Japanese. The problem was that the two battle lines were far too close to allow the navy planes to drop their bombs with any confidence of avoiding friendly troops. The outcome was that 17 marines died or were wounded in the attack. On 4 August, the command post of the 3rd Battalion of the 21st Marines was demolished by bombs from two B-25s. Not content with this, the two planes then strafed American personnel in the area. While the marines were suffering these blue-on-blues, the army had its hands full fending off American attacks themselves. On 28 July, a company of the 305th Infantry was bombed and strafed by US planes just after they had fought their way to the summit of Mount Tenjo, on southern Guam. This company only avoided destruction when one of its number, risking his life in the process, managed to spread out an identifying panel visible from the air. Further bombing and strafing incidents occurred to units of the 305th and 307th near Mount Santa Rosa and Yigo.

So frequent were the air attacks on friendly troops that the ground forces eventually lost all confidence when US aircraft were called in to support them. Shrader reports the following exchange between General Krueger and General Kenney, which seems to sum up the feelings of infantrymen everywhere during the Second World War: 'ground-pounders' were 'trigger-happy'.

> I must insist that you take effective measures to stop the bombing and strafing of our ground forces by friendly planes . . . These repeated occurrences are causing ground troops to lose confidence in air support and are adversely affecting morale.[48]

A tragic blue-on-blue occurred during the Korean War to British troops from the Argyll and Sutherland Highlanders. On 23 September 1950, the Argylls had just captured Hill 282 from the communist North Koreans and had called in air support against nearby enemy troop concentrations. They identified their own positions with recognition panels visible from the air but when the American Mustangs arrived they ignored the signals and plastered the British position with napalm. Seventeen members of the Argylls were killed and 76 wounded. Furthermore, they were forced to evacuate the hill that they had fought so long and hard to capture. Hill 282 was reoccupied by the communists but Major Kenneth Muir and his 30 surviving men promptly fought their way back up the hill and retook it, Muir dying in the moment of victory. For his courage and leadership Muir was awarded a posthumous Victoria Cross.

The problems of close ground support by the US Air Force,

which had produced so many friendly casualties in the Second World War, were even greater in Vietnam as a result of the acutely hostile environment. The planes were faster and more deadly in performance and, in their ground-support role, they were assisted by attack helicopters, yet the mainly jungle terrain of the battle zones made blue-on-blue incidents even more likely than in previous wars. The increased speed of their aircraft and the need for almost instant responses to a swiftly changing battle situation made pilot errors even more costly. Added to the problems of identifying friendly forces was the factor of mechanical malfunction by the increasingly complex hardware. Helicopters were particularly prone to technical failure. On 3 March 1968, near the village of Go Vap, a blue-on-blue incident resulted from a helicopter hitting an air pocket, causing the nose of the craft to dip violently. Unfortunately, this unplanned manoeuvre occurred just as the crew were firing two rockets in support of an American platoon from the 9th Infantry Regiment, which was caught in a communist ambush. Just three Americans were wounded in the incident, but the way in which it occurred was disconcerting for troops entirely dependent on the usually reliable UH-1 helicopters for ground support.

One part of the air war in Vietnam constituted an enormous example of friendly fire for the United States Air Force, the consequences of which are only now being fully appreciated. Operation Ranch Hand, during which Agent Orange was sprayed repeatedly in Vietnam over jungle or over food crops, was designed to defoliate the jungle so that enemy troops could not hide and also to destroy food crops that might be used by the enemy. Defoliants had been briefly used in warfare before, by the British in the Malayan Emergency for example, but no power had ever possessed America's potential to destroy the very food on which their enemy depended. From 1962, military pressure built up to begin a defoliation campaign known as Operation Ranch Hand although Dean Rusk saw it as a blunder. 'The way to win the war basically is to win the people. Crop destruction runs counter to this basic rule, he said, as it is impossible to differentiate friendly from enemy crops. At first, defoliation was introduced carefully, to avoid harming friendly peasants, but mistakes soon proliferated as defoliant spread in the wind. By 1967 – in which 1.7 million acres were sprayed – public disquiet was reaching epidemic proportions. The Vietcong claimed that the defoliant used by the Americans – Agent Orange – was not only poisonous but was a biological time bomb.

Agent Orange was a mixture of two herbicides: 24D and 245T and was given its name because there was an orange stripe around the barrels in which it was kept. The dioxin contaminant in Agent Orange was what caused the most concern to human health, causing cancers, immune deficiency, reproductive and developmental problems, endocrine, disruption, nervous system damage and many other health difficulties as well. Even though the two herbicides were domestically used in the United States, the type of Agent Orange that was used in Vietnam was high in the most toxic dioxin. Dioxins are among the most toxic chemicals ever made by man: molecule by molecule, they are very persistent, bioaccumulating so that, even in 2000, more than thirty years after their first use, doctors reported elevated dioxin levels from Agent Orange in Vietnamese blood.

There is no doubting the military advantages that initially flowed from Operation Ranch Hand yet, because it failed to research its own weapons adequately, the United States found that American soldiers on the ground were beginning to succumb to their own chemicals. The American military services claimed total ignorance of the danger posed by carcinogenic dioxins. The chemical companies had apparently known of these dioxins but had said nothing because their removal would have increased the cost of production. The fact that Agent Orange would harm both friendly and enemy soldiers who encountered it was conveniently overlooked. In the late 1960s, when the American military discovered that laboratory animals had developed cancer in tests when exposed to Agent Orange, they stopped its use in Vietnam. But it was already far too late: Agent Orange had become a devastating form of friendly fire.

In the confused fighting of a jungle battlefield, it was the problem of identification of friendly troops that provided the greatest difficulties for the jet and helicopter pilots in Vietnam. Friendly and enemy troops could and frequently did occupy almost exactly the same grid references, requiring pinpoint accuracy in bombing runs, something which was often beyond the capability of the pilots. Both planes and pilots were being asked to perform beyond their technological and human limitations.

In one case, cited by Charles Shrader, the ground troops – members of the Vietnamese Civilian Irregular Defence Group – marked their position in the thick jungle by using green smoke. Two B-57s were called in to give ground support but one strafed the designated target and managed to hit friendly troops, killing four men and wounding 28. The reason for this error was not simply the poor visibility afforded by the jungle but the fact that prior to his attack, the pilot was given numerous changes of target area and bearing. This new data clearly confused him and led to human error. Thus even though the pilot had the assistance of an airborne forward air controller, it was still possible for him to be overloaded with data to the point where he, rather than the technology he controlled, malfunctioned.

The involvement of forward air controllers in ground support should have decreased the incidence of friendly fire in modern wars. However, the introduction of another fallible human element into the decision-making process of air-to-ground operations, though essential in view of the technical demands of flying and fighting a state-of-the-art combat plane, had added another factor to an already complex chain. The chances of poor co-ordination between air controller and pilot and the transmission of flawed data has been at the root of a large number of blue-on-blue incidents in Vietnam and more recently in the Gulf. Literally, the more minds that are involved in taking a decision about where and when to drop bombs, fire rockets or strafe ground troops, the more chances there are for human error. Shrader cites an example from Vietnam in 1968. An FAC controlling the mission of an F-4D aircraft armed with an M-117 bomb, marked a target just over 200 yards from friendly troops. It was too tight for marking, particularly as the friendlies had put up no smoke for guidance, and the FAC's guidance rocket went 75 yards west of the intended target. The pilot now made two errors of his own, to compound the FAC's inaccurate rocket guide. He misinterpreted the position of the friendly troops and incorrectly estimated the position of the target, which lay between the friendlies and the inaccurate rocket guide. The result was that the bomb landed squarely in the middle of the US troops, killing three men and wounding 12 others.

The performance of the helicopter gunship, first used in Vietnam and then in every US operation since, has revolutionized ground-support operations. However, Vietnam was by some way the worst environment for such a weapon to be employed effectively. The jungle terrain made observation almost impossible and also shrouded enemy anti-aircraft guns. Nevertheless, the helicopter offered such advantages in mobility and the increased accuracy of its firepower that its success was assured in spite of the occasional blue-on-blue incidents that were a consequence of its unusual design characteristics. As Shrader has pointed out, the helicopter was as capable of misidentifying targets as the fixed-wing aircraft and its pilots just as liable to human error, yet its rotary blade and its proneness to instability in high winds carried with it particular problems for its pilots and the ground troops it was supporting. On 27 August 1967, a CH-47 helicopter was supporting units from the 12th Infantry, who were engaged with enemy forces. As the helicopter moved over a company of the 2nd Battalion, its door gunner was shot and killed by enemy fire. But the gunner was in the act of firing as he was killed and his grip on the trigger did not relax, so that he sprayed bullets into the friendly troops below. This unfortunate incident was a consequence of the nature of the helicopter as an aerial gun platform and could hardly have occurred in the case of any other aerial weapon. Even more unusual was the incident involving a fractured traverse rod on a door gun, which caused the helicopter gunner to fire into his own cockpit, wounding the pilot.

One element of friendly fire in the air that has always remained the closest of closely guarded secrets is the degree to which human irresponsibility has played a part in blue-on-blues. Foot soldiers since 1939, perhaps even earlier, have not always been convinced that their airmen colleagues have been as careful as they could be when it came to supporting the infantry. The all-embracing category of 'human error' has usually been enough to deter the investigator from pursuing individual motivation when it came to friendly fire. Yet what evidence there is does tend to suggest that some aerial blue-on-blues have resulted from drug- or drink-related carelessness on the part of pilots and aircrew, or at least that over-exuberance and youthful high spirits have occasionally played their part. Shrader suggests that two examples from Vietnam, which resulted in a number of deaths, may have been caused in these ways. During August 1969, near the town of Pleiku, a UH-1H helicopter crewed by inexperienced personnel on their first flight responded to a command from the crew chief to fire on the source of some smoke rising above the trees. The helicopter went straight into action without any attempt at identifying the target and fired straight into an American unit. In 1971, another UH-1H helicopter was shot down by American infantry from Fire Support Base 'Mary Ann', near Chu Lai. According to Shrader, indiscipline was the major cause of this disaster, in which the ground troops may have engaged the helicopter 'for a lark'. A percentage – however small – of the military personnel of any army will be gung-ho, trigger-happy, will love killing for its own sake, will commit atrocities, kill prisoners, rape women, torture suspects, frag their own officers, take drugs, be drunk on duty, will run away when the first shot is fired, and so on. However well drilled and professional an army, the stress of operational conditions will bring out the best in some men and the worst in others. While human beings engage in warfare they will always face two enemies: the enemy who points the guns and rockets their way, and the enemy within, the selves that they did not know they possessed until their lives were placed in the balance day after day. In military terms the US invasion of Grenada in 1983, known as Operation Urgent Fury, was 'a close run thing'. It skirted the edge of farce. The Americans even bombed a lunatic asylum by mistake.

Air strikes by Corsair IIs were used against Cuban and Grenadian People's Republican Army positions east of the town of St George's. Unfortunately the fighter-bombers attacked Fort Matthew, an old Briish colonial fortress which was being used as a mental asylum. As bombs and rockets exploded in and around the fort dozens of pathetic inmates ran screaming into the streets of the town. Although the fort was clearly marked as a hospital on the American maps, the pilots had confused it with other hill fortifications nearby. The consequences were that the Corsairs killed 21 helpless people and wounded hundreds of others. It was a shocking and thoroughly discreditable incident.

At 1600 hours on 27 October, a scout platoon from the 3rd Battalion of the 325th Regiment was brought under sniper fire in the south of Grenada. Shots also passed over a jeep carrying the Air Naval Gunfire Liaison Company, whose task was to co-ordinate naval and air support for ground troops, notably the 3rd/325th. A chief warrant officer in the jeep spotted the house from which he thought the firing was coming and decided to call for support. Unfortunately he was not in contact with the 3rd/325th at that time and so on his own initiative he called in a Spectre gunship, only to be told that none was available. He then made contact with the flight leader of four A-7s and gave the target details, which were a white house with a red roof, on a ridge north of a drive-in cinema. He gave his contact pilot a bearing if 260 degrees from the sugar mill.

The A-7s made three passes over the target area and the chief warrant officer was satisfied that they had located the target. But when the A-7s began their bombing run it seemed to him that they were coming in on the wrong heading. The lead pilot was heard to say on his intercom that he could see people near he house. The ground officer knew this was wrong and called the pilots to abort the mission but it was already too late. As he spoke, the leading aircraft opened fire on the wrong building, which turned out to be Colonel Stephen Silvasy's 2nd Brigade Tactical Operations Centre (TOC), employed in co-ordinating the ground operation. The A-7 pilots had fired not into a white building with a red roof, north of the drive-in cinema, but into a grey building to the west of the drive-in. In the operations centre 17 men were wounded, including Sargeant Sean Luketina, who later died of gangrene, his legs having been crushed. So out of touch was the chief warrant officer on the ground that he called for the A-7s to make another run and when they refused and returned to the carrier *Independence*, he called in A-6 Intruders, which dropped bombs – fortunately duds – around the stricken operations centre. This was too much for Lieutenant-Colonel George Crocker and his men of the 1st/505th, who were in that area and who then contacted their air liaison officer to cancel any further air support.

A Cuban officer commented on the US forces he encountered, 'Their tactic is to destroy everything with their planes and artillery first and then see what's left.' As one Grenadian soldier, Keith Phillips, more succinctly put it in an interview for Channel 4 TV in 2000, 'They're just a bunch of bullies.' The Lind Report, written in the aftermath of Operation Urgent Fury, drew particular attention to what was referred to as 'the cowboy syndrome' among the airborne troops and the Rangers.

In numerous military situations in the thirty years since the Vietnam War, from the Gulf War through Yugoslavia to

Afghanistan, US military personnel emboldened by overwhelming technological superiority and complete dominance of the skies, have contributed to incidents of friendly fire through just such a gung-ho attitude. President Ronald Reagan, at the end of the Grenadian fighting in 1983, gave a thoroughly unhelpful politician's verdict on the operation, congratulating America's returning legions with the hollow words: 'Our days of weakness are over. Our military forces are back on their feet and standing tall.' But this was misleading and dishonest. All the service chiefs knew that Operation Urgent Fury had been hobbled by poor and faulty intelligence, which had been at the root of the friendly fire that occurred on Grenada and became an increasingly significant aspect of every US operation thereafter. The 'cowboy syndrome' on Grenada, combined with deficiencies in military intelligence, were just two of the contra-indications of America's love affair with its state-of-the-art military technology.

E M Forster's story, 'The Machine Stops', demonstrates the dangers inherent in too much reliance on technology so that it exceeds human capacity to control it or to operate it its absence. The tragedy that engulfed USS *Vincennes* and Iran Air Flight 655 in the Persian Gulf on 3 July 1988 was a direct result of just such an interaction between technological failure and human error.

Just twelve months before, in the same area of the Persian Gulf, an American frigate, USS *Stark*, was accidentally struck by two missiles from an Iranian jet which her radar had picked up but which Captain Brindel had regarded as posing no threat. Every US naval commander in the Gulf took one look at the fate of Brindel, who suffered forced retirement and a reduced pension, and made the firm decision that the same would not happen to them. As a result, guns and missile systems were on 24-hours' hair-trigger and a policy of 'shoot first and ask questions later' was the order of the day. Without this background it is difficult otherwise to understand how a ship carrying the most up-to-date instruments in the world as the *Vincennes*, known in the US Navy by the title 'robocruiser', could make the error that resulted in the shooting down of Flight 655.

USS *Vincennes* was operating with a taskforce of US warships in the Persian Gulf. Just after dawn on 3 July, she received news that another American ship, the frigate *Montgomery* was under attack and she immediately set off to the rescue, cutting through the water at over 30 knots. Another message from the *Montgomery* reported that she was in action with thirteen Boghammer speedboats. The *Vincennes* ordered her crew to battle stations and the cruiser's helicopter was launched to investigate. Meanwhile, however, the *Vincennes* was ordered to stay out of the immediate action by Rear Admiral Tony Less, an order which the ship chose to ignore. Admiral Less was furious and radioed the *Vincennes*, ordering her in no uncertain terms to keep out of the action.

Meanwhile, the pilot of the *Vincennes*'s helicopter sent to investigate the action around USS *Montgomery*, flew too close to the fighting and came under fire from the Iranian speed-boats. Hearing the report of this attack, the robocruiser took offence. Ignoring the fact that she was violating international law, she set off at full speed into Iranian territorial waters, pursuing the Iranians who had fired on her chopper. Admiral Less, trying to follow the action as it developed, again refused the robocruiser permission to engage the enemy boats. There was no need for billion-dollar ships to engage speedboats.

While this unnecessary engagement was brewing up, an Iranian airbus, Flight 655, was leaving the airport at Bandar Abbas for the short flight to Dubai, carrying 290 passengers across the Persian Gulf. As the airliner took off it was detected by the radar of the frigate, USS *Sides* and by the *Vincennes* which inexplicably reported that it was an F-14 fighter. The tactical officer on the *Sides* was not convinced that it was a fighter and tried to contact the pilot but, erroneously in view of the fact that this was a civilian aircraft, both he and the *Vincennes* used the Military Air Distress frequencies. Not surprisingly they got no reply from the English-speaking

Iranian pilot, who had actually been educated in the United States. Normally, when an Iranian warplane was caught on American radar and realized that missiles were locking in, it turned about and retreated. In this case, the pilot took no notice but kept climbing, apparently offering no threat whatsoever to the American ships. The captain of the *Sides* concluded that the plane was an old airliner and could be ignored.

Unfortunately, human intuition of this kind was not as welcome on the *Vincennes* as it had been on the *Sides*. Deep within the darkened information centre of the cruiser a different conclusion had been reached: Bandar Abbas doubled as both an airport and a military airbase and therefore anything coming out of there must be presumed to be hostile. And, to make matters worse, the airliner was heading directly over the *Vincennes*. Human error now proved the Achilles heel for the vessel's state-of-the-art electronics. One of the crew used the Aegis system to query the identity of the plane flying towards them, revealing that it was an airliner. He then checked a list of scheduled commercial flights but missed Iran Air Flight 655. The Iranians had been known to use an airliner to mask the presence of a fighter. Who could afford to wait to see whether this was such an occasion? Shooting first left one with a dead body and questions about responsibility and guilt to be answered afterwards. Shooting second left one only with a dead body – your own.

Warning signals were sent to the unknown plane but still there was no response. If the plane came nearer than twenty miles from the ship, she knew how to respond. However, in the combat information centre one of the crew had picked up the code of a commercial airliner. Simultaneously, the Aegis system proclaimed that the airbus was, in fact, an F-14 fighter and, rather than slowly rising, it was in fact descending toward the *Vincennes* as if planning to attack. That was what was needed for the robocruiser to protect itself. Within seconds two missiles were heading upwards carrying death to the 290 passengers on the Iranian airbus.

The technology aboard the robocruiser knew nothing about excuses or cover-ups: it was amoral. It was left to the crew to decide the rights and wrongs of this appalling tragedy. The first response, of course, was to conceal the evidence and this would be done by shifting the blame as much as possible on to the victims. The *Vincennes*, it was alleged, had been in international waters and why had Iranian Flight Control sent an airliner over the head of a warship engaged in a battle? Why, furthermore, was the airliner descending rather than ascending and why were the Iranians surprised at what happened when they often masked their fighters by flying them behind airliners? Why, in addition, did the pilot not respond to the warnings issued by the robocruiser? Good questions, all of them.

The crew of the *Stark* had been criticized for allowing the Iranian jet to fire first, even accidentally. So, even if the *Vincennes* had been wrong to shoot down an airliner, at least there would be no dead Americans being brought home wrapped in body bags. The captain of the *Stark* had been forced to leave the navy for not firing. Surely it would be wrong to dismiss a commander who did fire? Probably the best thing to do, and certainly the most popular and patriotic, was to give the crew of the robocruiser combat medals. After all, they had been in combat. Incredibly, the air warfare co-ordinator was awarded the Commendation Medal for his 'ability to quickly and precisely complete the firing procedure'.

It is probably unique for an important aspect of military technology to become the subject for cartoon coverage by American TV but that was certainly the case with the problem of American pilots misidentifying their targets. During an episode of *The Simpsons* two American fighters are shown pursuing a hot-air balloon bearing the image of the Springfield Elementary School Principal, Seymour Skinner. The radar screen in one of the cockpits identifies the target as 'Iraqi fighter' plane and the pilot launches an interceptor missile. The missile immediately changes course and shoots down the accompanying American fighter. As the pilots parachute to safety they argue over the allocation of military funding and are finally seen fighting once they are on the ground.

If this problem had remaining within the realm of TV cartoons no harm would have been done but as so often with *The Simpsons*' targets there is far more to it. In spite of the fact that the radar misidentifies its target as does the interceptor missile, the pilot never for one moment makes the obvious identification of a balloon by using his own eyesight. Relying on technology alone he perpetrates a fratricidal attack on his companion. Technology here serves to enlarge the human error by removing the normal sense of responsibility that the human will always draw on in dealing out death in warfare. There is a lesson here for the American military: if the cartoonists can get it right then why cannot the dollar-burning captains of America's military industry?

In 1991, in the aftermath of the Gulf War, the United Nations imposed a 'no-fly' zone in the north of Iraq, along the 36th Parallel, to prevent Iraq using her air force against the Kurdish population which had fled northwards to escape persecution by Saddam Hussein's regime. The Americans had made it clear that any Iraqi planes that crossed into the zone would be shot down by US fighters operating from their base at Incirlik in Turkey. As a result, for more than two years a precarious peace prevailed in the area. The only planes that were seen in the air-exclusion zone were Allied, almost exclusively American, and few incidents were recorded of Iraqi planes attempting to test America's resolve.

In view of the numerous blue-on-blue incidents that had occurred during the Gulf War, the Americans had developed a five-step failsafe system to prevent accidental engagements between friendly aircraft flying in the zone. However, on 14 April 1994, near Aqrah, there occurred one of the most inexplicable examples of aerial amicide ever recorded. On that morning, two American Black Hawk helicopters, carrying more than twenty UN officials and observers from America,

Britain, Turkey and France, as well as five Kurdish translators, left the Iraqi border town of Zakho to fly to Salahuddin, the headquarters of the Kurdistan Democratic Party. It was a routine flight, one that had been made many times in previous months, and there was nothing about it that should have attracted the attention of the two F-15 fighters which, identifiying the American helicopters as Iraqi, shot them out of the sky without warning, killing all twenty-six people aboard, including Lieutenant-Colonel Jonathon Swann of the Royal Artillery and Captain Harry Shapland of the Irish Guards. In spite of the five-step failsafe system the Americans were operating to prevent such blue-on-blues, human error once again proved impossible to anticipate and overcome.

Explanations for the disaster proved elusive. One Kurdish leader commented, 'I can't imagine how the Americans can have made the mistake that they [the Black Hawks] were Iraqi helicopters. It means that they still don't know the Iraqis or the territory. You would never see Iraqi helicopters in this area. This is too far for the Iraqi planes to come. The American planes would shoot them down long before they got there.'

Once again the accusation of 'trigger-happiness' so frequently levelled at American pilots was hard to avoid. Yet in this case the Pentagon was baffled. Many previous blue-on-blues could at least be explained by poor weather conditions or by the stress of battle, but this one had no such excuse. In the first place, the fighter pilots had the assistance of an AWACS aircraft which should have been able to provide them with precise information about anything flying in their sector of patrol. Secondly, F-15s had very little to fear from helicopters and could take their time to identify their opponents before there was any need to open fire. Given such information as the AWACS could provide and all the time they needed to make an identification, it is almost impossible to believe that the fighters can have made a mistake. Yet they did, and at a cost of twenty-six lives. What was particularly baffling was that the AWACS plane carried state-of-the-art computers and the F-15s were equipped with an IFF device, which enabled them to 'identify friend or foe'. These devices were in full working order on the day of the incident, yet they failed to prevent the blue-on-blue. Even in the event of computer malfunction there was nothing to prevent either the fighter pilots or the AWACS plane contacting the Black Hawks to request radio identification. And in the final extremity the pilots had high-powered binoculars with which they could confirm identification. In fact, we know that the two F-15s passed the helicopters twice in bright sunny conditions, and the pilots could not, therefore, reasonably claim that identification was difficult. Yet the Chairman of the American Joint Chiefs of Staff, General Shalikashvili, later claimed that visual identification was made after the IFF check had received no friendly response. Apparently the two Black Hawks were flying at low altitude and were wrongly identified as Soviet-built Hind helicopters of the Iraqi Air Force. This says little for the professionalism of American training as the Black Hawk and the Hind are extremely dissimilar. Reports also indicate that the F-15s were observing from 20,000 feet, but this is hardly a justification for such an error; after all, with their enormous speed advantage over the choppers, there was no reason for them to fire first before making a thorough investigation. In the end we are left with the problem we started with: human error. In the case of so many American examples, notably aerial ones, a dangerous degree of 'trigger-happiness' seems to be an ever-present feature, along with an unwillingness to take the risk or the trouble of investigating the identity of a target before firing.

In the *Star Wars* movies, according to Earl Tilford Jr, it is the evil empire that obliterates its enemies from the safety of the Death Star. However, as Tilford demonstrates in an article for the *US Army College Quarterly*, in the post-Cold-War world there is only one candidate for the role of evil empire – the United States. There is no doubt whose side the cinema audiences are on when Luke Skywalker – an American super-hero in the tradition of the men of 1776 or rebel freedom fighter/terrorist of some extra-terrestrial *jihad*? – destroys the evil of technology, inhuman and distant, with low technology and spiritual force. If, therefore, the USA adopts the impersonal approach to war, killing at a distance through overwhelming technological superiority while being unprepared to risk any of her own soldiers even in support of her interests and ideals, then there is a danger that she will be held in contempt by adversaries and – if the truth be known – by friends alike.

Tilford Jr maintains that the notion that airpower can make war bloodless for the United States and NATO is fraught with danger for the future because if potential enemies believe that the fear of suffering casualties constitutes a vulnerable centre of gravity for the so-called free world, they will exploit that vulnerability. This was clearly at the root of Iraqi policy during the negotiations between Saddam Hussein and April Glaspie just prior to the invasion of Kuwait. This may also be true of the terrorist strikes on New York and Washington on 11 September 2001. America's enemies will devise strategies that inflict maximum casualties on her and her allies. According to Tilford, no credible foreign policy can be used to build a lasting international security system as long as the United States seeks to impose its will on other nations but is unwilling to shed the blood of her own people. If US objectives in Kosovo were not worth the life of a single American soldier or aviator, why were they worth the lives of so many Albanian Kosovars, indeed so many Serbs?

General Sir Michael Rose makes very much the same point when he argues that the political imperative that grew out of the Bosnian war and of American losses in Somalia, notably in Mogadishu, was casualty limitation at all costs. Moreover, the air warriors and the immense industrial muscle that supports them, is always trying to get a bigger slice of the budget by saying that they can win any war without recourse to ground troops. But by concentrating on airpower alone NATO, which was constrained by rules to fly at a particular altitude and use certain sorts of weapons systems, actually killed three times more innocent civilians, both Kosovo Albanians and Serbs, than they did members of the Serb military. Rose is not alone in believing that this calls into question the entire NATO strategy which came close to violating the Geneva and the Hague Protocols.

Deception by the Serbs led to many errors by NATO aircrew. On one occasion a line of heavy mortars pointing at Sarajevo turned out to be Bosnian haystacks, which were piled in circles around a pole in the middle. Travelling at 450 mph haystacks can apparently look like mortars. On another occasion NATO aircrew nearly engaged a French tank which they identified as a Soviet T55 and only human observers on the ground saved it from being destroyed. Essentially, troops were not deployed on the ground in Kosovo because of the old fear of having casualties: the Gulf War, and to a certain extent Bosnia, have persuaded people that you can engineer change in these situations without the risk of casualties.

Rose's summing up of his experiences in Bosnia and Kosovo is that you have to put troops on the ground and have to be prepared to risk casualties if you are going to retain any sort of credibility as a war-fighting or even peace-keeping organization. If NATO makes it clear that it is not going to be prepared to accept casualties, it will have credibility neither in peace nor war. It is interesting that the United Nations peace-keepers in Kosovo suffered 300 killed during its mission, without complaints from any of the governments involved, yet NATO can accept none in a war.

The bombing of the Chinese embassy in Belgrade stands as a symbol of the blunders that have accompanied US high-technology war since Vietnam. The official explanation for this disaster was that the wrong information had been provided by the CIA, which had identified the embassy as a Yugoslav weapons warehouse so that the mistake was made at an early stage of initial target selection. NATO insisted that their maps were not inaccurate or outdated and that they had known in advance where foreign embassies were situated in the Serbian capital. Yet so complex was the web of explanations that emanated from NATO headquarters that it was difficult to get near the truth. In the first place, the Chinese embassy had been situated in the same building for the previous four years so if there had been an intelligence failure it had been a very large one. The location of the embassy was even marked on English-language tourist maps so at least those wishing to get a visa to visit China were in no danger of making their application to the Yugoslav Directorate of Military of Supply and Procurement. And if visiting tourists knew this much one is stretching imagination too far to believe that the CIA did not. The embassy was listed in the local telephone directory and journalists of many countries knew its whereabouts and had daily contacts with it. Moreover, the USA had at its disposal a high-technology surveillance system budgeted at $29 billion.

Or am I missing the point? If one cannot accept the bombing of the Chinese embassy as a mistake, then one is left to wonder why NATO thought it could persuade the world to accept it as a mistake. The handling of the bombing by NATO after the event was perhaps even more inept than the 'mistake' – had it been a mistake – was in the first place. Military experts from throughout NATO hastened to assure a worried world that targets for bombing raids were not selected so casually that the sort of mistake apparently made by the Americans was possible. The US people were assured that at least two sources of information were always used to confirm a target. However, nobody replied with the obvious question. If the Chinese embassy could not have been bombed by mistake, was it fair to assume that it had been bombed on purpose? While President Clinton was referring to the bombing as a 'tragic mistake', more and more experts provided evidence that such a mistake was impossible. Was Clinton lying or did he genuinely not know how the bombing had taken place? If so then one is left questioning the motivation of senior military commanders in NATO and in the Pentagon.

Mike Head has raised an intriguing question on this apparent bombing blunder on the Internet in 2000: 'If the embassy building was indeed mistaken for the Directorate of Supply and Procurement, why was it only selected as a target in the seventh week of NATO's air assault? If it were an identifiable military target why had it not already been hit during one of the 18,000 bombing missions against Yugoslavia?'

The bombing of the Chinese Embassy occurred at a time when relations between the United States and China were declining as a result of the Kosovo crisis. China, as it happens, was representing Yugoslav diplomatic interests in Washington and the news had just broken that a Chinese spy had obtained American nuclear secrets. More significant, however, was the division within the American government over President Clinton's attempts to get a settlement of the Yugoslav situation through Russian intervention. There were many Americans who feared that Clinton might accept a 'dangerously flawed deal' with the Yugoslavs in an attempts to escape from an unpopular and difficult war. If the Russians could be alienated by some incident involving the United States – a mistaken bombing of the Chinese embassy for example – then their peace plan with Serbia would break down and NATO would be forced to fight to win a complete victory in Kosovo. The message to China would then be quite clear: however soft a touch Clinton might appear to be, there were forces within the United States that would stop at nothing to maintain US economic and military policy.

I have explained elsewhere that an aerial campaign by itself speaks to the enemy not of strength but of weakness. It indicates a fear of casualties and an unwillingness to involve land troops with all the risks that that involves. The impersonality of aerial technology removes the old adage 'don't fire until you see the whites of their eyes' which, in a sense, encapsulates the primitive element in fighting, the imposition of individual willpower over an enemy. An aircrew cannot be persuaded of its defeat if it never sets eyes on the enemy, ten or fifteen thousand feet above his homeland.

Part III

Maintaining Discipline

13

Intentional Friendly Fire

Fear is the natural state of the soldier. We know from ancient writers that Greek warriors often urinated involuntarily as the enemy battle line bore down on them. Their natural inclination was to run away, to avoid the danger that was before them, but most, through an exercise of willpower, stayed in line and fought. It was not that these men who did not run had not wanted to, but that they had been able to control the instinct for self-preservation. Some factor, perhaps a greater fear of failure or disgrace, or of letting their comrades down, had kept them in the place of danger. They had shown courage but, as we know from modern research, courage is no absolute. On another day, in another place, a 'brave' man can run away. In his book *The Anatomy of Courage*, Lord Moran has written that 'Courage is willpower, whereof no man has an unlimited stock; and when in war it is used up, he is finished. A man's courage is his capital and he is always spending. The call on the bank may be only the daily drain of the front line or it may be a sudden draft which threatens to close the account.' In 1914, it was the task of military discipline to support a soldier's own self-discipline, so that when the latter began to waver, he found support in the chilling imperative of the gun pointed at his back or at his head. From that point onwards, war consisted for each individual soldier of balancing a chance against a certainty: the chance of death or mutilation at the hands of the enemy against the certainty of death and disgrace at the hands of his own colleagues; a grisly form of friendly fire that has rarely earned more than a footnote in military memoirs.

In his important book *Morale*, John Baynes has shown that military discipline has always had two purposes. In the first place, as we have seen, it prevents a soldier giving way in circumstances of great danger to a natural instinct for self-preservation. It shows him where his duty lies, even if it should cost him his life in doing that duty. In the second case, it maintains order within the army itself, so that neither in its parts nor as a whole does it abuse its power. It is the first aim that most concerns the writer on friendly fire, for it is in situations where the instinct for self-preservation has prevailed over the soldier's duty that it is necessary for military discipline to reveal itself in all its stark simplicity. As one writer has put it, 'The avenue to the rear' must be absolutely closed in the soldier's mind, and 'military discipline serves to buttress the individual in his struggle with his own fears.'

A private from the time of the American Civil War spoke for every soldier who has ever gone into battle when he wrote, 'The truth is, when bullets are whacking against tree trunks and solid shot are cracking skulls like egg shells, the consuming passion in the heart of the average man is to get out of the way. Between the physical fear of going forward, and the moral fear of turning back, there is a predicament of exceptional awkwardness, from which a hidden hole in the ground would be a wonderfully welcome outlet.' Every soldier needs to overcome such fear in battle if he is to be of any military value at all. Successful armies throughout history have been those that have overcome this fundamental problem. The Romans, for example, exercised a severe military discipline, as Gibbon described:

. . . it was impossible for cowardice or disobedience to escape the severest punishment. The centurions were authorized to chastise with blows, the generals had a right to punish with death; and it was an inflexible maxim of

Roman discipline, that a good soldier should dread his officers far more than the enemy . . . In his camp the general exercised an absolute power of life and death; his jurisdiction was not confined by any forms of trial or rules of proceeding, and the execution of the sentence was immediate and without appeal.[49]

In the army of the Prussian king, Frederick the Great, the Roman ideal was imitated, perhaps even exceeded. Frederick himself agreed with Gibbon in saying that the common soldier must fear his officers more than the enemy. Prussian officers would strike their men for even the most trivial lapses, inflict torturous field punishments like riding the wooden horse, brand or flog them, or make them run the gauntlet. For more serious offences, there were capital punishments, such as shooting, hanging or breaking on the wheel. Barbaric as this may sound, it was not a regime confined only to the Prussian army. The British redcoats of the eighteenth century were known throughout Europe as the 'bloodybacks' as a result of the British predilection for flogging. As sophisticated an officer as James Wolfe ordered that 'a soldier who quits his rank, or offers to flag, is instantly to be put to death by the officer who commands that platoon, or by the officer or sergeant in rear of that platoon, a soldier does not deserve to live who won't fight for his king and country.' A century and half later, in 1914, these identical words could have been spoken by many British officers on the Western Front, charged with transforming a massive civilian army into an efficient military machine. As one of them wrote, 'I, who am a soldier, know that it is difficult to leave the shelter of a shell-hole for a final rush in the face of a deadly shower of bullets and the certain knowledge that cold steel awaits. It is less difficult, however, if there is the knowledge that a loaded revolver for use against the enemy is also loaded for use against you if you fail to jump forward when the barrage lifts.' John Baynes cites an example of a British soldier panicking in 1915, shouting to the men around him, 'Get out! Get out! We're all going to be killed' just as the

Germans were launching a counter-attack. A sergeant promptly split his skull with a shovel he was holding and the panic ended instantly.

In the 1930s a senior British officer, Brigadier-General Frank Percy Crozier, caused an outcry in Britain by telling what he claimed to be the 'unvarnished truth' of the First World War. In two books, the second provocatively entitled *The Men I Killed*, Crozier spoke of the way in which the British troops had been kept at their posts not, as the popular press had always told the British people, to defend King and country or to punish the Huns for their atrocities in Belgium, but because they feared that if they did not go forward to face the German guns they would be killed by their own officers. Crozier elaborated on this theme by writing openly of the officers and men he had personally shot. It was at his command, Crozier claimed, that fleeing Portuguese troops were machine-gunned by their British allies in 1918. In these books it was Crozier's intention to shock and to force a complacent public to face the true cost of war and of victory. Nevertheless, by opening up the subject for general discussion, Crozier was also raising the whole question of discipline in wartime. Was it acceptable, in the pursuit of victory or the avoidance of defeat, for men to shoot their colleagues in the heat of battle or for the authorities to execute soldiers for cowardice and desertion? This aspect of friendly fire is every bit as worthy of investigation as incidents of an accidental nature.

Brigadier-General Crozier's claim that British officers were sometimes shot for cowardice in the thick of battle was a startling revelation at a time when courage was not just an attribute of military rank but a *sine qua non* for a whole social class in Britain that had ruled unchallenged for centuries. When Crozier wrote his books the truth about executions of British soldiers had not reached the general public, so that the idea of discipline imposed at the point of a gun was particularly shocking. It may have been believed of the German or Russian armies, but not of the British. Yet Crozier made no apologies for what he had done:

Strictly from the military point of view I have no regrets for having killed a subaltern of British infantry on that same morning I ordered our machine-guns and rifles to be turned on the fleeing Portuguese. It happened on the Stratzeel Road. It was a desperate emergency. I had to shoot him myself, along with a German who was running after him. My action did stem the tide; and that is what we were there for.

Vividly I still remember that scene. It might almost have been only yesterday. Never can I forget the agonized expression on that British youngster's face as he ran in terror, escaping from the ferocious Hun whose passions were a madness and who saw only red.

. . . Oh, I know you will ask why I killed that British subaltern. The answer is more obvious than easy. My duty was to hold the line at all costs. To England the cost was very little. To Colonel Blimp in his club and Mrs Blimp in her boudoir the cost was nothing. To me? Even if the effort did mean murder, the line had to be held.

There were other British soldiers there, the last of a remnant. Panic spreads so easily when the madness of a moment assails you. And a running man is a dangerous madness. Only, you don't stop to think once you've begun running.[50]

Another incident described by General Crozier indicates just how often these battlefield killings took place:

I remember an officer of birth and breeding of the special reserve – a captain, with experience at Gallipoli, it was said – who joined with a reinforcing draft after the Somme battle. By his talk and bearing I imagined him an efficient officer, but being always suspicious of the talking soldier I took the precaution of placing him under test as second-in-command of a company, under a most capable temporary captain of the new armies.

He objected. It was as well. For he turned out to be useless and afraid.

'What did you do exactly at Gallipoli?' I asked him one day, after finding him crawling on his stomach, in daylight well behind the lines, on his way up to his company, in an effort to avoid imaginary danger caused by the cracking of overhead, indirect rifle-fire. The firing had got on his nerves.

'I was on the staff,' he replied. And it then transpired that he had got no further than one of the islands and was, in effect, a 'bottlewasher'. I mentioned this fact to his captain, who told me that he had made up his mind to get the fellow bumped off in a scrap in No-Man's-Land . . . It was Montgomery speaking . . . who, it was whispered, had found it necessary to slay many of his side in order to restore reason and confidence [to] a reinforcing regiment from Yorkshire.[51]

Official statistics, only recently made available, show to what extent the British military authorities used the death penalty – or the threat of it – to maintain discipline in their largely civilian armies from 1914 onwards. Between 4 August 1914 and 31 march 1920, a total of 3,080 men were sentenced to death under the regulations of the Army Act of whom 312 were executed. Excepting those men punished for serious crimes like murder, rape or violence against civilians, the vast majority of those who were shot suffered for purely military 'crimes', such as desertion or cowardice. They were punished *pour encourager les autres*, or rather to instil sufficient fear into their fellow soldiers that they would endure the almost endurable in the knowledge that failure to do so would earn them certain death and ignominy at the hands of their fellows.

At the end of the First World War, the German commander, Field Marshal von Ludendorff, spoke with some envy of the severity of British and French military discipline compared with that in the German Army. 'The Entente no doubt achieved more than we did with their considerably more severe punishments. This historic fact is well established.' Certainly the British and French had many more executions than the Germans – the French during their 1917 mutinies shot an undisclosed number of mutineers to restore order – and the evidence from diaries and memoirs builds up a picture of numerous 'unofficial' executions during the heat of battle. One French general ordered his artillery to bombard his own trenches when his men refused to leave them, and there are many examples of British officers using death or the threat of death to move their men forward. Lieutenant-Colonel Lambert Ward recorded one occasion where a brigade of the 3rd Division had 'cracked to a man. You could not send them back to base, yet they were in such a state that they would willingly have taken ten years' penal servitude to stay out of the line. In these circumstances it was only fear of death that kept them at their posts.' Another British colonel was quite open about the fact that he ordered his machine-gunners to fire at some British troops who were in the process of surrendering in April 1918. As he said, 'Such an action as this will in a short time spread like dry rot through an army and is one of those dire duties which calls for immediate and prompt action.'

A large majority of the British soldiers executed during the First World War died to maintain discipline. Their 'crimes' were insignificant in the context of a civilian criminal code – desertion, cowardice, disobedience, striking a superior officer, sleeping at your post – yet in the context of maintaining morale in an army, the victims had not only to die but be seen to die, by their comrades. Their punishment was in no way retributive, only exemplary. British military authorities attempted to extend their draconian measures to the all-volunteer Australian force in France after 1916, but the Australian government refused to allow it. Most British officers regarded the Australians as undisciplined, untidy and disorderly soldiers. On the other hand, they were the best shock troops in the British Army, highly-rated by their German opponents. Their high morale and low desertion rates were not maintained by fear of the gun or the firing squad but by a healthy *esprit de corps*. It is significant that no British commander of the period seemed to grasp this fact and seek to re-create it in his own troops.

Early executions of British soldiers in 1914 were all of regulars, who had already seen service in the army before the war. The second man shot, Private George Ward of the 1st Battalion of the Royal Berkshire Regiment, was executed on the recommendation of his corps commander, Sir Douglas Haig, to act as an example to others. Ward's execution was, in fact, botched. As he was being taken out to be shot he broke away from the guard and tried to escape, being then shot in the back as he ran. He was fetched back on a stretcher and shot in the head by the sergeant of the guard to 'finish him off'.

One of the earliest volunteers to be shot was Private John Byers of the 1st Royal Scots Fusiliers, who had falsified his age to get into the army and was just sixteen when he died. Byers was posted to France only two weeks after enlisting, went absent without leave and was sentenced to be shot on 6 February 1915. Significantly, Byers's comrades who made up the firing squad were reluctant to shoot him and it is rumoured that he was only killed after a third volley. The effect on the men of the firing party was severe. An officer who had been an eyewitness at the execution later told a Labour MP, Ernest Thurtle, that 'When they came back, tough characters through they were supposed to be, they were sick, they screamed in their sleep, they vomited immediately after eating. All they could say was: "The sight was horrible, made more so by the fact that we had shot one of our own men." '

The most controversial part of the disciplinary process concerned those men who were suffering from extended exposure to artillery fire, known today as 'shell shock'. As the condition was at that time unknown to medical science, those sufferers who were examined before court martial were regarded as shirkers rather than men suffering from nervous exhaustion. Rifleman Bellamy, of the King's Royal Rifle Corps, had been serving in the trenches near La Bassée when the Germans exploded a mine under part of his battalion's trenches. The shock was tremendous and immediately afterwards

Bellamy refused to come out of his dugout and take up his position in the firing line. Bellamy told his sergeant that he felt too shaky to stand on the firestep. After a court martial on a charge of cowardice, Bellamy was referred to a medical board but they were unable to find any physical cause for his condition. As a result, on 16 July 1915 Rifleman Bellamy was executed at the village of Le Quesnoy, the first but certainly not the last man to fall victim to the psychological effects of shell fire.

The first man to die for striking an officer was Private Fox of the 2nd Battalion of the Highland Light Infantry. The incident occurred while his unit was in a rest area behind the lines and revolved around a kit inspection. Fox had only recently received tragic news from his home in Scotland and had been drinking on the night before the offence. On the morning of 10 April 1916, his company commander upbraided him for the dirty condition of his boots, prompting Fox to start swearing and then step forward and kick the officer in the knee. He was arrested on a charge of 'When on active service striking his superior officer, being in the execution of his duty.' In spite of all the extenuating circumstances, Fox was sentenced to death and shot on 12 May. It was a savage punishment that reflected the pressures the army authorities felt in maintaining discipline in a British army growing to an unprecedented size. It is significant that recommendations for mercy by the courts were being ignored by the Commander-in-Chief, Sir Douglas Haig, with great regularity at this stage of the war.

In his diary, Captain L Gameson, a medical officer with the British Fifth Army near Lille in 1918, describes two 'accidents' that occurred to him during his supervision of two separate executions. At the first, of two Cape Coloured from the 1st Battalion of the Cape Coloured Labour Corps, Gameson had the following close escape:

> The firing party of twelve I think, then took up their positions facing the stakes. They were given final instructions, and words of encouragement which manifestly they

needed. The loaded rifles were grounded. The party filed out of sight. A sergeant loaded some of the rifles with blanks – he said – no man would know whether he was partly reponsible for the killing . . . As he picked up one rifle it went off. The bullet zipped by my head; it passed, so I estimate, precisely just over my left shoulder where that structure joins the neck. A stray piece of wire, with one end fixed in the ground, had in some way discharged the rifle. 'My God, sir!' the scared sergeant shouted, 'it nearly got you.'[52]

Gameson was even luckier to survive another potentially fatal accident that occurred at the execution of Private F Alberts on 13 May 1918:

Again I came unpleasantly near to being shot myself; this time with a revolver.

The squad's aiming had been bad. I dashed in immediately after the volley and at once told the sergeant on the opposite side of the moribund victim that the man still lived. With a revolver, he shot the man through the skull at its thinnest part. I repeat that I stood on the opposite flank of the victim. The sergeant fired before I had any chance to remove myself. The bullet went clean through and buzzed by my head as I bent over the semi-unconscious man tied to his stake. I told the sergeant it was much to his credit that he was so rattled by our sordid work as to be irresponsibly careless; perhaps the firing squad had been rattled.[53]

Since the end of the American Civil War, only one American soldier has been shot for desertion. First World War executions in the United States Army had been for murder, often linked to mutiny, or for offences like rape. Private Eddie Slovik, shot by a firing squad from the 109th Infantry Regiment of the 28th Division, died on the morning of 31 January 1945 in the village of St Marie aux Mines, in Alsace. He was shot because he ran away, as thousands of American soldiers had run away on battlefields in Europe and the Pacific. But he was selected to be an example to others of what would happen to men who gave way to their fears. It was his misfortune to desert at a time when American fortunes were low in Europe, when the battles in the Hürtgen Forest and the Ardennes were stretching the will power of commanders and there was a need to stiffen morale.

On 24 October 1944, the 28th Division had moved in to replace the 9th Division in the Hürtgen Forest. The 28th was commanded by the tough Major-General Norman Cota, who was determined to succeed in taking the village of Schmidt in the middle of the forest, which the 9th had been unable to do. But Cota's tough talking was going to cost the lives of thousands of his men and the only one whose name would be remembered was the one who funked it – Eddie Slovik. Slovik was going to become famous as the only man shot for desertion by the US Army in the Second World War.

The 28th Division had made a bad start in Hürtgen. The 'American Luftwaffe' did what it could to help them by carrying out a bombing of the forest but all they managed to do was to hit Cota's men, killing and wounding 24 of them. Yet when 'Dutch' Cota said he meant business he was not joking and in just two days the 28th Division took the village of Schmidt. But unknown to Cota, the Germans were planning a counter-attack with Mark IV tanks, immune to their own mines. These tanks powered their way through the forest and ripped into the Americans. Soon everyone was running: it seemed as if the whole division was racing madly through the trees. 'It was the saddest sight I have ever seen,' said one officer, 'down the road from the east came men from F, G and E Companies: pushing, shoving, throwing away equipment, trying to outrace the artillery and each other, all in a frantic effort to escape. They were all scared and excited. Some were terror stricken.' Officers were seen running with the men – even a battalion commander reported himself sick with combat fatigue. It was a catastrophe for the 28th Division and for General Cota. And someone had to take the blame. The men had run: one of them must suffer to encourage the others – Eddie Slovik. Eddie Slovik was chosen to take the blame.

On the other side of the hill, the Germans were using their own draconian methods to maintain discipline. During the entire war they shot 10,000 Eddie Sloviks. Commuting the death penalty for deserters did not provide them with a comfortable stay in prison, out of the fighting. Instead, they were formed into special punishment units and sent on 'Ascension Day missions' or suicide runs, from which few ever returned.

During its time in the Hürtgen, the 28th Division suffered 45 per cent casualties. But even that was not enough for the American High Command. As had happened so often during the First World War, soldiers were being sent to fight in impossible terrain because their commanders were too far behind the front and knew nothing of the conditions. At Supreme Headquarters in Paris it is said Eisenhower was out of touch with events at the front. He appeared complacent, while American lives were uselessly thrown away. Even Eddie Slovik's pitiful appeal to Eisenhower asking for clemency fell on deaf ears. Perhaps he never even read these words:

Dear General Eisenhowser [sic],

How can I tell you how humble [sic] sorry I am for the sins I've committed. I didn't realize at the time what I was doing or what the word desertion meant. What it is like to be condemned to die. I beg of you deeply and sincerely for the sake of my dear wife and mother back home to have mercy on me. To my knowledge I have a good record since my marriage and as a soldier I'd like to continue to be a good solider.

Anxiously awaiting your reply, which I earnestly pray is favourable. God bless you and in [sic] your Work for Victory.[54]

Instead, Eisenhower steeled himself to do something that had not been found necessary even in the First World War. His confidence had been shaken by the German resistance in the

Ardennes. Too many US soldiers thought the war was already over. They needed proof that there was no way home but through victory. So Eisenhower confirmed the death sentence on Slovik. Thousands of Americans had deserted their posts and run away – were running away at that moment – from the enemy, and so Eddie Slovik must stand for all of them.

On 31 January 1945, Private Eddie Slovik was shot. Most of his colleagues present thought he deserved to die. They had no compassion for the men who ran away. As one of the firing squad later commented:

> I think General Eisenhower's plan worked. It helped to stiffen a few backbones. When the report of the execution was read to my company formation, that effect was good. It made a lot of guys think about what it means to be an American. I'm just sorry the general didn't follow through and shoot the rest of the deserters instead of turning them loose on their community. I want my children to be raised to believe that their country is worth dying for . . . and that if they won't fight for it, they don't deserve to live.[55]

Mutiny in the British or American armies has been a very rare event in modern times. Yet mutiny can take many forms and one that has become more widespread in the twentieth century is known as 'fragging', that is the murder of officers or NCOs who show an over-eagerness for seeking contact with the enemy or for undertaking other dangerous missions, or even for being dangerously useless. During the First World War, young British officers – often no more than eighteen-year-old lieutenants, fresh from public school – had to order their men to go 'over the top' in the face of a withering enemy fire. It was relatively simple for the officer to be shot in the heat of battle so that his men could remain in their trenches for lack of anyone to lead them. Statistics for this form of assassination are unavailable for the First World War, yet it remains an open question as to what proportion of the extremely heavy casualties among junior officers were caused by their own men.

In the Vietnam War it has been estimated that as many as 20 per cent of officer fatalities were the result of fragging, either through shooting or more often by an apparently misdirected fragmentation grenade.

The murder of unpopular officers, often in action, has been widely documented even as far back as Roman times. Richard Holmes reminds us of the Pannonian mutiny of AD 14, during the reign of the emperor Tiberius. One officer who was killed by his own men was the centurion Lucilius, who was nicknamed 'another-please' from his unpleasant habit of breaking his vine-staff on the backs of his men. Christopher Duffy tells us that during the eighteenth century, wounded Spanish officers were often robbed and murdered by their own men and that even in the well disciplined English army of the time, an early form of fragging did take place. A famous example from the period involved a major of the British 15th Regiment of Foot at the battle of Blenheim in 1704. The man was an infamous martinet who had treated his men harshly in the past and was thoroughly hated. Aware of this he addressed his men before the battle, saying that if he should fall in the coming fight at least let it be by an enemy bullet. A soldier replied that they had more to think about than him at that moment and so the regiment went into battle. After victory had been won he turned to his men, raised his hat and called for a cheer, only to fall with a bullet through his head.

During the Napoleonic Wars, French soldiers were not slow to express their opinions of their officers, and to follow them up if necessary with more direct action. Richard Holmes gives an example of one unpopular Napoleonic general being fired on by his own men, while a general sent to enlist men for the National Guard was actually killed. In 1807, after the abortive British assault on Buenos Aires, rifleman Harris recounts how many of General Craufurd's men were calling the Commander-in-Chief, General Whitelocke, a traitor and looking for an opportunity to shoot him. At the battle of Quatre Bras, just two days before the battle of Waterloo, the commander of the 92nd Foot, Colonel Cameron of Fassfern, was shot dead by a man he had recently had flogged. In the American Civil War, the democratic and undisciplined nature of many of the troops meant that they were less willing than European soldiers of the time to follow an incompetent officer. When Colonel Adelbert Ames – a West Pointer of high ability – took over the 24th Maine Regiment, his regime of hard drilling so annoyed his troops that even as sound a man as Sergeant Tom Chamberlain wrote to his sister, 'I swear they will shoot him the first battle we are in.' In fact, Chamberlain was wrong and the men of the 24th grew to admire their colonel when they understood what he was trying to achieve. But many Union officers, in particular, did not live long enough to win the affection of their men.

During the First World War, one notably unpopular sergeant was dispatched by a grenade down his trousers, as General Crozier relates:

A British NCO had been bullying some of his subordinates. As there appeared to be no way of dealing with the case there, aggrieved men decided to deal with the matter in their own way. As the essence of crime, from the criminal's point of view, is to leave no trace, they decided to get rid of their tormentor in the manner which they thought most suited to that purpose.

A Mills bomb has a local but very violent explosive effect. They decided that the Mills bomb should therefore be their agent. Pulling out the pin from the bomb which held the lever in check and which, in its turn, ignited the charge which exploded after the lapse of some seconds, one of them – they had previously drawn lots for the job – pushed the bomb down the back of the NCO's trousers after which they made off at lightning speed to avoid the explosion.

Fortunately the poor man was isolated and entirely alone or others would have been killed – but he, ignorant till too late of what had happened, was, figuratively speaking, hoist by his own petard, for he, of course, became a battle casualty.

There was no trace whatsoever left of this NCO while, of course, there was no evidence available.[56]

In his autobiographical work, *Goodbye To All That*, the poet and writer Robert Graves gives an account of one of the few documented cases of 'fragging' in the British Army, which he later retold in his poem 'Sergeant-Major Money'. On 20 January 1915, the 2nd Battalion of the Welsh Regiment, to which Graves was attached, was in the trenches near Béthune. The weather was appalling and to liven their spirits that evening, two soldiers – Lance-Corporal William Price and Private Richard Morgan – got drunk and shot the company sergeant-major, a man named Hughie Hayes. In fact, Hayes died by mistake as Morgan and Price had been intending to kill their platoon sergeant, an unpopular man who had been making their lives a misery.

As Richard Holmes has explained in his book *Firing Line*, fragging is merely a symptom of a general breakdown of discipline and the 'phenomenon of collective combat refusal' which, until quite recently, was met with the most draconian of reactions by the military authorities, ranging from the Roman 'decimation' of mutinous units to the British use of machine guns on their own troops and those of their allies in 1918. Although fragging is clearly a reaction by the rank and file of an army that has deep roots in military history, it only came to public attention during the Vietnam War. Apparently fragging reached a peak in 1971 with as many as 333 confirmed incidents and a further 158 possible examples. Even these figures give only a partial idea of the extent of the problem. Historian Richard Gabriel estimates that a more accurate figure would be 1,016 fraggings and suggests that as many as 20 per cent of officers killed in the Vietnam War were in fact victims of their own men, evidence if any were needed of the most serious large-scale disintegration of discipline in American military history. Yet according to Charles Anderson:

Every soldier, marine, sailor or airman who fragged a unit

leader believed at the time of the incident that he acted with more than ample justification. Such a view may sound incredible now but anyone who has seen combat and perceived what it does to one's thinking can appreciate the extreme difficulty, perhaps even the folly, of making value judgments on the thoughts and actions of men in a combat environment.[57]

In a sense the problem was compounded by the widespread presence of television cameramen and newspaper reporters in the rear areas, who were willing to take up the grouses that were typical in any army. Soldiers felt that they were not the helpless victims of a military system. Instead, ordinary GIs had access to the whole machinery of civilian life, no more than a phone call away. For the first time in military history civilian soldiers were able to have direct contact with the public at home, telephoning their folks and in direct contact with their loved ones. This had important consequences for the maintenance of discipline in the American forces. Once a soldier felt that he had a way out through the yearly rotation of troops, he could see light at the end of the tunnel in the way that troops in the First World War, serving for the duration, with only rare chances of home leave, never could. This had few beneficial effects on military efficiency. Instead, many soldiers in Vietnam failed to identify positively with their units or their officers, and subsequently lacked the *esprit de corps* that was common in early American wars. It was more a question of counting the days, rather than trying to do your best for your company or your friends. This weakened the traditional bonds between soldiers and their small-unit commanders. It meant that they were unwilling to take any risks and resented it when an officer was too ready to commit them to dangerous operations.

In turn, this made things very difficult for young, inexperienced officers, who felt themselves dragged in two directions at once. Concern for the welfare of their own men was a fundamental responsibility of any officer, but how did one square this with the officer's responsibility to achieve whatever military task that he might be given, even if this was likely to prove costly to his men. This problem was felt most acutely by young officers, whose experience in man management was necessarily limited and whose desire to please their superiors was often paramount. This could result in the alienation of the soldiers in an officer's unit, increasing tension on both sides and making fragging a possible outlet for the men's frustration. Certainly for most American soldiers in Vietnam, an officer's willingness and ability to avoid casualties was a far better guide to his credentials as a leader than any outdated concepts of duty and heroism.

C W Bowman of the 25th Infantry Division described the arrival of a new CO, who was bad news from the start:

> Toward the end of my tour, our morale did drop because we got a new CO. Officers only spent six months in the field before they were moved back to the rear. We got a new captain in, and he was Gung Ho John Wayne. But it wasn't the place to play John Wayne because Charlie was real good at suckering people into ambushes . . . Charlie tried his trick one day and we tried to tell the CO what was going on. But he didn't want to hear it, so we were suckered into a minefield. Gary stepped on a Bouncing Betty. It blew his leg off.[58]

Dan Vandenberg expressed his contempt for the fussy officers, who made their men's lives hell over little things. It was officers of this kind as well as the gung ho variety who brought out the worst in the American soldier. Men like this officer sometimes ended up with a bullet in the back or a fragmentation grenade for company:

> Some of the very few officers I came into contact with were totally incompetent. They were more concerned with how you looked, how your uniform was, or how you hair was cut. The petty chicken-shit stuff that they tried in the

United States they tried to enforce in Nam – which is a way to get a bullet in your back. We had enough to worry about staying alive. As far as shaving, we were lucky enough to have water to drink . . .[59]

Officers who harassed their men, even by issuing malaria pills or insisting that they wear their flak jackets and helmets, were in danger of provoking a violent reaction. Whether this can be construed as amicide is a moot point. That it was deliberate rather than accidental is undeniable, which would tend to separate it from the majority of friendly-fire incidents that we have studied in this book. Yet it is also undeniable that the wounding or killing of officers by their own men does qualify as friendly fire in that such acts were committed by men who were fighting on the same side in the conflict. Moreover, fragging should never be regarded simply as murder. Developing the point that Charles Anderson made above, the men responsible for the fragging are convinced that what they are doing is not a crime but a military necessity. Because of the poor relationship that exists between themselves and their officer, and because there is no way within the system that they can achieve their aim of removing him without harming him, it becomes necessary to sacrifice the individual in the interests of the unit. Combat conditions provide their own compulsion and their own justification.

Afterword

Victory in war does not always go to the side that makes the fewest mistakes. Neither the Germans nor the Japanese were in the same league as the British and the American when it came to blundering during the Second World War. Instead, as John Ellis has shown in his new book *Brute Force*, victory went to the big battalions of industry, not infantry. Amicide may not have been an Anglo-Saxon monopoly between 1939 and 1945, but there are times when one can be forgiven for thinking it was. Fiascos like the airborne operation over Sicily, Operations Cobra and Totalize, and the bombing of Switzerland, are more than simply the inevitable consequences of war on a previously unimaginable scale. From an ordinary GI in the Aleutians, firing at shadows in the trees, to the navy flak gunner shooting his fellow Americans as they parachute down over the Sicily beaches, one is dealing with fear and the hysteria to which it can so easily lead. In Paul Fussell's *Wartime: Understanding and Behaviour in the Second World War*, the writer claims that American anti-aircraft gunners were so shaky that during the early days of the Normandy campaign their guns had tags attached to their triggers saying 'This gun will only be fired under command of an officer.' For Fussell, this fear was at the root of a disastrous incident in 1988, when an Iranian airliner was shot down by American navy gunners, who feared that it was a hostile combat plane. Apparently the airliner had shown up on the radar of the USS *Vincennes*, which had shot first and investigated afterwards. The result was an amicide of 290 civilians. In 1992, during NATO exercises, the US Navy was at it again. The aircraft carrier *Saratoga* fired missiles at an imaginary foe and hit the bridge of a Turkish destroyer, killing a number of Turkish sailors. 'Technical error' was how the US Navy explained the blue-on-blue; 'human error brought about by panic or fear' was almost certainly the true cause.

Since the Gulf War there has been a concerted effort in the United States to develop an electronic tagging system to identify friendly vehicles during combat. It is hoped that these gadgets will prevent the sort of blue-on-blue incidents that involved aircraft firing on Coalition forces. It is evidence of a positive attitude on the subject of amicide. Even more so is the acknowledgement by the Pentagon that errors by American serviced personnel were reponsible for the deaths of the twenty-six passengers and crew of the two Black Hawk helicopters shot down in northern Iraq in April 1994. The pilots of the two F-15 fighters involved and the crew of the AWACS plane in the vicinity at the time of the tragedy may face prosecution, and the US Government has agreed to pay compensation to the families of the UN personnel killed, including the two British officers. Unfortunately, such a response has not been forthcoming from the Americans in the case of the Gulf War blue-on-blue which cost the lives of nine British servicemen. The Pentagon acknowledges neither guilt in this case nor need for compensation.

In conclusion, I contend that the message of two thousand years of friendly fire is that in the final analysis it is men who make mistakes, through the stress that war imposes, and that this stress is fundamentally linked with fear on their part: fear of death and mutilation, and fear of failure and humiliation. When men are afraid they will always shoot first rather than identify a target, or drop bombs too early rather than risk the flak. Mistakes will be reduced when men have less to fear. But then that would not be war, and they would not be men.

Notes

1   Lieutenant-Colonel C R Shrader, 'Friendly Fire: The Inevitable Price', *Parameters* Autumn 1992, p. 29.
2   John Keegan, *The Face of Battle*, Penguin 1978, pp. 100-101.
3   Jean Froissart, *The Chronicles of England, France and Spain*, Dent 1906, p.45.
4   Blaise de Monluc, ed I Roy, *Military Memoirs*, Longman 1971, p. 69.
5   Christopher Duffy, *The Military Experience in the Age of Reason*, Routledge 1987, p. 211.
6   John Green. *A Soldier's Life 1806–1815*, EP Publishing, p. 17.
7   T H McGuffie, *Rank and File*, Hutchinson 1964, p. 44.
8   Christopher Hibbert (ed), *The Recollections of Rifleman Harris*, Leo Cooper 1970, pp. 26-7.
9   T H McGuffie, *Rank and File*, Hutchinson 1964, pp. 234-5.
10 T H McGuffie, *Rank and File*, Hutchinson 1964, p. 254.
11 P Griffith, *Rally Once Again*, Crowood Press 1987, p. 89.
12 P Griffith, *Rally Once Again*, Crowood Press 1987, p. 89.
13 P Griffith, *Rally Once Again*, Crowood Press 1987, p. 111,
14 R U Jackson and C C Buel (eds), *Battles and Leaders of the Civil War*, Vol I, Castle 1883, p. 235.
15 G Regan, *Someone Had Blundered*, Batsford 1987.
16 G Regan, *Someone Had Blundered*, Batsford 1987.
17 L Macdonald, *1915*, Headline 1993, pp. 502-3.
18 T Norman, *The Hell They Called High Wood*, Patrick Stephens 1984.
19 L Macdonald, *1915*, Headline 1993, pp. 307-8.
20 L Macdonald, *They Called It Passchendaele*, Michael Joseph 1978, p. 197.
21 L Macdonald, *They Called It Passchendaele*, Michael Joseph 1978, p. 198.
22 C E W Bean, *Offical History of Australia in the War of 1914-18*,m Vol IV, Angus and Robertson, Sydney 1942, p. 887.

23 J Ellis *The Sharp End of War*, David and Charles 1980, p. 18.

24 J Ellis *The Sharp End of War*, David and Charles 1980, p. 267.

25 Lieutenant-Colonel C R Shrader, *Amicide: The Problem of Friendly Fire in Modern War*, Combat Studies Institute, Fort Leavenworth USA 1982, p. 5.

26 Lieutenant-Colonel C R Shrader, *Amicide: The Problem of Friendly Fire in Modern War*, Combat Studies Institute, Fort Leavenworth USA 1982, p. 90.

27 J Ellis *The Sharp End of War*, David and Charles 1980, p. 95.

28 J Ellis *The Sharp End of War*, David and Charles 1980, p. 19.

29 J Ellis *The Sharp End of War*, David and Charles 1980, p. 20.

30 J Ellis *The Sharp End of War*, David and Charles 1980, p. 92.

31 G McKay, *In Good Company*, Allen and Unwin, Sydney 1987, p. 137.

32 General N Schwarzkopf, *It Doesn't Take a Hero*, Bantam, New York 1993, p. 232.

33 G McKay, *In Good Company*, Allen and Unwin, Sydney 1987, p. 114.

34 E Bergerud, *Red Thunder, Tropic Lightning*, Westview, Boulder USA 1993, p. 130.

35 E Bergerud, *Red Thunder, Tropic Lightning*, Westview, Boulder USA 1993, p. 141-2.

36 E Bergerud, *Red Thunder, Tropic Lightning*, Westview, Boulder USA 1993, p. 131.

37 E Bergerud, *Red Thunder, Tropic Lightning*, Westview, Boulder USA 1993, p. 160.

38 E Bergerud, *Red Thunder, Tropic Lightning*, Westview, Boulder USA 1993, p. 179.

39 H McManners, *The Scars of War*, HarperCollins 1993.

40 H McManners, *The Scars of War*, HarperCollins 1993.

41 C Whiting, *Slaughter Over Sicily*, Leo Cooper 1992.

42 C Whiting, *Slaughter Over Sicily*, Leo Cooper 1992.

43 C Whiting, *Slaughter Over Sicily*, Leo Cooper 1992.

44 General G S Patton, *War As I Knew It*, W H Allen 1948.

45 Carlo D'Este, *Decision in Normandy*, Collins 1984, p. 341.

46 Max Hastings, *Overlord*, Michael Joseph 1984, p. 254.

47 Carlo D'Este, *Decision in Normandy*, Collins 1984, p. 402.

48 Lieutenant-Colonel C R Shrader, *Amicide: The Problem of Friendly Fire in Modern War*, Combat Studies Institute, Fort Leavenworth USA 1982, p. 54.

49 J Baynes, *Morale: A Study of Men and Courage*, Cassell 1967, p. 182.

50 Brigadier-General F P Crozier, *The Men I Killed*, Michael Joseph 1937, pp. 54-5.

51 Brigadier-General F P Crozier, *The Men I Killed*, Michael Joseph 1937, pp. 69-70.

52 J Putkowski and J Sykes, *Shot at Dawn*, Wharncliffe Publishing 1989, p. 304.
53 J Putkowski and J Sykes, *Shot at Dawn*, Wharncliffe Publishing 1989, p. 305.
54 C Whiting, *The Battle of Hürtgen Forest*, Leo Cooper 1989, p. 170.
55 C Whiting, *The Battle of Hürtgen Forest*, Leo Cooper 1989, p. 228.
56 Brigadier-General F P Crozier, *A Brass Hat in No Man's Land*, Cape 1930, pp. 208-9.
57 Richard Holmes, *Firing Line*, Penguin 1987, p. 330.
58 E Bergerud, *Red Thunder, Tropic Lightning*, Westview, Boulder USA 1993, p. 134.
59 E Bergerud, *Red Thunder, Tropic Lightning*, Westview, Boulder USA 1993, p. 303.

Bibliography

The following works have been most useful to me during the writing of this book and I have referred to many of them in the text.

M Adkins, *Urgent Fury*, 1989.

J Baynes, *Morale: A Study of Men and Courage*, Cassell 1967.

CEW Bean, *Official History of Australia in the War of 1914–18* Angus and Robertson, Sydney 1942.

E Bergerud, *Red Thunder, Tropic Lightning*, Westview, Boulder USA 1993.

O Bradley, *A General's Story*, Simon and Schuster, New York 1983.

C Carlton, *Going to the Wars*, Routledge 1992.

FP Crozier, *A Brass Hat in No Man's Land*, Cape 1930.

FP Crozier, *The Men I Killed*, Michael Joseph 1937.

Carlo D'Este, *Decision in Normandy*, Collins 1984

M Cumming, *The Starkey Sacrifice*, Sutton 1996.

Sir P de la Billière, *Storm Command*, HarperCollins 1993.

Blaise de Monluc, ed I Roy, *Military Memoirs*, Longman 1971.

C Duffy, *The Military Experience in the Age of Reason*, Routledge 1987.

RL Eichelberger, *Our Jungle Road to Tokyo*, Viking, New York 1950.

J Ellis *The Sharp End of War*, David and Charles 1980.

Jean Froissart, *The Chronicles of England, France and Spain*, Dent 1906.

P Fussell, *Wartime: Understanding and Behaviour in the Second World War*, Oxford University Press 1989.

R Graves. *Goodbye to All That*, Penguin 1960.

P Griffith, *Rally Once Again*, Crowood Press 1987.

VD Hanson, *The Western Way of War*, Oxford University Press 1990.

M Hastings, *Overlord*, Michael Joseph 1984.

C Hibbert (ed), *The Recollections of Rifleman Harris*, Leo Cooper 1970.

R Holmes, *Firing Line*, Penguin 1987.

J Keegan, *The Face of Battle*, Penguin 1978.

L Macdonald, *1915*, Headline 1993.

L Macdonald, *They Called It Passchendaele*, Michael Joseph 1978.

D MacShane, *Friendly Fire Whitewash*, Epic 1992.

SLA Marshall, *Pork Chop Hill*, Morrow, New York 1956.

T H McGuffie, *Rank and File*, Hutchinson 1964.

G McKay, *In Good Company*, Allen and Unwin, Sydney 1987.

H McManners, *The Scars of War*, HarperCollins 1993.

C Mercer, *Journal of the Waterloo Campaign*, London 1877.

Lord Moran, *The Anatomy of Courage*, Constable 1945.

T Norman, *The Hell They Call High Wood*, Patrick Stephens 1984.

GS Patton, *War As I Knew It*, WH Allen 1948.

D Prior and T Wilson, *Command on the Western Front*, Blackwell 1992.

J Pukowski and J Sykes, *Shot at Dawn*, Wharncliffe 1989.

GB Regan, *Someone Had Blundered*, Batsford 1987.

Norman Schwarzkopf, *It Doesn't Take a Hero*, Bantam, New York 1993.

CR Shrader, *Amicide: The Problem with Friendly Fire in Modern War*, Combat Studies Institute, Fort Leavenworth USA 1982.

Earl H Tilford Jr, 'Operation Allied Force and the Role of Air Power', in *Parameters*, US Army War College Quarterly, winter 1999–2000.

C Whiting, *Slaughter Over Sicily*, Leo Cooper 1992.

C Whiting, *The Battle of Hürthgen Forest*, Leo Cooper 1992.

D Winter, *Haig's Command*, Viking 1991.

L Wolff, *In Flanders Fields*, Penguin 1979.

Index

A General's Story (Bradley), 211
A-10 Tankbusters, 9, 16–18
Agent Orange, 226–8
Air Warfare:
  American amicide incidents during
    the Second World War, 179–81
  amicide statistics concerning, 179
  attacks on Belgium, 214–15
  battle of the Bulge, 215
  between Salm and Ourthe Rivers,
    215
  British amicide incidents during the
    Second World War, 177–8
  First World War, 171–6
  German amicide during the Second
    World War, 178–9
  in Grenada, 231–3
  Korean War, 225
  near Grandménil, 215
  near Laval, 214
  near Mortain, 213
  Operation Cobra, 200–15
  Operation Ladbroke, 184–9
  Operation Totalize, 212
  Operation Tractable, 213
  in the Pacific, 224–5
  near Troisgots, 213
  Vietnam War, 226–31
  See also Ground Warfare
Alexander, Alexander, on
  carelessness during Napoleonic
  Wars, 58–9
Allen, Captain, on

battle fought on San Juan Hill, 76
American Civil War: 67–74
  battle of Ball's Bluff, 74
  battle of Chancellorsville, 72
  battle of Gettysburg, 68
  battle of Seven Pines, 69
  faulty loading of weapons during, 68
  First battle of Bull Run, 68–9
  Fragging incidents during, 248
  'Stonewall' Jackson's fatal accident
    during, 72–3
  unintentional killing of officers
    during, 72–3
  Union soldier training, 69–70
Amicide:
  contributing factors concerning,
    7–10
  disciplinary, 11
  human error and, 9–11
  statistics concerning, 7
  throughout history, 3–7
Ammianus Marcellinus, 30
Anatomy of Courage, The (Lord
  Moran), 247
Anderson, Charles, on fragging, 262–3
Anderson, General Frederick, 205
Andrews, Benjamin, on Union soldier
  training, 67
Anzacs, 101
Artillery:
  First World War, 86–8
  Second World War, 125–6
  See also Weapons

273

Ashbourne, Admiral Lord, 187
Austrian army at Karansebes, 54–6

Balbo, Marshal Italo, 181
Barrilleaux, Melvin, 133
Battles:
  Adrianople, 30
  Agincourt, 33–4, 38
  Albuera, 62
  Ball's Bluff, 74
  Barnet, 36–7
  Blenheim, 260
  Bulge, the, 215–16
  Bull Run, first, 69
  Busaco, 62
  Cannae, 4,
  Chancellorsville, 72
  Crecy, 37–8
  Crewkerne, 45
  Delion, 31
  El Alamein, 125
  Eylau, 61
  Gettysburg, 68
  Hastings, 35
  Kasserine Pass, the, 180
  Kolin, 47
  Lake Trasimene, 32
  Leipzig, 57
  Loos, 94–101
  Majuba Hill, 5
  Messines, 111–14
  Oudenarde, 46
  Passchendaele, 114–21
  Reonville, 60
  Roosebeke, 33
  Schmidt, 133–4
  Seven Pines, 69
  Somme: 101–9
    attack on Pozieres, 102–3
    attack towards Delville Wood and
      Longueval, 106–7
    incident at High Wood, 108–9
  Stamford Bridge, 35
  Talavera, 60
  Towton, 36
  Villers-Brettoneaux, second, 120–1
  Vimeiro, 60

  Wagram, 62
  Waterloo, 63–6
  Ypres, second, 94
  Zorndorf, 48
Bayerlein, General,
  on Operation Cobra incident, 210
Baynes, John,
  on failure in coordination during
    Second World War, 93, 249
Bean, Charles, 88, 110
  on battle of Poelcapelle, 113–114
  on British artillery, 117
Bedell-Smith, general, on Normandy
  terrain, 200
Belgium, US air attacks on, 214
Bergerud, Eric, 162
Bernard, Colonel, 90–1
'Black Day of the British Army', 108
Black Hawk helicopters, 237–9
Blair, Herbert, on Operation Husky
  incident, 193
Blamey, Jack, 148
Borden, Robert, 120
Bougainville, occupation of, 148–9
Bourke, Captain, 81–2
Braddock, General Sir Edward
  campaign on Monongahela River,
    10, 49–53
Bradley, General Omar
  on incident near Troina, 197–9
  on inexperienced troops, 145
  and Operation Cobra, 200–215
British Military:
  on discipline, 249–56
  Expeditionary Force, 91–2
  First Armoured Division, 12
  66th Division, at battle of
    Poelcapelle, 114–17
Brooke, Lieutenant-Colonel Alan, 119
Browning, General Frederick, 196
Brute Force (Ellis), 266
Bryan, CDB, 161
Buckingham, Duke of, 42–3

Cadiz, expedition to, 42–3
Cambridge, Duke of, 84
Camperdown, HMS, 77–84

Cannons, 39–40
Carleton, Charles, on English Civil
 Wars, 42
Carne, JP, 154–5
Carter-Campbell, George, 93
Chamberlain, Tom, 261
Chinese Embassy in Belgrade, US
 bombing of, 241–3
Churchill, Winston:
 on tanks, 103
 on U-boats,136
 on bombing of Le Portel, 182–3
Clark, John, on march to Kabul, 66–7
Clinton, President William, 242–3
Connors, Lieutenant, at Normandy,
 131
Corey, William, 126
Corsair IIs, 231–2
Cota, General 'Dutch', 257
Crozier, General Frank Percy:
 on British military discipline, 250
 on Fragging during the First World
 War, 252–3
Cunningham, Admiral, 185, 196
Cushman, Horace, on amicide in the
 Pacific during the Second World
 War, 142

Daun, Marshall, 47
de la Billiere, General Sir Peter, on
 amicide casualties, 13–14, 18–19
de Monluc, Blaise, on amicide incident
 during Habsburg-Valois Wars, 39
D'Este, Carlo on Operation Ladbroke,
 186–7
Dioxins, 226–8
Dönitz, Admiral, 137–8
Duffy, Christopher:
 on fragging during eighteenth
 century 260
 on poor fire discipline among
 eighteenth century soldiers, 47
Dunn, John, 152
Duxbury, Brett, 15

Edward IV, king of England, 36–7
Eichelberger, General, on battle of

Brinkman's Plantation, 141–2,
 145
Eichen, Sidney, on Operation Cobra
 incident, 209
Eisenhower, General Dwight:
 on Operation Husky amicide
 incidents, 194
 on Slovik execution, 258–9
Elliott 'Pompy', on attack on Pozieres,
 102
Ellis, John, 266
English Civil War:
 battle of Crewkerne, 45
 battle of Marston Moor, 45
 incident at battle of Edgehill, 45
 siege of Basing House, 41
 siege of Farnham Church, 44
 siege of Limerick, 44
Enterprise, USS, 181
Eugene, Prince, 46

F-15s, 237–9, 267
Face of Battle, The (Keegan), 33
Fairfax, Sir Thomas, 45
Falklands War, 165–8
 amicide near San Carlos Water,
 166–8
Firing Line, (Holmes), 262
First Afghan War, 66
First Bishops' War, 43
First World War:
 air amicide incidents during, 171–6
 artillery, 86–8
 battle at Calvary, 89
 battle near Rossignol, 88
 battle of Loos, 94–101
 battle of Messines, 111–14
 battle of Passchendaele, 114–21
 battle of Poelcapelle, 114–18
 battle of Samogneux, 89–91
 battle of the Somme, 101–9
 British attack at Neuve Chapelle,
 92–3
 fragging incidents during, 261–2
 incidents at Authuille, 92
 second battle of Villers-Brettoneux,
 120–1

second battle of Ypres, 94
tanks, 103–8
Froissart, 38
Forster, EM, 233
Fortescue, Sir Faithful, 45
Fragging:
British incidents of, 260–2
incidents during American Civil War, 261
incidents during Napoleonic Wars, 260
incidents during First World War, 261–2
incidents during Vietnam War, 262–5
Franco-Prussian War, 60
Frederick the Great, king of Prussia, 41, 46–8, 249
French, Sergeant, on Falklands War amicide incident, 168
French military:
discipline, 253
invasion of Algeria, 66
Friendly Fire. *See* amicide.
Friendly Fire (Bryan), 161
Friendly Fire Whitewash (MacShane), 7

Gabriel, Richard 262
Gameson, L, on military executions, 255–6
Gavin, Colonel James, 189, 194
German military:
discipline, 252–3
49th Infantry Division amicide incident, 134
25th Panzer Grenadier Regiment amicide incident, 134.
Gershwin, george and Ira, 217, 222
Gibbon, Edward, 248–9
Gilbert Islands, invasion of, 146
Gilford, Lord, 80–1
Giraudoux, Jean, 89
Goebbels, Josef, 139
Going to the Wars (Carlton), 42
Goodbye to All That (Graves), 99, 262
Gordon, Alexander, on carelessness during Napoleonic Wars, 58

Goring, Lord George, 45
Gough, General Sir Hubert, 114
Graves, Robert, on poison gas attack at the Battle of Loos, 99
Greek battlefield, ancient, and weapons, 29–32
Green, John, on carelessness during Napoleonic Wars, 57
Grenada, invasion of, 231–3
Griffith, Paddy:
on faulty loading of weapons during American Civil War, 69
on fire discipline, 70
Grimes, Captain, at the battle of San Juan Hill, 75–6
Ground warfare:
Afghan war, 66
American Civil War, 67–75
ancient, 29–32
Austrian army at Karansebes, 55–6
campaign on Monongahela River, 49–53
English Civil War, 41–5
Falklands War, 165–8
First World War, 86–112, 171–6
Franco-Prussian War, 60
French invasion of Algeria, 66
Hundred Years War, 33–8
Korean War, 152–7
medieval, 33–40
Napoleonic Wars, 57–66
Peninsular War, 60–61
Prussian Wars, 46–8
Second World War, 122–51, 177–225
Spanish-American War, 74–6
Vietnam War, 157–65, 226–31
Wars of the Roses, 36–7
See also Air warfare
Guam, occupation of, 149
Guderian, General Heinz, 179
Gulf War, 3, 5–6, 12–25
See also Operation Desert Storm

Hapsburg-Valois Wars, 39
Haig, Field Marshal Sir Douglas:
at battle of Loos, 94–101

at battle of Passchendaele, 114–20
at battle of Somme, 102–11
Haig's Command (Winter), 120
Hanson, Victor Davis, on ancient
    Greek battlefield, 29, 32
Harris, Rifleman, on battle of Vimeiro,
    59–60, 260
Harvey, Captain Michael, 155–6
Hayes, Ralph, 22
Hawkins–Smith, Commander, 80–1,
    83
Helicopter gun ships, 229–31
Hicks, Brigadier, 184
Hill, General AP, 72–3
Hitler, Adolf, 138
Hobbs, General Leland, 128–9
Holmes, Richard, 11, 60
Hopkinson, General, 187–8
Hornby, Sir GP, 79
Horner, General 'Chuck':
    advice to pilots in Gulf War, 19
    and Operation Desert Storm
        incidents, 12–25
Hunt, 'Kiwi', 165–6

Imboden, John:
    on carelessness during the American
        Civil War, 71
Iranair Flight 655, 233–6

Jackson, General 'Stonewall', fatal
    accident of, 67, 73–4
James II, king of Scotland, 39–40
Japanese, amicide incidents, 141–5
Jellicoe, John, rescued from *Victoria*
    amicide incident, 83
Joseph II, Holy Roman Emperor, 54–6
Ju87–Stuka dive-bombers, 178

Karansebes, Austrian army at, 54–6
Keegan, John, on battle of Agincourt,
    33–4
Kelley, Gerard, 146–7
Kerr, Admiral, 85
King, Patrick, on the battle of
    Poelcapelle, 115–17
King, Admiral, in U-boat war, 138–40

Kiska, invasion of and amicide
    incident, 143–4
Komosa, Adam, on Operation Husky
    incident, 192
Korean War:
    air amicide during, 225
    attack on Pork Chop Hill, 156–7
    'Glorious Glosters' at Imjin River,
        154–6
    Hill 282 incident, 225
Kosovo, amicide in, 240–1

Landsknechte, 38–9
Lathbury, Brigadier, 194
Le Massacre de notre Infanterie
    1914–18 (Percin), 87
Lee, General Robert E, on news of
    Jackson's accident, 73
Lees, General Oliver, 199
Leigh-Mallory, Trafford, and
    Operation Cobra incidents, 162–3,
    211–12
Le Portel, RAF bombing of, 182–4
Less, Admiral Tony, 234
Lewis, Norman, on fighting around
    Salerno, 124
Lind Report, on US invasion of
    Grenada, 232
Livermore, William, on battle of Ball's
    Bluff, 74
Lloyd George, David, 120
Lohse, Major, investigation of amicide
    incident at Normandy, 131–2
Longstreet, 'Old Pete', wounding of, 74
Ludendorff, Field Marshal Eric von,
    252–3

McCullum, Sergeant, on Falklands War
    amicide incident, 167
McInnis, Ellis, at Normandy, 130–1
McKay, Gary:
    at Courtney Rubber Plantation, 158
    on shells fired in thick foliage, 161
    on use of drugs during Vietnam War,
        160–1
McManners, Hugh, on Falklands War
    amicide incidents, 165–8

MacShane, Denis, on Hayes case, 22
Makin, invasion of and amicide
    incidents, 146–8
Malmedy, US attack on, 214
Marlborough, Duke of, 46
Markham, Admiral, 78–84
Marshall, General George, 140, 221
Marshall, SLA, 10, 156
Maximilian I, Holy Roman Emperor,
    38
Mellenthin, General von, on air
    amicide incident in Poland, 178
Men I Killed, The (Crozier), 250
Mercer, Cavalié, on incident at battle
    of Waterloo, 63–4
Middle Ages:
    battlefield, 33–6
    weapons, 34–6
Millis, Walter, on battle of San Juan
    Hill, 75
Missile misdirection, 36–7
Montgomery, General Bernard, 125,
    199
Montgomery, USS, 234
Morale (Baynes), 248
Muir, Major Kenneth, 225

Napoleon I, emperor of France, 61–4
Napoleonic Wars:
    battle of Eylau, 61
    battle of Leipzig, 57
    battle of Wagram, 62
    battle of Waterloo, 63–6
    carelessness during, 58–60
    fragging incidents during, 260
New Georgia, amicide incidents on,
    145
Nielson, Carl, on Vietnam War amicide
    incident, 151

Oberembt, amicide incident at, 134–5
Oman, Sir Charles, on 'trampling', 38
Operation Cobra:
    postponement of, 206
    preparations for, 204–5
Operation Desert Storm:
    American losses from amicide

during, 7
amicide incidents during, 23–4
conflict of evidence concerning
    amicide tragedy, 18–21
death of British soldiers by amicide
    during, 15–16
Operation Drumbeat, 135–40
Operation Husky, 190
Operation Ladbroke, 184–7
Operation Ranch Hand, 226–8
Operation Totalize, 212
Operation Tractable, 213
Operation Urgent Fury, 232

Papua, campaign in Buna, 148
Parry Island, landing at, 148
Peninsular War:
    battle of Albuera, 62
    battle of Busaco, 62
    battle of Talavera, 60
    siege of Badajoz, 62
Pennsylvania, USS, 181
Percin, General, on French artillery
    amicide incidents, 9, 87–9
Philip VI, king of France, 37
Phillips, Keith, on fighting in Grenada,
    232
Poelcapelle, battle of, 114–17
Poison gas:
    problems in employing, 93–7
Polybius, 31
Pound, Admiral Sir Dudley, 138
Prussian Wars:
    battle of Kolin, 47
    battle of Zorndorf, 48
Pullen, John, on carelessness during
    American Civil War, 70
Pulteney, General, at High Wood, 107
Pyle, Ernie, on Operation Cobra
    incident, 208

Rally Once Again (Griffith), 68
Rawlinson, General Sir Henry:
    at battle of Loos, 94–101
    using tanks on the Somme, 104–7
Recollections of Rifleman Harris,
    59–60, 162

Red Thunder, Tropic Lightning (Bergerud), 162
Ridgway, General Matthew, 185–97
Romans, military discipline, 249, 260
Roosevelt, President FDR, 136, 138
Rose, General Sir Michael, 240–1
Rusk, Dean, 226

Saddam Hussein, 5–7, 237–9
St Clair, General, 54
St Cyr, Marshal, 62
Saint-Rémy, Lieutenant, 174–5
Saipan, invasion of, 149–50
Sans Pareil, HMS, 80
Scars of War, The (McManners), 165
Schwarzkopf, General Norman, 6, 13, 19, 161
Second World War:
 air amicide incident near Laval, 214
 air amicide incident near Mortain, 213
 air amicide incident near Troisgots, 213
 airborne operations over Sicily, 184–90
 Allied advance through Italy, 125–6
 American air amicide incidents during, 179–81
 amicide incident on island of Kiska, 143–4
 artillery in, 124–5
 assaults on the Gothic Line at Monte Altuzzo, 126
 battle of Brinkman's Plantation, 145
 battle of the Bulge, 215
 battle of the Kasserine Pass, 180
 battle of Schmidt, 133–4
 British air amicide incidents during, 177–8
 Buna, campaign in Papua, 148
 fighting around Salerno, 124
 fighting between Salm and Ourthe rivers, 215
 German air amicide incidents during, 178–9
 Grandménil air incident, 215
 Hollandia amicide incident, 145
 invasion of Gilbert Islands, 146
 invasion of Sicily, 184
 morale during, 123
 New Georgia amicide incidents, 145
 Normandy invasion, 122, 200
 Oberembt amicide incident, 134–5
 occupation of Bougainville, 148–9
 occupation of Guam, 149
 Operation Cobra in Normandy, 200–212
 Operation on Saipan, 149–50
 Operation Totalize, 212
 Operation Tractable, 213
 Parry Island landing, 148
 Undeclared war between Switzerland and the United States, 217–223
'Shell-shock', 254
Sherman, General, on fire discipline in battle, 69
Shrader, Charles:
 on air amicide incidents in North Africa, 179–80
 on air amicide incidents in Pacific, 224–5
 on airborne operations over Sicily, 197–9
 on amicide incidents during Vietnam War, 162, 226–31
 on assaults at Monte Altuzzo, 126
 on human errors, 168
Siborne, Captain William, 63
Sicily, invasion of:
 amicide incident near Troina, 197–99
 amicide incident at Venafro, 199
Sides, USS, 234–5
Simpsons, The, 236
Slaughter over Sicily (Whiting), 186
Slovik, Eddie:
 execution of, 259
 letter of Eisenhower, 258
Smith, General Rupert, 14
Spaatz, General:
 on Operation Cobra incident, 201–2, 210
 during US attacks on Switzerland, 218–19, 222

Spears, Sir Edward, on air amicide
    incidents during the First World
    War, 173
Stalin, Josef, 139
Stark, USS, 236
Storm Command (de la Billiere), 18
Swinton, ED on First World War
    tanks, 103–4
Switzerland:
    US attacks on railway junction at
        Noirmont, 221
    US attack on Thayngen, 221
    US attack on Zürich, 222
    Schaffhausen raid, 217, 219

Tanks, First World War: limitations,
    104
Tedder, Sir Arthur, 195, 201
'Three-rank' formation, 41, 46
Thucydides:
    on Athenian night attack at
        Epipolae, 30
    on battle of Delion, 31
Thurtle, Ernest, 254
Tiberius, Emperor, 260
'Trampling', 38
Tryon, Admiral, 76–85
Tucker, Colonel Reuben, 185, 191
Turkish Brigade in Korean War, 153
Twentieth Maine, The (Pullen) 70

Vandenberg, Dan, on Vietnam War
    amicide incidents, 163
Vandenberg, Hoyt, on Operation
    Cobra incident, 205–6
Vaquette, Boromée, 92
Victoria, HMS, sinking of, 76–85
Vietnam War:
    Agent Orange, use of in, 226–8
    air amicide incident near Chu Lai,
        231
    air amicide incident near Go Vap,
        226

air amicide incident near Pleiku, 231
Courtney Rubber Plantation
    incident, 158
Fragging incidents during, 262–5
helicopter gunships used during,
    229–31
Operation Ranch Hand, 226–8
statistics concerning Fragging during,
    262
Vincennes, USS, 233–6

Wabash River, battle of, 54
Warrior IFVs, attack on, 14–17
*Wartime: Understanding and
    Behaviour in the Second World
    War,* (Fussell), 266
Washington, George, 53
Weapons:
    ancient Greek, 31–2
    cannons, 31–40
    faulty loading of, 68
    medieval, 33–9
    poison gas, 97
    See also Artillery
Wellington, Duke of, 63–4
Western Way of War, The (Hanson),
    29
White, Lieutenant, on releasing poison
    gas, 100
Whitelocke, General, 260
Whiting, Charles, on operation
    Ladbroke, 187
Wilson, A, amicide experience, 111
Wimbledon, Viscount, 42–3
Winter, Denis, on battle of
    Passchendaele, 120
Wolfe, General James, 10, 249
Woolf, Leon, 115

Zürich, US bombing of, 222